Anorexia Nervosa

Anorexia Nervosa
A Comprehensive Approach

edited by

Meir Gross, M.D.

Head, Section of Child and Adolescent Psychiatry
Cleveland Clinic Foundation

 **The Collamore Press**
D.C. Heath and Company
Lexington, Massachusetts
Toronto

Published simultaneously in Canada and the United Kingdom

Printed in the United States of America

International Standard book number: 0–669–04307–9

Library of Congress Catalog Card Number: 80–68892

61,933

Library of Congress Cataloging in Publication Data
Main entry under title:

Anorexia nervosa.

  Bibliography: p.
  Includes index.
  1. Anorexia nervosa—Addresses, essays, lectures.
I. Gross, Meir, 1936–
[DNLM: 1. Anorexia nervosa. WM 175 A615]
RC552.A5A575   616.85'2   80–68892
ISBN 0–669–04307–9   AACR2

To the memory of my patient, Carol S. Haus,
who was taken away so unexpectedly
by an accident

Contents

Preface
and Acknowledgments

Anorexia nervosa and bulimia usually occur during adolescence or early adult life, when looks and sexual attractiveness are of paramount importance. This is a period in the growing person's life in which changes occur in the body and its physical appearance. A new awareness of physical change and a preoccupation with appearance sometimes lead to attempts at controlling the body in various ways, such as by skipping meals, inducing vomiting, abusing laxatives or diuretics, or using over-the-counter diet pills. Abuse of amphetamines to reduce appetite also is prevalent as a way to control the growing body.

Nowadays, overweight, aging, and ill health are considered moral lapses that one ought to "do something about." We hear: "It's a disgrace the way she's let herself go!" "Don't eat that—you'll get fat and ugly!"

Some of us remember an ample, gentle grandmother reading fairy tales, rocking us to sleep, and waking us to the heavenly aroma of kugel baking in the woodburning kitchen stove. Her dress modestly covering her ankles, she busied herself sprinkling cloves, pine needles, and apple peelings on the hot stove so that the whole household could enjoy the fragrance. Paradise lost: nowadays, grandma weighs 96 pounds, works out at Vic Tanny's, and serves TV dinners. "Just call me Tillie," she tells her grandchildren, "I wanna feel young!"

Since the end of World War II, Americans have become obsessed with appearances. Hollywood fantasies still dominate our lives. The vitamin and health food market is booming. The weekly *New York Times* best-seller list usually includes three or four diet books and one or two on improving sexual performance. Elderly people are regularly being swindled by dance studios, exercise parlors, and "youth" doctors.

The Me Generation seems to have little interest in anything below the surface. There is no meaningful conversation in the home; children grow up in front of the television set rather than interacting with loving parents and grandparents. Millions of young couples are simply living together, without the commitment of marriage. Children are considered a burden—even a disaster to the would-be beauty queen. The flat belly is all. Given this society and these values, the increase in anorexia nervosa and bulimia is hardly surprising.

Anorexia nervosa and bulimia have caught the attention of the mass media lately. Many magazines devote large coverage to the problem: stories about girls who suffer trying to keep slim—becoming ill and needing professional help—or stories about cured patients, who present their insights into the process of getting better and their feelings about having gone through it. The interest of the public in dieting and in the possibility of becoming anorectic or bulimic is so great that lay people often have more detailed information about the illnesses than many practicing physicians do.

Education about nutrition is lacking in many medical schools. There also is insufficient awareness among practitioners that emotional stress or conflict can lead to self-starving or purging and, consequently, to anorexia or bulimia. Furthermore, it seems that many practitioners cannot see the relationship between the current preoccupation with slimness and thinness and the adolescent's choice of self-starvation as a way to avoid life's responsibilities and the process of growing up.

It is not unusual for a very thin girl to see a gynecologist because her menstrual periods have ceased for a few months or altogether, and yet no diagnosis of anorexia nervosa is made. It is not unusual for a school coach whose students are weighed routinely to comment that a few of them are too heavy or have overly large stomachs or thighs, leading a few of the youngsters to a very strict diet or into prolonged periods of actual fasting.

This book is intended to fill the void in the professional's awareness of the enigma of anorexia nervosa and bulimia. Better understanding of the illnesses from both medical and psychological perspectives will undoubtedly benefit the increasing number of youngsters who are heading toward these severe conditions.

This book is directed toward all professionals who work with youngsters, including pediatricians, general practitioners, family doctors, internists, gynecologists, psychiatrists, nutritionists, psychologists, social workers, nurses, professionals in sports medicine, and educators. Parents of patients and patients themselves might also find the information in this book valuable for understanding the psychopathology of anorexia and bulimia and the medical treatment for them.

This book was initiated by requests for written materials following a conference on anorexia nervosa and eating disorders, organized by the editor and sponsored by the Cleveland Clinic Educational Foundation. Speakers at this conference kindly contributed their papers in final form for the book.

I am grateful to the colleagues and friends who helped me bring this book to its present form—a compilation of their experience and knowledge—so that it could be shared by medical-science professionals, paramedical professionals, and all who attend to anorexia nervosa. Their willingness to contribute to this book will be much appreciated, I am sure, by the many patients and parents who might benefit directly and indirectly from their valuable experience.

Meir Gross, M.D.

Contributing Authors

Eugene L. Bliss, M.D.
Foundations Fund Research Professor of Psychiatry
University of Utah College of Medicine
Salt Lake City, Utah

William D. Carey, M.D.
Department of Gastroenterology
Cleveland Clinic Foundation
Cleveland, Ohio

Richard Chiulli, M.D.
Resident in General Surgery
Department of General Surgery
Cleveland Clinic Foundation
Cleveland, Ohio

Edmund J. Doering, M.D.
Clinical Instructor—Pediatrics
Case Western Reserve University
Cleveland, Ohio

Lynne M. Dorman, M.A.
Department of Psychology
Case Western Reserve University
Cleveland, Ohio

Paul G. Dyment, M.D.
Chairman, Department of Pediatric and Adolescent Medicine
Cleveland Clinic Foundation
Cleveland, Ohio

Gita P. Gidwani, M.D.
Department of Gynecology
Cleveland Clinic Foundation
Cleveland, Ohio

Grattan Giesey, M.S.S.A. (ACSW)
Department of Social Work
Cleveland Clinic Foundation
Cleveland, Ohio

Meir Gross, M.D.
Head, Section of Child and Adolescent Psychiatry
Chairman, Research Committee on Anorexia Nervosa
Cleveland Clinic Foundation
Cleveland, Ohio

Margaret Grover, R.N.
Hyperalimentation Nurse
Cleveland Clinic Foundation
Cleveland, Ohio

Patricia L. Howe Tilton
Executive Director and Founder, National Anorexic Aid Society
Columbus, Ohio

Enrique Huerta, M.D.
Section of Child and Adolescent Psychiatry
Cleveland Clinic Foundation
Cleveland, Ohio

Judy Johnson, B.A.
Group Leader and Member, National Anorexic Aid Society
South Bend, Indiana

Jerome F. Kiffer, M.A.
Clinical Biofeedback Therapist, Department of Psychiatry
Cleveland Clinic Foundation
Cleveland, Ohio

K. Miller Kovach, M.S., R.D.
Department of Dietetics–Clinical
Cleveland Clinic Foundation
Cleveland, Ohio

Michael G. McKee, Ph.D.
Psychologist, Department of Psychiatry
Cleveland Clinic Foundation
Cleveland, Ohio

Douglas S. Moodie, M.D.
Head, Department of Pediatric Cardiology
Cleveland Clinic Foundation
Cleveland, Ohio

Barbara A. Reece, R.N.
Head Nurse, Adolescent Psychiatric Unit
Cleveland Clinic Foundation
Cleveland, Ohio

John B. Reinhart, M.D.
Professor of Pediatrics and Child Psychiatry
University of Pittsburgh School of Medicine
Director, Division of Behavioral Science
Children's Hospital of Pittsburgh
Pittsburgh, Pennsylvania

Ezra Steiger, M.D., F.A.C.S.
Department of General Surgery
Chairman, Hyperalimentation Committee
Cleveland Clinic Foundation
Cleveland, Ohio

Frederick H. Strieder, M.S.S.A. (ACSW)
Department of Social Work
Cleveland Clinic Foundation
Cleveland, Ohio

Anorexia Nervosa

1 Introduction

Meir Gross, M.D.

Anorexia nervosa is a baffling disease, and its cure is elusive. It seems to have increased during the past decade, but it is not clear whether there are more cases now because dieting is so popular and because many American girls aspire to lose weight or because the disease is now more easily recognized. Recently, anorexia nervosa has become a common subject in the mass media. It is possible, therefore, that its popularity is creating a mass hysteria, in which anorectic girls become models for identification by other teenage girls. The disorder occurs predominantly in girls, in a ratio of 9:1, usually during adolescence and can affect one of every 250 girls between the ages of 12 and 18 years.

The typical anorectic girl has a body-image distortion. She feels fat or overweight even when her body is emaciated. She is preoccupied with her body size and frequently will gaze at herself in a mirror and be obsessed with her appearance. She will lose weight by reducing her food intake or by eating only food that is low in carbohydrates or fat. At times, she might induce vomiting to get rid of the food or might take laxatives, diuretics, or enemas. Most anorectic patients tend to overexercise in an obsessive, compulsive manner for long hours every day.

At the onset of the disease there is often evidence of a stressful life situation, such as conflict in the family or at school and peer-group pressure. These patients have a tendency to be perfectionists and usually have a history of being model children. About one-third of the patients may have begun dieting because they were slightly overweight but then adapted obsessive, compulsive eating habits, with weight loss as the primary goal. Once they succeed in losing weight, they continue relentlessly, to the point of severe emaciation. When a substantial amount of weight is lost, they become fearful of regaining it and resist any pressure from their parents to eat. This fear of gaining weight can reach phobic proportions.

Amenorrhea is a common feature of anorexia nervosa, often occurring before substantial weight has been lost; in most cases, amenorrhea occurs when 17% of body weight is lost. The term *anorexia* is a misnomer, since most of the patients do not lose their appetites until a late stage of the illness. When the weight loss becomes profound, hypothermia may occur. Pulse rate may become slow, blood pressure may be reduced, edema may be prominent, especially in ankles and legs, and lanugo may appear on the skin. Possible metabolic changes include abnormal liver function, abnormal protein levels, low white blood cell count, and reduced immunological resistance in the late stages of the disease. Loss of hair is seen occasionally.

The course of the disease may continue to death by starvation or by electro-lyte imbalance (especially in bulimic patients) that may produce cardiac arrhythmia or cardiac arrest. Sometimes patients die of infectious disease be-cause of deficits in their immunological systems. The results of several studies show a mortality rate between 15% and 21%. If the weight loss becomes severe, hospitalization is sometimes required to prevent death. There are, however, cases of spontaneous recovery. In many cases, anorexia nervosa occurs as a single episode, with full recovery thereafter, especially if treatment is given in the early stages of the disease. Some patients have episodic relapses, however, even with intensive treatment.

Denial of the illness is one of the major defense mechanisms of anorectic patients. Many fear growing up and use anorexia as a means to stop the process of growing. Many have delayed psychosexual development and cannot cope with the transition through adolescence. They fear the responsibilities of adulthood. Interest in sex is decreased, and very few anorectic patients are interested in dating or getting married during the course of the illness. Obsessive, compulsive behavior is characteristic. Some girls develop elaborate ritual behavior, such as counting to a certain number before eating or doing other things. Some become involved in compulsive hand washing, obsessive wishes for cleanliness, and the tendency to be perfectionist in whatever projects are undertaken. There also is a tendency toward orderliness, and changing the order of things in the kitchen, for example, might become a source of argument or tantrum.

Changes in personality and behavior are also apparent during the course of the illness. The patient might succumb to her feelings of hunger and even have bulimic episodes in which she may overeat—usually large amounts of carbo-hydrates. After binging episodes, because of severe guilt and the fear of gaining weight, she might induce vomiting. Because of the suppression of appetite or the attempt to suppress appetite, these girls become preoccupied with thoughts of food most of the day. Many of them may undertake elaborate preparation of food for the family but rarely eat the food themselves. Most of them even avoid sitting near the dinner table with the family. Anorectic patients usually eat alone—eating very slowly, cutting their food into many small pieces, and not finishing the meal. Some hoard food—concealing it in their bedrooms so that they feel secure in having the food—but never eat it.

Although anorexia nervosa can be diagnosed easily in the late stages, there are still mistakes or delays in diagnosis. Despite its recent popularity, there are still cases that are not being diagnosed in time. Sometimes diagnosis is delayed two or three years. These patients may have been seen by a gynecologist because of lack of menstrual periods, and they even may have undergone elaborate endocrinological studies by pediatric endocrinologists, with no confirmed diagnosis. The following case is an example of missed diagnosis that allowed progression of the disease.

Susan, aged 22, was mildly overweight during adolescence. After getting married at age 18, she began a reducing diet. Six months later, her menstrual periods stopped, and she did not menstruate for about two and a half years. She consulted a gynecologist, who did an elaborate work-up and gave her an injection of progesterone, hoping to trigger the periods. Another gynecologist was consulted, and again an elaborate evaluation of hypothalamic functioning was made; the results were normal. Another attempt to induce periods by hormonal therapy was unsuccessful. After two years of amenorrhea, an endocrinologist was consulted and the endocrinological system was checked and found to be normal. Because the patient wished to become pregnant, she finally came to the Anorexia Nervosa Clinic of the Cleveland Clinic at the suggestion of family members who realized that she was losing too much weight. When seen at the clinic, her weight loss was not so apparent, as she looked good being thin. Severe cachexia was not evident, and no physician would have suspected anorexia nervosa. Only close family members, who knew her before the weight loss, realized how much weight she had lost. It was evident that her menstrual periods stopped because of loss of weight. By taking a psychological history, it became evident that she had all the obsessive, compulsive characteristics of anorexia nervosa, including avoiding meals with her husband; she liked to cook but never ate with family members.

Her consultations with the gynecologists and endocrinologists were part of the denial process. Unconsciously, she probably knew that the amenorrhea could be caused by her successful loss of weight. When anorexia nervosa was diagnosed, she was able to give up the denial and admit to the anorectic habits she had never before mentioned to a physician. She was willing and motivated to receive psychotherapy to gain the necessary weight, resume menstruation, and become pregnant.

Because this patient did not look too thin, and was even attractive, anorexia nervosa was not suspected. This emphasizes the need for taking a good history, including the initial weight. A good history could have prevented the elaborate endocrinological and gynecological studies. It could have helped the previous physicians diagnose the condition correctly earlier, without need for hormonal therapy to trigger menstrual periods.

It is important for physicians to be aware of the criteria for diagnosis of anorexia nervosa. The *Diagnostic and Statistical Manual of Mental Disorders* (DSM-III) of the American Psychiatric Association lists the following criteria.

1. Intense fear of becoming obese, which does not diminish as weight loss progresses.
2. Disturbance of body image, such as claiming to feel fat even when emaciated.
3. Weight loss of at least 25% of original body weight; if under 18 years of age, weight loss from original body weight plus projected weight gain expected from growth charts combine to make the 25%.

4. Refusal to maintain body weight over a minimal normal weight for age and weight.
5. No known physical illness that would account for the weight loss.
6. Amenorrhea.

It is important to rule out other physical conditions that might lead to weight loss, such as terminal malignancy or gastrointestinal-tract disorder (terminal ileitis, tuberculosis of the gastrointestinal tract). Suprasellar or hypophyseal tumor should also be ruled out. Loss of appetite due to severe depressive illness should also be considered, as well as a schizophrenic disorder in which there are bizarre eating patterns. Some girls might binge and vomit but not have severe weight loss. In such cases, a diagnosis of bulimia might be justified. Only if the weight loss in the bulimic patient surpasses 25% of original body weight is the diagnosis of the bulimic type of anorexia nervosa, or bulimarexia, justified.

The treatment of anorexia nervosa is elaborate and complicated because most of the patients are very resistant to treatment and refuse to give up their denial. They might also be resistant to changes in their obsessive, compulsive habits. Because of the resistance, it is important that the therapist be highly sensitive to the needs of the patients but still be firm and able to resist the typically manipulative behavior of these patients. There is no single therapy that is always completely successful in the treatment of this disorder. It is important to tailor the treatment modality to the specific problems of each patient. The best results are being achieved in large medical centers in which special remedial programs for anorexia nervosa are established. The therapist in charge of the treatment should work with a team in which there is complete collaboration among all team members, so that the patient will not be able to manipulate one therapist against the other. Frequent meetings of team members are important to assess progress in therapy.

The Cleveland Clinic Center admits 70 to 100 new patients with anorexia nervosa each year. Many former patients who live in the Cleveland area continue to help other patients through the local Anorexia Aid Society. The patients have monthly group meetings, and separate meetings are held for parents. During the meetings, the patients discuss their difficulties and problems and encourage resistant anorectic persons to initiate treatment. This type of help is similar to that given in other self-help groups, such as Alcoholics Anonymous. Professionals are invited to give talks about eating disorders and to advise parents in how to relate to their anorectic children. The growth of the Anorexic Aid Society as a self-help group is encouraging, since part of their goal is to enhance the recognition of the problem by professionals and lay people so that the diagnosis will be made earlier. Usually, the sooner the diagnosis is confirmed, the better the prognosis. Treatment can be more successful when the denial mechanism and obsessive, compulsive habits are not yet deeply imbedded into the personalities of the patients and they are therefore more ready to give up these habits.

2

History of
Anorexia Nervosa

Eugene L. Bliss, M.D.

A young woman thus afflicted, her clothes scarcely hanging together on her anatomy, her pulse slow and slack, her temperature two degrees below the normal mean, her bowels closed, her hair like that of a corpse— dry and lustreless—her face and limbs ashy and cold, her hollow eyes the only vivid thing about her—this wan creature whose daily food might lie on a crownpiece, will be busy—yet on what funds God only knows.[1]

Such is the terse description of anorexia nervosa, a disorder that has perplexed and intrigued physicians for centuries. It has long been realized that the basic disturbance is the patient's adamant refusal to eat, but why anyone should adopt so perverse a behavior has not been well understood.

Some very early reports of cases can be found, but the first detailed descriptions by reputable scientists were those of Hobbes in 1668 [2], Reynolds in 1669 [3], and Morton in 1689 [4]. Included in Morton's description of consumption resulting from bleeding, gonorrhea, and diabetes and "happening to nurses from giving of suck beyond what their strength will allow" were two cases of psychogenic malnutrition. Not until the late nineteenth century, however, when Gull in England and Laseque in France both published series of cases [5, 6], was an interest in this condition stimulated in Europe. Many papers followed, chiefly by the French and English, near the turn of the century, and during this period the description of the disorder was delineated. At first it was clearly realized that anorexia nervosa was a psychogenic malnutrition. Only later was confusion introduced and an organic basis for the disorder advocated. In part, the biological thesis was due to the temper of the times—a dedication to morbid pathology and medical disease. Another factor was the description of panhypopituitarism by the German pathologist, Simmonds, who noted that several of his cases had become cachectic terminally. Although it was later demonstrated that pituitary disease is not usually accompanied by malnutrition except terminally, the harm had been done, and medical people continued to associate cachexia with pituitary disease and pituitary disease with anorexia nervosa. Because of this, and because amenorrhea was so frequently a part of the disorder, every possible endocrinopathy was attributed to anorectic patients, and, accordingly, they were treated with every available endocrine preparation. Some investigators, who were concerned with the inner workings of the mind, focused their attention on the psychodynamics of anorexia nervosa in an effort to understand the mental vagaries of these patients.

By the early twentieth century, the clinical features of the disorder were well defined. It was known that sporadic cases occurred at all ages, but the vast majority were clustered in the late teens and early twenties. Most cases were found in females, although a small percentage occurred in males. The mechanism of weight loss was a reduction in caloric intake, although the malnutrition could be attributed to extreme overactivity in a few cases. The typical anorectic patient ate parsimoniously, often consuming less than 500 calories a day. Some followed unusual diets with eccentric choices of food, such as evaporated milk curds or bread toasted rock hard. Many lost their appetites, but some did not; some induced vomiting or went on sporadic eating binges like the sprees of alcoholics, only to suffer remorse later, leading to lengthy periods of semistarvation. Others, intent on being slim, hid their food or disposed of it surreptitiously. Finally, some anorectic patients became virtually addicted to cathartics in an effort to purge their intestines of unwanted nutriments.

Whether the technique was semistarvation, exercise, vomiting, or self-induced diarrhea, the purpose was the same—to reduce calories in order to reduce weight. As strange as these strategies might seem, they were reasonable when viewed from the perspective of the patient, who was determined for personal reasons to lose weight or was afraid to eat because food passing through the gastrointestinal tract induced intolerable discomforts and fears.

Many patients displayed remarkable energy despite their cachexia. As Sir William Gull stated: "It seemed hardly possible that a body so wasted could undergo exercise so agreeably" [5]. Others, however, were initially neurasthenic and weak, and all patients became feeble when their weights reached critically low levels.

Finally, there was a plethora of physical findings, including amenorrhea, constipation, hypotension, bradycardia, and mild anemia—all, or almost all, features of the cachectic state and attributable to the physiology of malnutrition. In the early psychiatric literature, these patients were classified under a variety of designations, implying a heterogeneity of psychiatric disorders. Some were considered hysterics or obsessional neurotics, a few were thought to be schizophrenic, but most were identified as depressed, unhappy adolescents with a pathological fear of obesity.

The typical story was that of the obese adolescent who was chided by friends for her overweight and then began a diet that ran amok. She developed the fear that she had little control over her appetite—if her eating were not relentlessly curbed, gluttony and obesity might return. As a result, she maintained a diet of semistarvation to avoid the risk of a relaxation of restraints, which might lead to the disaster of obesity.

Although this is a simplified description, it summarizes the main features of the anorexia nervosa syndrome—known since the turn of the century, but continuing to perplex physicians [7].

References

1. Allbutt, T.C., and Rolleston, H.D. *A System of Medicine*. London: Macmillan and Co., 1908.

2. Hobbes, T. Letter 1668. In S.J. Gee, *Medical Lectures and Clinical Aphorisms*. London: Oxford University Press, 1908.

3. Reynolds, J. *A Discourse on Prodigious Abstinence*. London, 1669.

4. Morton, R. *Phthisiologica—or A Treatise of Consumption*. London, 1694.

5. Gull, W. Anorexia nervosa (apepsia hysterica, anorexia hysterica). *Trans. Clin. Soc. Lond.* 7:22–31, 1874.

6. Laseque, C. De l'anorexie hysterique. *Arch. Gen. Med.* 1:385, 1873.

7. Bliss, E.L., and Branch, C.H.H. *Anorexia Nervosa. Its History, Psychology and Biology*. New York: Paul B. Hoeber, 1960.

3

Theoretical Perspectives on Anorexia Nervosa

Lynne M. Dorman, M.A.

Several theoretical models have been used to conceptualize the etiology of the anorexia nervosa syndrome. The classic psychoanalytical conception of anorexia nervosa draws an analogy between eating behavior and sexual instincts. Psychoanalytical concepts emphasize aggressive and libidinal drive fixation at the oral level of psychosexual development, regression in instinctual drives, and symptom formation around oral conflict occurring in young women who are unable to confront the demands of mature genitality. Classically, refusal of nourishment was believed to represent a defense against oral-impregnation fantasies, whereas bulimia was considered a breakthrough of unconscious desires for gratification. This viewpoint is somewhat restrictive, however, in its description and application.

More recently, authors working within the psychodynamic framework have expanded their notions to include a recognition of various ego deficits, particularly as they relate to early developmental factors. Hilde Bruch focuses on the primary role of specific perceptual-cognitive defects in ego functioning [1]. She contends that the main issue underlying the anorectic patient's "relentless pursuit of thinness" is the struggle for control and for a sense of identity and personal effectiveness. Bruch ascribes the blame for the anorectic person's development of a helpless self to the family's (primarily the mother's) failure to transmit an adequate sense of self-efficacy to the child.

Normal development involves the child's initiation of behaviors as well as response to external stimuli. Healthy development depends on a balance of appropriate responses by the mother to the clues coming from the child and on adequate stimulation from the environment. Bruch explains that, if the signals emitted by the hungry child are responded to appropriately by the mother, the child attunes to hunger as a distinct sensation. If the mother responds to the child's nutritional needs in an unsatisfactory manner (oversolicitous, neglectful, or inhibiting), the child does not learn to differentiate between the hunger sensations and the other sources of bodily discomfort. Hence, the child grows up lacking a discriminating awareness of physiological sensations and without a sense of control over the sensations. This sort of behavorial transaction, frequently observed in the developmental histories of anorectic patients, results in serious intrapsychic disturbances in hunger awareness, which generalize to disturbances in other ego functions. The child is deprived of the feeling that she is in control of her life. She feels helpless, enslaved, and exploited by internal growth urges and opposing external demands. Panicked and overwhelmed, she turns to her body to exercise control and attempts to gain respect and a sense of self by literally altering her body size [2].

Other clinicians working within the psychodynamic framework emphasize that early maternal deprivation produces permanent defects in the ego structure of anorexia nervosa patients, leaving them ill-prepared to cope with the adjustment to adulthood.

Sours has attempted to integrate the developmental notions of Margaret Mahler, regarding intrapsychic separation and individuation, into his explanation of how anorexia nervosa evolves [3]. He focuses on the crisis of the rapprochement stage as the critical period of the separation-individuation struggle. The child is believed to be bonded to a demanding, domineering mother who achieves self-gratification through the passive submission and perfection of the child. The youngster is incapable of disentangling herself from the dyadic attachment, which promotes fusion rather than nurturance. Sours states that the suppressed affects are bound up in somatic form, which fosters confusion in the individual in interpreting internal and environmental experiences.

Masterson considers that borderline personality organization underlies the anorexia nervosa syndrome such that the anorectic person is fixated at the oral-narcissistic stage of development [4]. As in Sour's conception, he links the pathological condition to a failure in empathy during the rapprochement subphase. The child is caught in a bind between her own developmental drive for individuation and autonomy and the withdrawal of the mother's emotional supplies that are required for growth. In an attempt to cope with the anxiety generated from the conflict, the child utilizes ego-splitting, denial, and primitive-idealization defense mechanisms. The young child turns her back on her emerging individuality, which threatens her maternal support. Even after separation, the child clings to her mother in an effort to be protected from the return of feelings of abandonment into awareness. Some of the qualities delineated as part of the anorectic syndrome are the following borderline characteristics: failure of development of an integrated self-concept, chronic overdependence on external objects alternating with distancing, depression, rage, fear, guilt, helplessness, lack of impulse control, anxiety tolerance, and development of sublimatory channels. The eruption of primitive affect states and self-aggressive strivings connected with early negative introjections is commonly observed in the anorexia nervosa patient [5].

In partial agreement with this postulation, Kramer emphasizes the child's contribution to the disturbed mother-child interaction and to her own inherent pathology [6]. Kramer ascribes the pathology to the "strength of the child's drives, harshness of its ambivalence, and reaction to its distorted fantasies" (p. 577), rather than to the faulty nurturance of the overbearing mother. In any event, inadequate mastery at this stage is believed to detrimentally affect the adolescence of these individuals, thus fostering the psychopathological condition that leads to development of the anorexia nervosa syndrome.

From a rather different perspective, the open-systems model employed by the structural family therapists broadens the focus from the sick child to the sick child within his family [7]. Minuchin and his colleagues have generated the family model which postulates that three factors in conjunction are necessary for the genesis of severe psychosomatic illness in children. First, the child must be physiologically vulnerable. Next, the family can be described as having the following four transactional characteristics: enmeshment, overprotectiveness, rigidity, and lack of conflict resolution. Finally, the sick child is seen to play an important role in the family's pattern of conflict avoidance. The role is considered to be an important source of reinforcement for the child's symptoms.

The selection of psychomatic symptoms is believed to be related to the family's history and organization. More specifically, in families with an anorectic child, other family members frequently worry about table manners, follow food fads, and are overconcerned with diet. The child develops a family organization that is fertile for the emergence and utilization of the adopted symptom.

The anorexia nervosa syndrome is activated by any number of possible events that upset the family homeostasis. Often the precipitating event revolves around an issue of normal development, which family members ignite into a major developmental crisis. Since any change, regardless of its magnitude serves to threaten the usual family transactional patterns, all the family members become mobilized in an effort to protect the system and to coerce the fluctuating member back into her original role. The target child (the anorectic child), feeling the stress within the system, responds with the symptoms, which are employed as a detouring device for the family's problems. The family members unite in concern, and thus the anorectic symptoms are reinforced and perpetuated [7].

A number of hypotheses can be advanced from the theoretical notions regarding the etiology of anorexia nervosa. It is believed that certain demographic and family variables may be correlated with specific personality traits.

According to Bruch's conceptualization, a positive correlation may be predicted between depression in the anorectic patient and the ages of the parents. This formulation is based on the notion that the anorectic child who has older parents often emerges from a well-established, overcontrolled home environment, which leaves the child with a sense of helplessness, entrapment, and ineffectiveness in her own environment.

In reference to psychoanalytical theories, one would expect to discover a repression of sexual drives and regression to a more infantile level in patients who are unable to deal with the onset of mature genital adjustment. One would typically expect these conflicts in young anorectic patients at the prepubertal or pubescent stage of development. Thus, among the younger patients, one could predict an attitude of naivete, immaturity, and self-centeredness, as well as a denial of psychological discomfort.

The theoretical and clinical literature frequently associates eating and dieting patterns with impulse-control issues. Therefore, the anorectic patients with rigid dieting behavior who lose weight by simple starvation tend to be viewed as highly controlled, rigid, and compulsive individuals. Bulimic patients (individuals who maintain an alternating pattern of gorging and starving), however, tend to have attitudes of rebelliousness, aggressiveness, and immaturity, as well as exhibitionist and acting-out behaviors.

According to the family-interactional perspective, large, enmeshed families generally transfer the blame to a sole member of the family in order to maintain homeostasis. The anorectic child, who becomes the scapegoat, becomes socially alienated, aloof, and isolated. One would expect to find a high degree of introversion and alienation among anorectic children in this type of family.

In keeping with the foregoing concepts, the following hypotheses are set forth:

1. A positive correlation exists between age of parents and depression in anorexia nervosa.
2. A negative correlation exists between age of onset of anorexia nervosa and hysterical personality traits.
3. A positive correlation exists between simple starvation-dieting behavior and rigid, moralistic personality features.
4. A positive correlation exists between bulimic behavior and acting-out, antisocial tendencies.
5. A positive correlation exists between large family size and degree of social alienation in the anorectic person.

Although numerous studies have indicated that an early age of onset is generally associated with a better prognosis, it is often difficult to document the precise age of onset because the definition of exactly what signifies the onset is unclear. Since the age of onset is primarily a subjective determination made by the anorectic person and her family, it is likely to be identified differently because of such reasons as denial and uncertainty.

The patient's age at consultation with the physician, psychologist, psychiatrist, and so forth, appears to be a less ambiguous measure and, in conjunction with the duration of the disorder, gives a better indication of the prognosis. It seems that the younger the patient, the better the chance for recovery, if only because the symptoms are generally less inbred than they are in the older patient. The longer the symptoms persist, the worse they become. According to Crisp, the disorder serves and exists to separate the person from biological and social growth [8]. As the person becomes more isolated within her biologically immature state, she becomes more alienated from effective peer relationship, and it becomes more difficult for her to negotiate the tasks of adulthood [9,10].

One of the major reasons that chronicity confers a worse natural prognosis is that different sorts of behaviors often develop during the course of the illness. It has been noted that a long-standing pattern of abstinence may eventually develop into a more malignant pattern of bulimia, vomiting, and purging. Several studies have distinguished noticeable differences between anorectic patients who exclusively limit their caloric intake and those who have developed a pattern of binging and vomiting (bulimic patients). The latter group generally is reported to be premorbidly obese. Consequently, bulimic patients never achieve as low a weight as the restricters do. These women tend to have more labile moods and to feel more out of control. They rely on laxatives, diuretics, and vomiting to reduce their weight, which appears to be an external manifestation of their lack of control. They tend to exhibit more destructive, impulsive behaviors, as manifested by suicide attempts, self-mutilation, and kleptomania. Although the bulimic patients, like the restricters, steadfastly pursue a thin body image, they deal with their drives in an extreme, pathological fashion. This may be partly due to their constitutional tendency to be obese or to unhealthy personality attributes or ego deficits. In any case, this pattern tends to be associated with a more severe pathological condition. Thus, it is possible to make several hypotheses based on these previous findings:

1. Younger patients demonstrate a less severe psychopathological condition.
2. The longer the duration of the illness, the greater the psychopathological condition.
3. A pattern of binging and vomiting is related to a greater psychopathological condition.

References

1. Bruch, H. *Eating Disorders: Obesity, Anorexia Nervosa and the Person Within.* New York: Basic Books, 1973.

2. Bruch, H. *The psychiatric differential diagnosis of anorexia nervosa.* In J.E. Meyer, and H. Feldman (Eds.), Anorexia Nervosa-Symposium in Gottigen, Stuttgart, West Germany, Georg Thieme, 1965.

3. Sours, J. The anorexia nervosa syndrome: Phenomenologic and psychodynamic components. *Psychiat. Q.* 43:240, 1969.

4. Masterson, F. Primary anorexia nervosa in the borderline adolescent: An object-relations review in borderline personality disorders. In P. Hartocollis (Ed.), New York: International Universities Press, 1977.

5. Kernberg, O.F. *Borderline Conditions and Pathological Narcissism.* New York: Jason Aronson, 1975.

6. Kramer, S. A discussion of the paper by John A. Sours on: The anorexia syndrome. *Int. J. Psychoanal.* 55:577, 1974.

7. Minuchin, S., Rosman, B.L. and Baker L. *Psychosomatic families: Anorexia Nervosa in context,* Cambridge: Harvard University Press, 1978.

8. Crisp, A. Diagnosis and outcome of anorexia nervosa: The St. George's view. *Proc. R. Soc. Med.* 70:464, 1977.

9. Theander, S. A psychiatric investigation of 94 female patients. *Acta Psychiatr. Scand. [Suppl.]* 6:214, 1970.

10. Morgan, H.G., and Russell, G.F.M. VAlue of family background and clinical features or predictors of long-term outcome in anorexia nervosa: Four years follow-up study of 41 patients. *Psychol. Med.* 5:355, 1975.

4

The Role of the Primary-Care Physician in the Diagnosis and Management of Anorexia Nervosa

Edmund J. Doering, M.D.

This chapter will discuss the initial diagnostic approach we have used in the last five years to evaluate 300 adolescents and young adults who have presented to the Cleveland Clinic with weight loss, amenorrhea, or other symptoms suggestive of anorexia nervosa. Of the 300 patients, 240 were found to have anorexia nervosa. In addition, the chapter will discuss my role as a nonpsychiatric physician in the initial management and ongoing care of these patients.

Forms of Anorexia Nervosa

We have found it useful to subclassify patients with abnormal eating behavior and weight loss with or without amenorrhea. We recognize a classic form of anorexia nervosa, characterized by the development of secondary amenorrhea in a teenage female near the time of onset of severe weight loss and abnormal eating behavior. Our psychiatric colleagues have further subdivided this group of teenagers into compulsive, hysterical, and schizoid personalities, although I do not have the expertise to do this myself. The weight loss in classic anorexia nervosa may be so rapid that patients have a 20% to 25% loss in body weight within two or three months of the onset of weight loss. At this point, they may have missed only one or two menstrual cycles and thus do not fulfill the stricter diagnostic criteria for anorexia nervosa. Alternatively, weight loss may be gradual, extending over a period of a year or two, and amenorrhea may have existed for as long as two years. It is our impression that patients with the former characteristics respond more rapidly to treatment than those with the latter.

Anorexia nervosa in a prepuberal female results in a "failure-to-thrive" syndrome. Both height and weight deviate from expected growth curves; bone age falls behind chronological age; and thelarche often does not occur. In such patients, we have observed that intrafamilial conflict about eating behavior is practically universal.

Anorexia nervosa may occur in boys, both before and after puberty. We have found significant psychopathological conditions in addition to abnormal eating behavior in a higher percentage of boys than girls with anorexia nervosa. Amenorrhea excepted, the behavior and physical symptoms of anorectic boys are similar to those of anorectic girls. It is our impression, however, that boys respond more rapidly and more completely to therapy and thus should be separately categorized.

Similarly, we have identified a group of women whose anorectic behavior, weight loss, and amenorrhea began in the third and fourth decades of life. By definition, these women have no history of amenorrhea or anorectic behavior during adolescence, and their symptoms often develop rather insidiously. Weight loss in this group of patients tends to be less extreme than in the younger patients. Perhaps because of the more protracted abnormal eating behavior, therapy may be more difficult.

Bulimia (binge overeating), which is usually associated with self-induced vomiting, may occur in any of the previously mentioned forms of anorexia nervosa. Bulimic patients may develop profound and life-threatening abnormalities of electrolyte levels and acid-base balance. Additionally, we believe that bulimic patients may be at higher risk of developing drug or alcohol dependency in their later years.

The final category in which patients may be placed is secondary anorexia nervosa. Schizophrenia may present rarely with severe weight loss and amenorrhea. Although depression is common in patients with anorexia nervosa, a careful history might reveal that significant depression preceded the onset of weight loss or amenorrhea. We consider that such patients have a primary affective disorder with secondary anorexia nervosa.

The clinical picture of a typical anorexia nervosa patient is helpful, but we must remember that the diagnosis rests on the phobia that produces the abnormal eating behavior, not on the eating behavior itself or the resulting signs and symptoms of malnutrition. The typical patient would be a 13- to 15-year-old, white, upper-middle-class female who had had the onset of normal menses a year or more prior to the onset of weight loss. Within two or three months, secondary amenorrhea would occur, and the weight loss would continue, despite parental and peer pressure to gain weight. The initial history would reveal little family conflict other than that surrounding the eating behavior of the anorectic child. The parents would state that the patient's early life was entirely normal and that, if anything, she was an extremely well-behaved young lady who was always willing and able to please her parents. The parents would admit to having rather high expectations for their children. They would report that the patient tended to eat alone, to cut her food into extremely small pieces, to eat very slowly, and to be preoccupied with food, nutrition, and food preparation. The patient would admit to being extremely orderly, if not compulsive, in her daily life. Her undergarments would be neatly folded and stacked in a bureau drawer, rather than thrown in, as is the norm at this age. Such a girl might jog for miles every day, despite minimal caloric intake. She would be perceived by her peers as a loner, and she would report constipation and intolerance of cold. On physical examination, we would expect to find that the patient had rather flat affect, but impeccable grooming. Further examination would reveal an emaciated frame with bony landmarks protruding through thin subcutaneous tissues. There would be a marked reduction in muscle mass, as evidenced by skin redundancy, and lanugo over the trunk and extremities, dystrophic hair and nails, hypothermia, bradycardia, hyporeflexia, and possibly mild to moderate hepatosplenomegaly. After their examinations, some patients would look the physician straight in the eye and say that they were still concerned that they were too fat. Practically all such patients would say that their thighs, breasts, lower abdomens, or some other anatomic features were too big or too fat.

No single patient will ever exhibit all the foregoing historical and physical features of anorexia nervosa. The initial history and physical examination, however, should give an overall impression of whether the patient's personality and physical characteristics are consistent or inconsistent with the diagnosis of anorexia nervosa.

Diagnostic Criteria

The official diagnostic criteria for classic anorexia nervosa are presented in table 4-1. These diagnostic criteria were intended for the use of researchers. To compare evaluation or treatment techniques, one must be sure to compare like cases. A 26-year-old woman who fulfills the other criteria has anorexia nervosa, but it would be inappropriate to compare her response to therapy with that of a 14-year-old girl. We believe that overly restrictive diagnostic criteria, when

Table 4-1
Diagnostic Criteria for Anorexia Nervosa

1. Age of onset less than 25 years
2. Anorexia, with accompanying weight loss of at least 25% of original body weight
3. A distorted, implacable attitude toward eating, food, or weight that overrides hunger, admonitions, reassurance, and threats (for example, denial of illness and failure to recognize nutritional needs; apparent enjoyment of losing weight, with overt evidence that food refusal is a pleasurable indulgence; a desired body image of extreme thinness, with overt evidence that it is rewarding to the patient to achieve and maintain this state; and unusual hoarding or handling of food)
4. No known medical illness that could account for the anorexia and weight loss
5. No other known psychiatric disorder, with particular reference to primary affective disorders, schizophrenia, obsessive-compulsive and phobic neurosis (on the assumption that, although it may appear phobic or obsessional, food refusal alone is not sufficient to qualify for obsessive-compulsive or phobic disease)
6. At least two of the following manifestations: amenorrhea, lanugo, bradycardia (persistent resting-pulse rate of 60 beats per minute or less), periods of overactivity, episodes of bulimia, vomiting (may be self-induced)

inappropriately applied, may delay the onset of treatment, to the detriment of the patient. Thus, a girl with a 20-pound weight loss must not be denied appropriate therapy until she loses another 5 pounds.

Differential Diagnosis

The differential diagnosis of anorexia nervosa includes all psychiatric and physical problems that are capable of producing severe malnutrition, amenorrhea, or abnormal eating behavior. Our experience with 300 patients has demonstrated that it is the careful history, not the physical examination or laboratory and roentgenographic results, that provides the diagnosis. The physical, laboratory, and roentgenographic examinations serve to exclude or diagnose coexisting medical problems and to define the clinical severity of malnutrition.

Environmental stress (such as that caused by the first year away from home at college, fear of pregnancy, or simultaneous dieting with exercise) may produce amenorrhea, loss of appetite, and weight loss without anorexia nervosa. The histories of patients suffering such stress will reveal that their primary concern is loneliness, fear of pregnancy, improved athletic or artistic performance, and the like, not preoccupation with food, food preparation, and weight loss. These patients are rarely proud of their ability to lose weight.

Gastrointestinal diseases, especially regional ileitis (Crohn disease), may coexist with anorexia nervosa. Irritable-bowel syndrome, cyclic vomiting, and malabsorptive states may cause malnutrition, which in turn may result in secondary changes in mood and personality. Again, the history is crucial for establishing the correct diagnosis.

Severe hypothyroidism, thyrotoxicosis, panhypopituitarism (Simmonds disease), and juvenile diabetes mellitus may cause severe malnutrition. Polydipsia and polyuria may occur in anorexia nervosa patients who assuage their appetites by ingesting large volumes of water or diet drinks. It is time-consuming, complicated, and very expensive to use the endocrinology laboratory in diagnosing anorexia nervosa. Anorexia nervosa patients often have multiple abnormalities of endocrine hormone blood levels, and the unsuspecting clinician, armed with an inadequate history, may investigate one after another in aiming toward an elusive endocrine diagnosis. Because patients have low triiodothyronine and gonadotrophin levels, abnormal diurnal cortisol variation, and the like, much has been published on the endocrine abnormalities associated with anorexia nervosa, but these abnormalities are of little clinical usefulness in making a diagnosis of anorexia nervosa. Such tests do serve to exclude coexisting endocrine disease, however, especially severe hypothyroidism. Laboratory evaluation of patients with anorexia nervosa will be described and justified in the next section.

Leukemia, lymphomas, and other advanced solid tumors may produce malnutrition. There should be no difficulty, however, in distinguishing patients with these problems from patients with anorexia nervosa. Craniopharyngioma and other suprasellar tumors may rarely result in a syndrome indistinguishable by history, physical examination, and laboratory evaluation from anorexia nervosa. For this reason, it is mandatory that a lateral skull film or, preferably, a head CAT scan with contrast be done on all patients to exclude this possibility.

Other chronic diseases—such as cystic fibrosis, sickle-cell disease, chronic pyelonephritis, subacute bacterial endocarditis, Kartagener syndrome, juvenile rheumatoid arthritis, and systemic lupus erythematosus—may result in a wasted, malnourished, amenorrheic patient. These diseases should not produce historical data consistent with the diagnosis of anorexia nervosa unless the patient also has anorexia nervosa.

Hyperplasia of the juxtaglomerular apparatus with hyperaldosteronism and hypokalemic alkalosis (Bartter syndrome) may mimic psychiatric illness. The psychiatric illness, however, will have few, if any, of the psychiatric features of anorexia nervosa.

Drug and environmental-toxin exposure may result in extreme weight loss and, less commonly, amenorrhea. Amphetamine abuse, imipramine hydrochloride therapy for adolescent enuresis, methylphenidate hydrochloride therapy for hyperactivity, and heroin addiction are commonly encountered as causes of malnutrition. More rarely, exposure to ammonia, nitrogen oxides, and other environmental toxins may lead to weight loss.

Standard Laboratory and Roentgenographic Evaluation of Anorexia Nervosa Patients

From the foregoing differential diagnosis, we have been able to develop a list of laboratory and roentgenographic procedures that we believe are sufficient to exclude or diagnose coexisting medical problems as well as to establish the severity of malnutrition and acid-base and electrolyte disturbances resulting from anorexia nervosa (see table 4-2).

Hemoglobin level, white blood count, and differential white blood count are determined. Anemia is evaluated as it would be in any other patient. Anorectic patients tend not to be iron- or folate-deficient, and anemia, when present has been mild. Fewer than 10% of our patients are found to be anemic. The white blood count is often low, and an absolute granulocyte count of less than 2,000/ cu mm is not uncommon. Despite their neutropenia, our patients do not seem to be at increased risk for bacterial or fungal infection.

The sedimentation rate has been uniformly normal in patients without coexisting Crohn disease, acute infection, or other chronic inflammatory process.

A normal qualitative or semiquantitative stool-fat level excludes significant malabsorption. Protein malnutrition so severe as to produce malabsorption may

Table 4-2

Standard Roentgenographic and Laboratory Tests

1. Hemoglobin level, white blood cell count, and differential white blood cell count
2. Sedimentation rate
3. Qualitative or semiquantitative stool-fat level
4. SMA-18 or equivalent
5. Urinalysis
6. Purified protein derivative (PPD) or tine tuberculin test and chest roentgenogram
7. Triiodothyronine (T_3) and total thyroxine concentration (T_4) or free-thyroxine index
8. Morning and evening plasma cortisol, luteinizing hormone (LH), follicle-stimulating hormone (FSH), and prolactin assays
9. Head CAT scan with contrast
10. Complete gastrointestinal (GI) roentgenographic series, including small bowel
11. Pelvic examination
12. Electrodardiogram (ECG)

occur in anorexia nervosa, but this would be an extremely late finding, seen at a time when there should be no question about the diagnosis of anorexia nervosa. A fasting multichannel blood chemistry and electrolyte profile (such as the SMA-18) serves to exclude severe hepatic and renal disease and will usually reveal a serum cholesterol value that is either elevated or below normal but rarely within the normal range. The alkaline phosphatase level may be normal at a time when one would expect it to be elevated during the adolescent growth spurt. The calcium and serum albumin levels are often low in patients with significant vomiting. Other anorectic patients tend not to be protein-malnourished. Protracted vomiting also may result in significant hypokalemia and compensatory hypercarbia.

Patients with hypokalemia should have determinations of their urinary electrolyte levels. In the presence of hypokalemia, the urine potassium level should be negligible. A normal or elevated urine potassium level with hypokalemia is suggestive of Bartter syndrome or primary hyperaldosteronuria. Urinalysis and urine culture are performed routinely.

A chest roentgenogram and intermediate-strength PPD should exclude acute miliary or chronic active tuberculosis, to which patients with anorexia nervosa may have a slight predisposition.

A free-thyroxine index, a ratio of triiodothyronine (T_3) to total thyroxine concentration (T_4), or a T_4 determination should serve to exclude significant thyroid disease. Our anorectic patients have had a low T_3 level but usually a normal T_4 level. Those patients with a low T_4 level have had a normal thyroid-stimulating hormone (TSH) level, which serves to distinguish them from patients with hypothyroidism.

We routinely perform luteinizing hormone (LH), follicle-stimulating hormone (FSH), and prolactin assays. We expect the levels to be normal or low but are aware of the rare pituitary or hypothalamic tumor that might mimic anorexia nervosa.

Morning and evening plasma cortisol levels have been determined routinely on our patients. Patients who have lost more than 25% or 30% of their body weight have generally lost the normal diurnal cortisol variation. The cortisol level has not been low enough to permit any confusion with Addison disease or Simmonds disease.

We have performed an upper gastrointestinal roentgenographic series, small-bowel follow-through, and barium enema examination in all our patients. The yield from these gastrointestinal roentgenograms has been low, but the previously mentioned tendency for Crohn disease to coexist with anorexia nervosa provides justification [1].

A pediatrician or a gynecologist specializing in adolescence performs a pelvic examination on all our anorexia nervosa patients. Most of our patients have had numerous questions regarding fertility and eventual resumption of normal menses, and they appreciate the reassurance that a complete bimanual examination has been normal. In prepuberal females, we occasionally have performed a rectal examination alone. If a normal uterus and adnexa are palpable, a vaginal examination is not performed.

This laboratory and roentgenographic evaluation is completed in 48 hours for an inpatient and in 72 hours for an outpatient. Outpatient evaluation is undertaken in patients for whom outpatient psychotherapy is planned and whose malnutrition is not severe. All patients with bulimia and vomiting, a history of syncope, bradycardia less than 55 beats per minute, or weight less than 80 pounds are admitted to an adolescent medical-surgical inpatient unit for evaluation.

Initial Management

Following a thorough medical history, it has been possible to make a certain diagnosis of anorexia nervosa in the majority of patients. During the first office visit, this impression is discussed with the patient and parents. At least half of these families had already read Hilde Bruch's *The Golden Cage*, a well-written book that appears, however, to engender shame in anorectic patients and guilt in their parents. We attempt to explain the pathophysiology of anorexia nervosa in such a way as to assuage this shame and guilt. We recognize a typical family setting in which anorexia nervosa occurs. The parenting is aggressive and success-oriented, with pride and high expectations for the children's achievements. Such a family might be considered a prerequisite for a young woman who will one day attend law, medical, or graduate school, and we point out that this setting of aggressive, success-oriented parenting does not always result in anorexia nervosa. We then describe the poorly understood interaction between the cerebral cortex and the hypothalamus. We have found it convenient to invoke homunculi (the little men employed by scientists of the Dark Ages) in explaining how a genetic predisposition to an abnormally sensitive connection between the cortex and hypothalamus might result in the clinical disease anorexia nervosa. We encourage patients to be annoyed that their daytime hours are filled with time-wasting preoccupation with food, body image, and other anorectic behavior. We point out that there is no reason for them to be ashamed of this behavior, since it is not their fault that they have anorexia nervosa. The primary goal of initial management is to motivate prompt psychiatric intervention. We point out that untreated anorexia nervosa is a life-threatening illness; mortality figures available to the public, mostly from the older literature, range from 10% to more than 20%. We also point out that a delay in beginning effective psychotherapy results in an increased duration of expensive psychotherapy and, regrettably, decreases the likelihood of permanent or complete disease control. Most patients will promise that they can gain weight on their own, and the primary-care physician must emphasize confidently that only a mental-health professional can keep this problem from recurring. We have found that parents who feel significant guilt also feel responsible for solving the patient's problem on their own. Most patients readily tell their parents that the more nagging they receive about gaining weight, the easier it is for them not to eat. At this point, parents feel helpless; the teenager is terrified that she is crazy; and the time has come for the physician to provide confident, firm guidance. The parents need to feel that they are in good hands. Otherwise, their overwhelming need to be involved will surely sabotage the treatment effort. We explain to the parents that we understand their feeling of helplessness, since it is a feeling that we share. We tell them that nagging and forced tube feeding are equally destructive to the psychotherapeutic goal of the patient's attaining independence and self-confidence.

Thus, in addition to motivating prompt psychiatric care, one of the goals of the initial office visit is to educate the parents about the patient's eating behavior. We point out that it would be best if they did not mention food, dieting, weight loss, vomiting, and so forth, in any setting other than family therapy. We also direct them to the National Anorexic Aid Society, which has proved to be an invaluable support group for parents of anorectic patients.

Follow-up Management

After the laboratory and roentgenographic evaluation, the patient and the parents are fully informed of the results of the testing. If mild ventricular dilatation and cerebral cortical atrophy are evident on the CAT scan, these abnormalities are shown to the patient and parents, with the reassurance that they represent a reversible decrease in brain water or lipid levels. Similarly, neutropenia, endocrine abnormalities, and all normal test results are discussed fully, with the goal of putting to rest any fears that a significant nonpsychiatric problem might be overlooked. Initial psychiatric evaluation takes place during the medical evaluation. If there is no significant coexisting medical problem, primary management responsibility is transferred to the mental-health professional following the medical evaluation. This transfer of primary responsibility does not imply a termination of responsibility by the primary-care physician. Suicidal ideation is not uncommon during hospitalization for medical evaluation, and patients with significant acid-base and electrolyte disturbances may need aggressive nonpsychiatric management for weeks following transfer of primary management responsibility to the psychiatrist.

Patients with anorexia nervosa are uncommonly adept at manipulating adults. They have been practicing for weeks or months on their parents and seem to relish the challenge of being able to play a psychiatrist off against a pediatrician and the reverse. Close communication between the medical and psychiatric services is thus essential. Life-threatening arrhythmias, tetany, and severe hypokalemia obviously require emergency management. We reemphasize that all management decisions should be shared by the adolescent-medicine and psychiatry services and that major management changes should not occur without close liaison. We must remember that the primary goal of psychotherapy is to engender in the patient an ability to control the anorectic behavior. Forced feeding, tube feeding, and the like (as well as parental nagging) are counterproductive from a psychotherapeutic viewpoint. A dilemma exists, however, in that we have found that it is practically impossible for patients to respond to psychotherapy until they have gained some weight. The severely cachectic, malnourished anorectic patient is extremely resistant to psychotherapy until a behavior-modification contract has proved successful in producing this necessary initial weight gain.

Intensive Supportive Care

Patients who continue to lose weight during psychiatric hospitalization occasionally require additional somatic therapy. A smaller number of patients initially present with such severe complications of malnutrition that intensive medical support is required from the onset of psychotherapy. Patients with ileus and gastric distention, significant arrhythmias, sepsis, coagulopathies, and hypoproteinemia of a degree to produce significant edema require emergency nutritional support. In the past, such patients have been heavily sedated and fed by nasogastric tube. We have found that patients do not tolerate tube feedings without sedation and will do anything in their power to sabotage weight gain. After a period of sedation and tube feeding, we found, all too often, that patients would slide back to a state requiring reinstitution of tube feedings. Total parenteral nutrition is an alternative feeding technique in which all essential nutrients are infused through a central venous line to sustain patients who cannot or will not eat. Hyperalimentation costs $300 to $400 per day in most institutions and has life-threatening potential risks. Because of its cost and the risk of complications, we have reserved the use of hyperalimentation for patients in whom tube feeding has failed. Maloney and Farrell reported that four depressed and socially withdrawn anorectic patients with intractable weight loss all demonstrated lasting weight gains following hyperalimentation with follow-up psychotherapy [2]. They noted an improvement in mood and surprising cooperation from their patients with intravenous feeding. The problems of ileus and gastric distention are avoided by using this technique, and it is possible that well-designed clinical studies will demonstrate an expanded role for total parenteral nutrition in the management of anorexia nervosa.

Conclusions

The primary-care physician is important in the process of recognizing and managing anorexia nervosa. A delay in diagnosis or failure to motivate prompt psychiatric intervention may result in a protracted clinical course. The diagnosis rests on a careful medical, social, and dietary history. Physical, laboratory, and roentgenographic examinations are required to estimate the degree of malnutrition and to diagnose or exclude coexisting medical problems. Motivation toward prompt psychiatric intervention is aided by alleviation of patient shame and parental guilt. The primary-care physician should attempt to educate the parents about the patient's abnormal eating behavior and must maintain a close liaison with psychiatric colleagues to avoid being manipulated by the patient.

References

1. Grand, R.J., and Homer, D.R. Approaches to inflammatory bowel disease in childhood and adolescence. *Pediatr. Clin. North. Am.* 22:835–850, 1975.

2. Maloney, M.J., and Farrell, M.K. Treatment of severe weight loss in anorexia nervosa with hyperalimentation and psychotherapy. *Am. J. Psychiatry.* 137(3):310–314, 1980.

Annotated Bibliography

1. Drossman, D.A., Ontjes, D.A., and Heizer, W.D. Anorexia nervosa. *Gastroenterology* 77:1115–1131, 1979. Dr. Drossman and his colleagues provide an excellent academic review of the endocrinological and other medical effects of severe malnutrition.

2. Meyer, H. The underweight adolescent. *Clin. Pediatr.* 19:819–823, 1980. This article is an extremely practical and concise review of disease states, including anorexia nervosa, that lead an adolescent to be underweight.

3. Lucas, A.R. The meaning of laboratory values in anorexia nervosa. *Mayo Clin. Proc.* 52:748–750, 1977.

4. Hurd, H.P., Palumf., P.J., and Gharif, H. Hypothalamic-endocrine dysfunction in anorexia nervosa. *Mayo Clin. Proc.* 52:711–716, 1977. Dr. Hurd and associates report on the endocrine abnormalities discovered in 101 patients with anorexia nervosa at the Mayo Clinic. Dr. Lucas's editorial in the same issue emphasizes that laboratory studies are primarily helpful in documenting the degree of malnutrition and that there is no laboratory profile that is diagnostic or even typical of anorexia nervosa.

5. Speroff, L., and Redwine, D.B. Exercise and menstrual function. *Physician Sports Med.* 8(5):42–52, 1980. To my knowledge, this is the only study reported in the literature that attempts to document and correlate secondary amenorrhea with strenuous exercise and weight loss. Among 900 amateur runners surveyed, secondary amenorrhea occurred in more than 14% of 164 nonpregnant female joggers who had lost 10 or more pounds. The authors emphasize the similarities between this type of amenorrhea and that seen in anorexia nervosa.

6. Hogan, W.M., Huerta, E., and Lucas, A.R. Diagnosing anorexia nervosa in males. *Psychosomatics* 15:122–126, 1974. Of 155 patients seen at the Mayo Clinic from 1969 through 1971, 15 (9.7%) were males. The authors discuss the criteria for diagnosis of anorexia nervosa in males and the slightly different differential diagnosis.

5

Hematological Changes Induced by Anorexia Nervosa

Paul G. Dyment, M.D.

When evaluating patients with anorexia nervosa, physicians are often concerned because of abnormalities that show up in the routine blood count. The purpose of this chapter is to review the medical literature on the subject and to provide some practical suggestions for the practitioner.

In their classic studies of the effects of starvation during World War II, Keys and associates reported the common occurrence of both normocytic, normochromic anemia and mild leukopenia, either with a normal differential count or with a slight lymphocytosis [1]. In kwashiorkor, pure red-cell aplasia is frequently seen [2]. It is therefore not surprising that we find hematological changes in many patients with anorexia nervosa. These three states of malnutrition are very different, however: wartime starvation is due to both protein and carbohydrate depletion, kwashiorkor is due to protein insufficiency, and anorexia nervosa is usually characterized by both caloric and carbohydrate depletion. Undoubtedly, it is this peculiar dietary pattern in anorexia nervosa that results in a hematological picture different from that of the other two forms of semistarvation.

In 1972, Mant and Faragher in Australia reported one of the few prospective series of patients with anorexia nervosa with particular reference to the hematopoietic system [3]. They described six patients, most of whom exhibited abnormal blood findings. It should be noted that this group of patients was unusual: they were older than patients with anorexia nervosa in the United States (16 to 44 years, average 28 years), two had died, and only one patient recovered. Five patients had anemia, and anisocytosis and poikilocytosis were commonly seen. Some acanthocytes (or spur cells) were the most typical abnormality in all of the patients, and these cells were present in large numbers in three. As the patients recovered clinically, this morphological picture improved.

They performed blood-volume studies on four patients and reported either normal or increased red-cell, plasma, and total blood volumes, with relatively greater increases in the plasma and blood volumes.

Bone-marrow examinations showed hypoplasia in five of their six patients. A peculiar background gelatinous material appeared to surround the scattered marrow elements. Histochemical stains showed the characteristic pattern of an acid mucopolysaccharide: pink-purple with Romanowsky stains, pink with hematoxylin and eosin, positive to Alcian blue with higher pH, and positive to colloidal iron; the PAS stain was only faintly positive. Bone-marrow iron was absent or reduced in most cases, but the serum iron level was usually a low normal, with a lower than usual iron-binding capacity. They also saw prominent blue-green granules by Romanowsky stain in four patients' histiocytes; these did not stain with any histochemical agent and remain unexplained.

Leukopenia was present in three patients, granulocytopenia in four, and lymphopenia in all six. Two had mild thrombocytopenia (90 $\times$ $10^6/L$ and 130 $\times$ $10^6/L$).

In summary, these studies found anemia, lymphopenia, neutropenia, and acanthocytic changes of the red cells; the bone marrow was hypoplastic with a gelatinous and mucopolysaccharide material; and there were blue-green granules in the histiocytes.

Lampert and Lau in Germany studied ten young patients with anorexia nervosa, nine girls and one boy aged 10 to 16 years [4]. The blood studies were repeated when the patients had recovered sufficiently from the disease after hospitalization. Six patients had leukopenia ($< 5 \times 10^6/L$) involving both neutrophils and lymphocytes; four had thrombocytopenia ($< 105 \times 10^6/L$); and the seven patients who underwent bone-marrow aspiration showed a marked hypocellularity, with only a few megakaryocytes present but abundant gelatinous material. Despite this bone-marrow hypoplasia, which included erythroblastopenia in five patients, the peripheral blood hemoglobin level was normal. These changes disappeared within days to a few weeks, by which time there had been a considerable gain in body weight. No mention was made about red-blood-cell morphology, so it is not known whether acanthocytosis was present.

The results of an earlier nonprospective study of three patients were reported by Pearson in the United States in 1967 [5]. Two patients were anemic, one had a mild leukopenia ($3.5 \times 10^9/L$), and all had extreme marrow hypocellularity. Pearson also reported a prominent pink-staining (with Wright-Giemsa technique) mucoid material that was consistent histochemically with an acid mucopolysaccharide.

Cornbleet, Moir, and Wolff used extensive histochemical techniques to study the peculiar mucoid-appearing substance noted in all of these bone-marrow aspirates [6]. They concluded that the substance was an acid mucopolysaccharide consisting predominantly of hyaluronic acid and was probably a result of the generalized serous atrophy of fat that occurs in long-standing malnutrition. The one patient they studied had mild normocytic, normochromic anemia with many acanthocytes present and leukopenia principally due to neutropenia. It should be noted that bone-marrow hypoplasia without mucopolysaccharide accumulation occurs in protein malnutrition states [3].

Despite the bone-marrow hypocellularity in these studies, only some of the patients were anemic. Seidensticker and Tzagournis reported anemia in only 30% of patients with anorexia nervosa, and in most it was mild [7].

The acanthocytosis noted by Mant and Faragher was published in a single case report by Amrein and associates [8]. This patient died of sepsis, presumably secondary to a profound pancytopenia associated with anorexia nervosa (hematocrit, 26%; white blood count, 0.13×10^9/L; platelets, 90×10^9/L). Nearly all the peripheral red cells were acanthocytes, and the bone marrow was severely hypoplastic, with the fat space replaced by a gelatinous ground substance. Beta- and pre-beta-lipoproteins were undetectable on lipoprotein electrophoresis. The appearance of acanthocytosis in hereditary a-beta-lipoproteinemia is well known. The five patients described by Mant and Faragher who had acanthocytes did not have a total absence of beta-lipoprotein, but moderate decreases in beta-lipoprotein could not be assessed by their technique, so it is not known how common this association of acanthocytes and lipoprotein deficiency is in anorexia nervosa.

Conclusion

Despite the prevalence of anorexia nervosa, the hematological abnormalities induced by this condition have been reported in only a few cases. About half the reported patients have leukopenia, one-third have thrombocytopenia, and less than one-quarter have anemia. Bone-marrow hypoplasia occurs fairly consistently and is associated with a reduction in the bone-marrow fat and the appearance of an amorphous acid mucopolysaccharide. Acanthocytosis occurs commonly and may be associated with low levels of beta-lipoprotein. All these changes return to normal as the patient regains weight, and only rarely do they complicate the patient's clinical course.

The practitioner needs to be aware of the reported frequency of these abnormalities so that needless worry about them does not complicate their medical evaluation. I see no reason to do any blood studies other than a complete blood count. Mild degrees of anemia, thrombocytopenia, and leukopenia can then be accepted as being part of this condition, and further workup can be avoided. Profound neutropenia ($< 1 \times 10^9$/L) or thrombocytopenia ($< 50 \times 10^9$/L) should be investigated with a bone-marrow aspiration because of the possibility of a coexistent bone-marrow aplasia or malignancy, and a moderately severe anemia (hemoglobin < 10 gm/100 ml) should be investigated, just as any unexplained anemia should be.

References

1. Keys, A., Brozek, J., Henschel, A., et al. *The Biology of Human Starvation*. Vol. 1. Minneapolis: University of Minnesota Press, 1950. Pp. 248–272.

2. Adams, E.B. Anemia associated with protein deficiency. *Semin. Hematol.* 7:55–66, 1970.

3. Mant, M.J., and Faragher, B.S. The hematology of anorexia nervosa. *Br. J. Haematol.* 23:737–749, 1972.

4. Lampert, F., and Lau, B. Bone marrow hypoplasia in anorexia nervosa. *Eur. J. Pediatr.* 124:65–71, 1976.

5. Pearson, H.À. Marrow hypoplasia in anorexia nervosa. *J. Pediatr.* 71: 211–215, 1976.

6. Cornbleet, P.J., Moir, R.C., and Wolff, P.L. A histochemical study of bone marrow hypoplasia in anorexia nervosa. *Virchows Arch. [Pathol. Anat.]* 374:239–247, 1977.

7. Seidensticker, J.F., Tzagournis, M. Anorexia Nervosa—clinical features and long-term follow-up. *J. Chronic Dis.* 21:361–367, 1968.

8. Amrein, P.C., Friedman, R., Kosinski, K., and Ellman, L. Hematologic changes in anorexia nervosa. *JAMA* 241:2190–2191, 1979.

Anorexia and Gastrointestinal Disorders

William D. Carey, M.D.

Anorexia nervosa must be distinguished from a variety of diseases that can produce similar degrees of decreased food intake and weight loss. The diagnostic criteria for anorexia nervosa [1] are discussed elsewhere in this book, and excellent multidisciplinary reviews are available [2]. For the purpose of this discussion, we will consider that patients with diseases simulating anorexia nervosa have *organic disease,* whereas anorexia nervosa is a *functional disorder.* Since we can identify several definite hormonal and metabolic changes in anorexia nervosa, and since its specific causes are not known, we have to accept that this is an arbitrary distinction, representing our ignorance about the root cause.

Many gastrointestinal disorders are characterized by anorexia or weight loss. Despite the great advances in techniques of gastrointestinal diagnosis over the past several years, many disorders are elusive or uncommon and therefore difficult to diagnose unless they are thought of specifically.

Definitions

Anorexia and *weight loss* are not synonymous. Although anorexia will almost inevitably produce weight loss if it persists long enough, many disorders produce weight loss without anorexia (for example, nontropical sprue and diabetes mellitus). Another important distinction is between anorexia and food aversion. Although these terms are more closely synonymous, there are several specific disease states in which the patient's desire for food remains intact yet food ingestion is avoided because of the specific symptoms that food intake will produce. Patients with chronic intestinal vascular ischemia, for example, will develop severe pain within an hour or so after eating. Such patients may lose a great deal of weight despite their excellent appetites. The weight loss occurs because these patients would rather not eat than deal with the pain produced by ischemia. This is somewhat different from the anorexia of the cancer patient or the patient with anorexia nervosa, who more characteristically has no interest in eating or is easily satiated. This distinction does not always bear up, however, since some anorectic patients will readily vomit if induced to eat excessively. Also, the dysphoria produced by food ingestion and the perceived presence of

31

excess body weight is certainly a target symptom for these patients, just as abdominal pain is for the patient with ischemia.

Gastrointestinal Disease and Anorexia

With these definitions in mind, we will examine in detail some of the gastrointestinal diseases that might mimic anorexia nervosa, at least occasionally, and therefore should be distinguished by the examining physician.

Problems of Deglutition

Congenital abnormalities of the esophagus are nearly always detected in the neonatal period and rarely remain undetected into adulthood. Acquired disorders of swallowing, however, can occur in young adults and might be confused with anorexia nervosa. Primary neurological disorders that impair oral pharyngeal function include multiple sclerosis, poliomyelitis, and amyotrophic lateral sclerosis. Disorders of striated muscle that may affect deglutition include myasthenia gravis, oculopharyngeal myopathy, and myotonia dystrophica. Most of these diseases occur in a distinctive clinical setting, and confusion with anorexia nervosa will not occur. The young patient with multiple sclerosis or myasthenia gravis, however, may occasionally be seen by a pediatrician, internist, or gastroenterologist because of weight loss. The physician should be alert to a deglutition problem because of the symptoms produced, such as regurgitation of food through the nose and choking and coughing spells, suggesting aspiration. The patient with myasthenia gravis will also usually complain of progressive weakness and rapid fatigability. If only the muscles innervated by the cranial nerves are involved, however, the symptoms of muscle fatigue may be harder to elicit. Ptosis of the eyelids and dysphonia, with development of a peculiar nasal speech, are often highly characteristic. The use of edrophonium should restore muscle strength within 30 to 60 seconds. Electromyography may also be helpful. The detection of acetylcholine receptor antibodies is highly characteristic of this disorder [3]. Multiple sclerosis is a disease of young adults [4]. Although motor symptoms of clumsiness, stiffness, slowness, and weakness are common, these symptoms may be dismissed in the adolescent, especially if there is a disproportionate weight loss due to involvement of the nerves to the swallowing muscles. The diagnosis of multiple sclerosis rests on the clinical evaluation of the episodic nature of the disturbance and the multitude of neurological signs and symptoms produced by the spotty demyelinating disease. There are no specific laboratory tests to establish the diagnosis of multiple sclerosis. However, the cerebral spinal fluid protein reveals an elevation of the IgG in over 70% of patients. Other neuromuscular disorders of deglutition need not be considered here.

Disorders of the Esophagus

Most esophageal diseases have fairly characteristic symptoms, which allow for differentiation from anorexia nervosa. Achalasia usually occurs in young adults, although cases have been reported in children. The classic symptoms of dysphagia for both liquids and solids is explained by the observation that the lower esophageal sphincter has a high resting pressure and fails to relax during swallowing to allow the passage of esophageal contents into the stomach [5]. Regurgitation of retained food is another common symptom, and recurrent episodes of aspiration or recurrent pulmonary disease, such as bronchitis or pneumonia, may be found. Early in the course of disease, however, symptoms may be much more subtle than this. The patient may simply be a slow eater, for example. Because of peer pressure and other factors, this may result in an actual decrease in the amount of food consumed, with a denial of any specifically esophageal symptoms. Weight loss may occur, and the patient may be suspected of having anorexia nervosa. The diagnosis of achalasia can usually be made on the basis of a barium examination of the esophagus. The characteristic beaklike tapering of the distal esophagus is highly specific. Although cancer of the cardia occasionally may mimic achalasia, this is rarely a differential diagnostic point in the adolescent or young adult. Nevertheless, endoscopy with biopsy of the distal esophagus will virtually exclude cancer, and esophageal manometry will reveal the characteristic motor abnormality seen in achalasia. The treatment of this disorder is rupture of the hypertrophied muscles of the lower esophageal sphincter by balloon dilatation or a surgical myotomy [6].

Diffuse esophageal spasm occasionally may afflict adolescents and young adults. Chest pain is so commonly seen in this disorder, however, that it should not present a difficult differential diagnostic point with respect to anorexia nervosa. A benign stricture of the esophagus may prevent the passage of food into the stomach. Again, the cardinal symptom of dysphagia should be elicited. Unlike patients with achalasia, who complain of dysphagia for both liquids and solids, the patient with a stricture will note more difficulty with solids than liquids. Strictures occur in long-standing reflux esophagitis, so an additional clue is present if the patient reports that heartburn preceded the dysphagia by months or years. When swallowing becomes progressively difficult, weight loss obviously may ensue. A barium study of the esophagus should lead to a consideration of esophageal strictures when the diagnosis is obscure.

Esophageal webs and rings are different from strictures in that usually they are comprised only of mucosa and are very thin. These entities usually present in middle or later life. If the web occurs in the cervical esophagus and is associated with iron-deficiency anemia, the entity is called Plummer-Vinson syndrome. This disorder often occurs in neurotic females. The importance of Plummer-Vinson syndrome is its association with hypopharnygeal cancers [7]. An esophageal ring (Schatzki ring) occurs at the junction of the squamous and columnar mucosa in the lower esophagus. Rings that produce only a slight narrowing will remain asymptomatic and undiscovered unless a barium study of the esophagus is done for some other reason. If the ring produces sufficient narrowing of the lumen to produce dysphagia, however, weight loss may occur. The treatment of rings and webs is dilatation in most cases.

Tumors of the esophagus are unusual in the age group under consideration for anorexia nervosa. The cardinal symptoms, of course, are dysphagia and weight loss. Again, the barium study should be the determining factor.

Disorders of the Stomach and Duodenum

Peptic disorders of the stomach and duodenum are well-recognized clinical entities in the anorexia nervosa age group. The typical duodenal ulcer produces stereotyped symptoms, including a gnawing, hungerlike pain in the epigastrium that is relieved promptly by food ingestion or by antacids. Morever, the symptoms are usually periodic—symptomatic periods alternating with asymptomatic periods. Not all patients with ulcer disease have classic peptic symptoms, however. With the advent of upper intestinal endoscopy, it has become apparent that many ulcers are completely asymptomatic. Therefore, a broad range of symptoms can be encountered in the patient with peptic ulcer disease. Some patients have vague or atypical symptoms. Ulcers located in or near the pylorus may produce vomiting out of proportion to other abdominal symptoms [8]. The adolescent with vague abdominal pain but with prominent vomiting and weight loss because of ulcer disease may be thought to have anorexia nervosa. Since the typical anorectic patient has no abdominal pain, however, the presence of pain, even if it is atypical, should heighten the suspicion of a gastrointestinal disorder such as ulcer disease. Although upper intestinal endoscopy is more sensitive than barium roentgenography in detecting ulcers and other gastric lesions, the ease and lower cost of the roentgenographic examination make it the screening test of choice in a suspected anorectic patient.

Gastric tumors can cause anorexia and weight loss and usually also produce pain. They are very unusual in the adolescent and young adult, but we have recently seen a 21-year-old woman, with a 35-pound weight loss and food aversion, who had a highly anaplastic gastric carcinoma. She came to our clinic because her physician, who believed her symptoms were largely psychogenic, had urged her to get psychiatric therapy, which the patient refused. The upper gastrointestinal roentgenogram was clearly abnormal, which stimulated a search that ultimately established the diagnosis and surgical therapy.

Weight loss may occur on the basis of gastric-outlet obstruction. This is a common sequela of recurrent peptic-ulcer disease, with scarring of the antrum and pylorus to the point that food cannot pass. Physical examination will often reveal a succussion, indicating the presence of pools of food and liquid within the obstructed viscus. Again, an upper gastrointestinal roentgenogram should reveal the source of the problem in these patients.

Liver Disease

Acute viral hepatitis may be either clinical or subclinical in presentation. The majority of patients with viral hepatitis have nonspecific symptoms, which are often attributed to a flulike illness, or no symptoms at all. Those who develop icteric hepatitis will usually see their physicians promptly, and no diagnostic dilemma will occur. Those with anicteric hepatitis, however, may complain most prominently of fatigue, anorexia, and weight loss. The young female with these symptoms may be thought to have anorexia nervosa.

The convalescent period for viral hepatitis may be prolonged. Neurasthenia may exist for many months (up to a year) following an otherwise uncomplicated attack of viral hepatitis. The diagnosis of liver disease has become much easier, however, with the routine multichannel blood analyzers, almost all of which include a battery of liver-oriented tests.

Wilson disease, a disorder of copper metabolism, is a rare but treatable disorder characterized by liver and central nervous system symptoms [9]. It is a disease that affects adolescents and young adults. Approximately 20% of patients have neurological signs or symptoms. Such disturbances as childish behavior, personality changes, and frank psychiatric disturbances may be the earliest symptoms, and an occasional patient may also lose weight. Weight loss is not a cardinal feature of this disorder, however. The search for Kayser-Fleischer rings in the eye and associated liver-test abnormalities should help in seeking the correct diagnosis. A number of other chronic liver diseases may occasionally occur in young people but few are regularly characterized by weight loss or anorexia.

Pancreatic Disorders

The patient with pancreatic insufficiency will lose weight because of inadequate amounts of pancreatic enzymes, which aid in the digestion of food. When this occurs in an adolescent, the weight loss may simulate anorexia nervosa. An important clinical distinguishing point, however, is that the patient with pancreatic insufficiency should have some altered bowel function. Usually this consists of bulky, foul-smelling stools, which often are sticky and may actually contain oil globules. Also, appetite is well maintained in such patients. The young patient with familial pancreatitis and pancreatic insufficiency will also have abdominal pain, but some forms of pancreatic insufficiency are painless.

Cystic fibrosis is a multisymptom disease characterized by exocrine-gland dysfunction and altered function of mucus glands [10]. Approximately 80% of patients will have pancreatic insufficiency. Other prominent abnormalities are diffuse pulmonary-obstructive phenomena. The commonly used sweat-electrolyte test is useful in the diagnosis. Patients who maintain a low sweat sodium and chloride concentration (below 60 mEq/L) do not have cystic fibrosis. The closer the sodium concentration comes to being isotonic with respect to serum, the more likely it is that the patient has cystic fibrosis. Although this disorder is often detected in infancy, an occasional patient may reach adolescence or young adulthood before the diagnosis is made. The profound weight loss or failure to gain weight may simulate anorexia nervosa, but typically the appetite is very well maintained. In addition to sweat-electrolyte concentrations, an abnormal chest roentgenogram in a young person, steatorrhea, or other blood markers of malabsorption may all help in the diagnosis.

Small-Intestine Disease

Diffuse abnormalities of the small-bowel mucosa may result in malabsorption. Although the disease may first appear in infancy, many patients do not become symptomatic until adolescence, adulthood, or even old age. The typical symptom in the patient with nontropical sprue includes diarrhea, weight loss, and weakness [11]. The nature of the stools varies considerably among patients, however, and an occasional patient may complain of constipation. Usually, however, the disease involves passage of a very large stool, which may be pale or puttylike and which sticks to the side of the toilet bowl. Abdominal pain is conspicuously absent in these patients, which may only contribute to the confusion between this disorder and anorexia nervosa. Unlike the anorectic patients, patients with nontropical sprue usually have excellent appetites and report the loss of weight despite above-normal food intake. Nontropical sprue is caused by a sensitivity to gluten, which is present in wheat, barley, rye, and oats. The diagnosis may be established by the typical small-bowel biopsy and by improvement on a gluten-restricted diet. Because malabsorption occurs, a number of laboratory abnormalities often appear that alert the investigating physician. Occasionally, however, such patients present with evidence of isolated malabsorptive problems, such as iron-deficiency anemia or megaloblastic anemia due to folate deficiency.

Regional ileitis (Crohn disease) is a disease that often mimics other conditions [12]. The typical patient, who develops fever along with abdominal pain and weight loss and who, on physical examination, has a tender abdominal mass, is diagnosed correctly in the majority of cases. Like so many other gastrointestinal diseases, however, the protean manifestations of Crohn disease occasionally cause problems. Since weight loss is common (operating by a variety of mechanisms) the distinction between Crohn disease and anorexia nervosa may be difficult, especially if the weight loss is out of proportion to the abdominal pain. Features such as anemia, elevation of acute phase reactants, leukocytosis, prominent diarrhea, and extra intestinal manifestations such as erythema nodosum, arthritis, perirectal disease, and aphthous stomatitis suggest the possibility of Crohn disease. Since the disease often begins in childhood or adolescence, it should be considered in the differential diagnosis of the patient suspected of having anorexia nervosa. Similarly, inflammatory bowel disease involving the large intestine (whether it be Crohn disease or chronic ulcerative colitis) may occasionally mimic anorexia nervosa in that weight loss or failure to gain weight occurs.

Finally, parasitic infestations such as *Giardia lamblia* and *Strongyloides,* may occasionally cause weight loss and be confused with anorexia nervosa.

Medical Evaluation of the Anorexia Nervosa Suspect

Obviously, not all gastrointestinal tests can be done on every patient who has symptoms suggestive of anorexia nervosa. We believe, however, that a systematic evaluation of the gastrointestinal tract and the neuroendocrine axis is indicated in every patient before expensive and lengthy treatment for anorexia is undertaken. In order to exclude important disorders of the gastrointestinal tract, the following recommendations are made:

1. The physician must take a careful history and must distinguish among possible causes for weight loss. The anorectic patient loses weight because of food aversion and not because of pain or other symptoms that food intake might cause. The physician must ask the patient, both directly and indirectly, the reasons for decreased food intake. If the responses indicate a disordered perception of self or body, with the desire to be thin, anorexia nervosa is suggested. If, however, the patient complains of difficulty in swallowing or of food sticking or provoking abdominal symptoms, then the physician should suspect intestinal disorders.

2. Screening tests should be performed on suspected anorexia nervosa patients. These tests should include a complete blood count, screening tests for glucose, liver tests, kidney tests, protein analyses, and urinalysis. Specific tests of the gastrointestinal tract should include, at a minimum, a barium study of the upper intestinal tract, including views of the esophagus, stomach, and duode-

num. A small-bowel follow-through also should be done, and a proctoscopic examination and colon roentgenogram should be done in each case. Stools should be checked for ova and parasites. It is important that the stool be checked before any barium is introduced into the intestinal tract from above or below. It would be desirable to collect a 72-hour stool collection for fat analysis. This has proved impracticable in our experience, however, since patients refuse to consume a standard 100 gm fat diet, and stool collections have thus been inadequate because of poor patient compliance. A simple qualitative stool fat test should be performed, however. If all these tests are normal, the likelihood of the presence of significant organic gastrointestinal disease is minimal. If there are abnormalities on these studies, however, additional diagnostic tests should be considered on the basis of the particular abnormality uncovered.

Conclusions

The clinical diagnosis of anorexia nervosa is often very simple. Uncommonly, however, gastrointestinal disorders of various sorts may masquerade as anorexia. A careful history, physical examination, laboratory studies, and easily tolerated gastrointestinal studies will help to exclude such disorders and may also make the therapeutic milieu more successful, since the patient will be reassured that the symptoms are being taken seriously and that the diagnosis of anorexia nervosa rests on firm clinical grounds.

References

1. Feighner, J.P., Robins, E., Guze, S.B., et al. Diagnostic criteria for use in psychiatric research. *Arch. Gen. Psychiatry* 26:57-63, 1972.

2. Drossman, D.A., Ontjes, D.A., and Heizer, W.D. Anorexia nervosa. *Gastroenterology* 77:1115-1131, 1979.

3. Drachman, D.B. Myasthenia gravis. *New Engl. J. Med.* 298:136-142, 186-193, 1978.

4. McDonald, W.I. Pathophysiology in multiple sclerosis. *Brain* 97:179-196, 1974.

5. Cohen, S., and Lipshutz, W. Lower esophageal dysfunction in achalasia. *Gastroenterology* 61:814-820, 1971.

6. Nanson, E.M. Treatment of achalasia. *Gastroenterology* 51:236-241, 1966.

7. Wynder, E.L., Hultberg, S., Jacobsson, F., et al. Environmental factors in cancer of the upper alimentary tract: Swedish study with special reference to Plummer-Vinson (Patterson-Kelly) syndrome. *Cancer* 10:470-487, 1957.

8. Texter, E.C., Smith, H.W., Bundeson, W.E., et al. The syndrome of pylorique: clinical and physiologic observations. *Gastroenterology* 36:573–579, 1959.

9. Sternlieb, I., and Scheinberg, I.H. Wilson's disease. In R. Wright, K.G.M.M. Alberti, S. Karranss, et al. (Eds.) *Liver and Biliary Disease.* Philadelphia: W.B. Saunders Co., 1979. Pp. 774–778.

10. Waring, W.W. Current management of cystic fibrosis. *Adv. Pediatr.* 23:401–435, 1977.

11. Strober, W., Falchuk, Z.M., Rogentine, G.N., et al. The pathogenesis of gluten sensitive enteropathy. *Ann. Intern. Med.* 83:242–256, 1975.

12. Donaldson, R.M. Crohn's disease of the small bowel. In M.H. Sleisenger, and J.S. Fordtran (Eds.), *Gastrointestinal Disease.* Philadelphia: W.B. Saunders Co., 1978. P. 1052.

7

Gynecological Signs and Symptoms in Anorexia Nervosa

Gita P. Gidwani, M.D.

The reported sex incidence of anorexia nervosa has varied from a ratio of one male to fourteen females to a ratio of one male to twenty-four females [1]. In our experience, more female patients have anorexia nervosa. Before making the diagnosis of anorexia nervosa, therefore, clinicians and paramedical personnel, as well as parents and teachers, should be aware of the gynecological symptoms that may be present.

Amenorrhea—lack of menses—is the most common presenting symptom of anorectic girls who are seen by pediatricians, general practitioners, or gynecologists. Primary amenorrhea is defined as no menses until age 16. The patient usually shows retardation in the development of secondary sexual characteristics and appears to be a late bloomer. Examination often reveals that the patient is underweight but has normal external and internal genitalia. The vaginal mucous membrane shows absence of estrogen and pituitary gonadotropins; follicle-stimulating hormone (FSH) and luteinizing hormone (LH) are at prepuberal levels.

Secondary amenorrhea—the absence of menstrual periods after they had begun at the usual age of menarche—is also a common presenting complaint. What is interesting is that, in 20% to 65% of anorexia cases, absence of menses precedes actual weight loss [2]. This could be explained by the psychological stress that precedes the weight loss. Similarly, not all patients resume normal menstruation once they have gained an ideal body weight. The vaginal mucous membrane of the vagina and cervix is hypoestrogenic, glactorrhea is absent, and the levels of FSH and LH are low in the severe stage (see table 7-1).

The low gonadotropin levels differentiate these cases of amenorrhea from those of primary or secondary ovarian failure (high FSH and LH) and Stein-Leventhal syndrome (top-normal LH and an LH-FSH ratio of about 2:1). The amenorrhea does not respond to progestins in severe cases. Similarly, clomiphene citrate (Clomid) will not induce ovulation and menses in severe cases; as the patient gains weight, however, the cervical mucous shows ferning, and the patient may respond to progesterone and to Clomid before attaining normal menstrual patterns. Again, in severe cases, withdrawal bleeding will not take place with the administration usual doses of estrogen and progesterone (for example 1.25 mg of Premarin and 10 mg of Provera) or birth-control pills. Higher doses or continual priming with estrogen-progesterone, however, may finally induce with-

Table 7-1
Pituitary Gonadotropins in Patients with Anorexia Nervosa

Patient No.	Age (yrs)	Symptoms	Weight Loss (%)	LH/FSH (ImU/ml)	Prolactin (ng/ml)
1	21	Secondary amenorrhea	50	3.3/4.7	3.3
2	11	Primary amenorrhea	25	2.8/3.5	2.7
3	26	Secondary amenorrhea	50	5.8/10.3	25.0[a]
4	25	Secondary amenorrhea	25	2.4/5.2	9.3
5	17	Secondary amenorrhea	43	8.8/6.6	–
6	24	Secondary amenorrhea	40	3.4/2.4	–
7	15	Secondary amenorrhea	40	4.5/5.8	36.4[a]
8	18	Secondary amenorrhea	28	3.0/5.6	8.2
9	23	Secondary amenorrhea	50	10.0/10.6	2.0
10	19	Secondary amenorrhea	40	8.0/25.5	10.0

[a]Patient was receiving antidepressants before entering program.

drawal bleeding. Luteinizing hormone-releasing hormone (LHRH) may cause LH and FSH to rise to normal preovulatory levels, and ovulation may occur [3].

In prepuberal girls, LH levels show only minimal fluctuation above the baseline. Later, in early puberty, LH levels begin to be secreted in 15- to 30-minute bursts during the period of normal nocturnal sleep. Later, as puberty advances to adulthood, the secretory bursts persist and are distributed throughout the day. Katz, Boyar, and colleagues reported that patients with anorexia nervosa show LH patterns suggestive of prepuberal or early puberal girls [4]. It is believed that it is the abnormally functioning hypothalamus that accounts for the amenorrhea in anorectic patients.

Frisch and McArthur have proposed that each woman must attain a certain critical weight before cyclic gonadotropin secretions can occur [5]. As a girl grows and her body weight increases, the percentage of body weight that is adipose tissue increases. The degree of fatness, rather than absolute body weight, seems to be the critical determinant in the timing of menarche. Frisch has estimated that a body-fat content of at least 17% is required before menarche can occur. Therefore, it is easy to see why menstrual periods will not start while the patient is underweight.

The need for early recognition of anorexia nervosa cannot be overemphasized. Lack of menses may occur early in the full spectrum of symptoms of an anorectic patient, and thus all physcians must pay attention to a history of dieting and weight loss in women who consult them for secondary amenorrhea. The results of a Finnish follow-up study of 48 patients with anorexia nervosa, who had been followed during a mean period of 5 years, showed that anorexia nervosa is a serious condition that is difficult to treat effectively and has considerable mortality [6]. It was shown, however, that the prognosis for a later freedom from symptoms was four times as good in patients who were treated within the first three years after onset (58% symptom-free). Thus, in order to improve the prognosis, every woman with secondary amenorrhea and self-induced weight reduction who does not suffer other obvious primary psychiatric illness should be regarded as a potential anorexia nervosa patient.

Infertility or inability to conceive may be a presenting complaint of the anorectic patient. After a complete examination is done and gonadotropin values are obtained, the patient should be encouraged to see a psychiatrist and to increase her weight. Menotropins (Pergonal) therapy can be employed. In a study of 13 women with anorexia nervosa, Nillus and Wide were able to induce ovulation with prolonged LHRH treatment [3]. The progesterone levels were low, however, and they theorized that these women had inadequate luteal function. They suggested giving a combination of LHRH with human chorionic gonadotropin (HCG) so that these patients may have a normal pregnancy. Clinically, however, it seems that, unless the patient decides to increase her weight and see a psychiatrist, the treatment of her infertility will be a complex and expensive process with poor results.

Lack of libido and dryness of the vagina have also been described by our patients.

Management of anorectic patients with amenorrhea includes the following:

1. The causes of amenorrhea must be determined. Pregnancy, polycystic ovarian disease, hypopituitary conditions, pituitary tumors, ovarian failure, and thyroid abnormality must be ruled out. After the condition has been diagnosed, a simple explanation of the mechanism of amenorrhea should be given to the patient. This helps allay the patient's anxieties, such as "Blood backs up every month in my ovaries," or "I have a period that does not come outside," or "I am bloated."

2. Surveillance is necessary to be sure that a pituitary prolactin-secreting adenoma is not developing.

3. Small doses of estrogen can be used to aid secondary sex development in delayed menarche, or estrogen cream can be used locally for vaginal dryness.

4. Cyclical estrogen-progesterone, or birth-control pills should not be prescribed to induce periods, because they tend to interfere with the levels of pituitary gonadotropins.

5. The patient must be encouraged to see a psychiatrist so that the entire syndrome may be dealt with.

No long-term studies have been undertaken to determine the reproductive future of these anorectic patients. We hope to continue to study our patients to provide some data in this area.

References

1. Hogan, W.M., Huerta, E., and Lucas, A.R. Diagnosing anorexia nervosa in males. *Psychosomatics* 15:122-126, 1974.

2. Fries, H. *Anorexia Nervosa.* Vigersky R.A. (Ed.). New York: Raven Press 1977.

3. Nillius, S.T., and Wide, L. Effects and/or Onset of Prolonged Luteinizing Hormone-Releasing Hormone Therapy on Follicular Maturation, Ovulating and Corpus Luteum Function in Amenorrheoeic Women with Anorexia Nervosa. *Med. Sci.* 84:21-35, 1979.

4. Katz, J.L., Boyar, R.M., Roffwarg, H. LHRH responsiveness in anorexia nervosa: Intactness despite prepubertal circadian LH pattern. *Psychosom. Med.* 39:241, 1977.

5. Frisch, R. E., and McArthur, J. W. Menstrual cycles: Fatness as a determinant of minimum weight for height necessary for their maintenance and/or onset. *Science* 185:949, 1974.

6. Niskanen, P., Jaaskelainen, J., and Achte, K. Prognosen vid anroxia nervosa. *Nord. Psykiatr. Tidskrift.* 28:160-165, 1974 (no abstract in English).

8

Cardiac Function in Anorexia Nervosa

Douglas S. Moodie, M.D.

Anorexia nervosa is associated with a significant mortality, ranging from 15% to 20% [1]. Some of these patients die suddenly. Based on studies in adults, there is a possibility that patients with anorexia nervosa may be subject to significant ventricular arrhythmias, with an abnormal response to exercise, and thus may be predisposed to sudden cardiac death [2]. Adult studies have also suggested that the left atrium, left ventricle, and aorta are smaller than normal in patients with anorexia and that, because of small left-heart volumes, ventricular ectopy, relative hypotension, bradycardia, and a blunted heart-rate response may be noted with exercise [3]. Based on such alarming findings in adult anorectic patients, what can or should the physician who is caring for anorectic children do about evaluating their cardiac status—and are his anorectic patients at risk for cardiovascular abnormalities? In this chapter, we will describe the clinical cardiovascular findings in adolescent and young-adult patients with anorexia nervosa. Based on these cardiovascular findings, we will suggest the kinds of cardiac evaluations that should be performed routinely for these patients.

Study Population

We studied cardiac function in 12 patients with anorexia nervosa—10 females and 2 males. The patients' ages ranged from 13 to 25 years, with a mean of 17.6 years. Eight of the 12 patients were under 20 years of age. Table 8–1 briefly lists the major criteria used for the diagnosis of severe anorexia nervosa (see table 4–1 for more detail), and table 8–2 lists the minor criteria. All patients included in the survey had to fulfill all five major criteria and at least two minor criteria. Table 8–3 describes the cardiac-function studies performed in the 12 patients. Chest roentgenograms, electrocardiograms, and stress-exercise tests were per-

Table 8–1
Major Criteria for Diagnosis of Anorexia Nervosa

1. Age at onset: <25 years
2. Anorexia, with at least 25% loss of original body weight
3. A distorted, implacable attitude toward eating, food, or weight, overriding hunger, admonitions, reassurance, and threats
4. No known psychiatric disorder, with particular reference to primary affective disorders, schizophrenia, obsessive-compulsive and phobic neuroses

Table 8-2
Minor Criteria for Diagnosis of Anorexia Nervosa

1. Amenorrhea
2. Lanugo
3. Bradycardia (heart rate < 60 beats per minute)
4. Periods of overactivity
5. Episodes of bulimia
6. Vomiting (may be self-induced)

formed in all 12 patients. The exercise tests were all performed on a bicycle ergometer according to the protocol originally described by James [4].

Eleven of the 12 patients had M-mode echocardiograms and resting radionuclide left-ventricular ejection fractions, using the gated technique that has been described elsewhere [5]. Ten of the 12 patients had continuous, 24-hour electrocardiographic Holter monitor recording. Four patients had two-dimensional echocardiograms performed with an 80° phased-array sector scanner (Varian 3000), using a 2.25 MHz transducer. From the long- and short-axis views, ventricular volumes and left-ventricular mass were calculated, as described elsewhere [6].

Clinical Cardiac Findings

Electrocardiograms

Electrocardiograms revealed normal sinus rhythm in all patients (figure 8-1). Three patients had myocardial changes consisting of ST and T segment abnormalities (figure 8-2), and one patient had U-waves suggestive of hypokalemia. QT intervals were normal in all patients, and all patients had normal potassium levels.

Previous investigators had described electrocardiographic abnormalities in seven of nine patients with anorexia nervosa, consisting primarily of sinus bradycardia, T-wave inversion, or flattening of ST segments, and mild prolongation of the QT interval [7]. Many of the changes described in previous investigations could be secondary to hypokalemia. We have seen anorectic patients (not included

Table 8-3
Cardiac Studies Performed

Type of Test	Number of Patients
Chest roentgenogram	12/12
Electrocardiogram	12/12
M-mode echocardiogram	11/12
Stress-exercise test	12/12
24-hour Holter monitor	10/12
Resting radionuclide left-ventricular ejection fraction	11/12

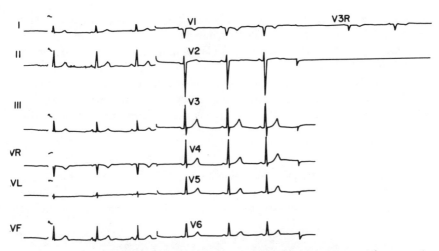

Figure 8-1. Normal electrocardiogram in a 14-year-old patient with anorexia nervosa.

in this study) who, because of cyclic vomiting with potassium loss, presented with marked hypokalemia, severe bradycardia, and premature ventricular contractions. These patients certainly are at significant risk for severe cardiac arrhythmias—that is, ventricular fibrillation and sudden death. An electrocardiogram (ECG) should be performed on any anorectic patient with significant cyclical vomiting. If the ECG demonstrates U-waves or flattened T-waves, a blood-potassium sample should be drawn immediately. The ECG provides a unique way of following the patient's blood-potassium level. Certainly, premature ventricular contractions in any patient with anorexia nervosa should alert the physician to the possibility of hypokalemia; in all our patients with normal

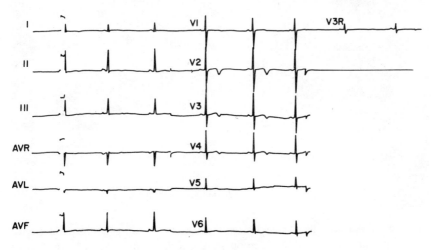

Figure 8-2. Electrocardiogram from a 14-year-old patient with anorexia nervosa.

potassium levels, the ECGs demonstrated normal sinus rhythm. A low blood
potassium may be the most lethal metabolic derangement in patients with
anorexia nervosa; we have seen potassium levels in the range of 1.3 to 1.7 mEq/L
in patients who have chronic vomiting with their anorexia nervosa. This may
account for many of the cases of sudden death described in the literature. It
seems, however, that most patients with anorexia nervosa who are not chronically
vomiting will have normal electrocardiograms, with no arrhythmias demonstrated.

Chest Roentgenograms

The chest roentgenograms in our study population demonstrated a cardiothoracic
ratio greater than 0.40 in only two patients. Ten patients had cardiothoracic
ratios less than 0.40 (figure 8-3). Two patients had cardiothoracic ratios less

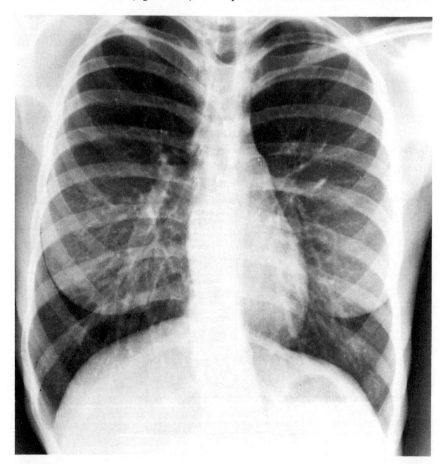

Figure 8-3. A-P and lateral chest roentgenogram in a 22-year-old patient with
anorexia nervosa, demonstrating what appears to be a very small
heart.

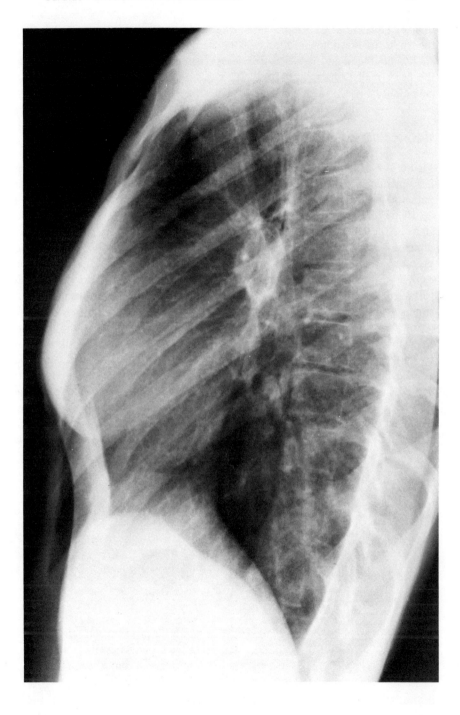

than or equal to 0.32. What is interesting to the primary-care physician is that the chest roentgenogram often will be described as normal in patients with anorexia nervosa, and yet, when the chest roentgenogram is carefully inspected, the heart really appears very small. This was a uniform pattern in most of our patients.

M-Mode Echocardiograms

Figure 8-4 demonstrates the results of the M-mode echocardiogram, comparing left-ventricular systolic, end-diastolic, and posterior wall dimensions in our patients to the patient's actual square surface area (normal data were as described by Henry and associates [8]). The systolic, diastolic, and posterior wall dimensions of the left ventricle all fall within the normal range. Left atrial and aortic dimensions were normal as well. Figure 8-5 compares the systolic, diastolic, and posterior wall dimensions to the patient's ideal square surface area, and again the cardiac dimensions are normal. One of our patients was noted to have mitral-valve prolapse and a small pericardial effusion. All other echocardiographic measurements were normal.

Although the chest roentgenogram demonstrates a small heart, the echocardiograms performed in our patients suggested that the internal dimensions of the heart were normal. This led us to speculate that patients with anorexia nervosa have either lost a great deal of pericardial fat or have a reduction in left-ventricular mass. In addition, we were somewhat surprised to find that only one patient in this group had mitral-valve prolapse. Mitral-valve prolapse is frequently described in young females, particularly those of the neurasthenic type. Anorexia nervosa patients are certainly within this general group, but mitral prolapse was unusual in our population.

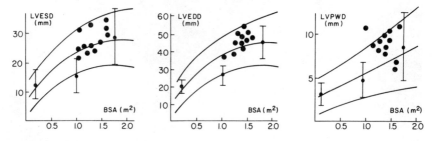

Figure 8-4. M-mode echocardiogram, comparing left-ventricular end-systolic dimension (LVESD), left-ventricular end-diastolic dimension (LVEDD), and left-ventricular posterior-wall dimensions (LVPWD), in millimeters, to the patient's actual square surface area.

Source: Moodie, D.S. and Salcedo, E. Cardiac function in adolescents and young adults with anorexia nervosa. *J. Adolescent Health Care* 2:3(1982). Reprinted with permission.

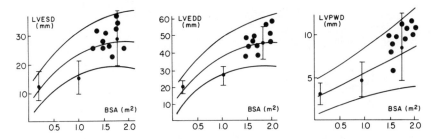

Figure 8-5. M-mode echocardiogram, comparing systolic and diastolic left-ventricular dimensions as well as posterior-wall dimensions to the patient's ideal square surface area.

Two-Dimensional Echocardiograms

Table 8-4 lists the left-ventricular mass measurements, as determined by two-dimensional echocardiography, and compares them with the cardiothoracic ratio on chest roentgenogram. A direct relationship exists between the left-ventricular mass measurements and the small heart size on roentgenogram. Figure 8-6 demonstrates that three of the four patients had a reduction in left-ventricular mass when compared to the patient's weight in kilograms. Three of

Table 8-4
Cardiac Function in Adolescents and Young Adults with Anorexia Nervosa (Two-Dimensional Echocardiography, Left-Ventricular Mass)

Patient No.	Measurement	Value
1	LV wall and cavity volume	9.64 ml
	LV wall volume	71.1 ml
	LV wall mass	74.65 gm
	C/T ratio	.35
2	LV wall and cavity volume	17.77 ml
	LV wall volume	134.89 ml
	LV wall mass	141.63 gm
	CT/ratio	.41
3	LV wall and cavity volume	11.17 ml
	LV wall volume	84.54 ml
	LV wall mass	88.77 gm
	C/T ratio	.35
4	LV wall and cavity volume	9.12 ml
	LV wall volume	66.2 ml
	LV wall mass	69.51 gm
	C/T ratio	.32

LV = left ventricle
C/T = cardiothoracic

Source: Moodie, D.S. and Salcedo, E. Cardiac function in adolescents and young adults with anorexia nervosa. *J. Adolescent Health Care* 2:3(1982). Reprinted with permission.

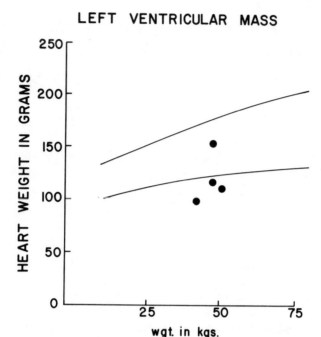

LEFT VENTRICULAR MASS

Figure 8-6. Comparison of heart weight to the patient's actual body weight, in kilograms.

Left-ventricular mass measurements were obtained from two-dimensional echocardiograms.

Source: Moodie, D.S. and Salcedo, E. Cardiac function in adolescents and young adults with anorexia nervosa. *J. Adolescent Health Care* 2:3(1982). Reprinted with permission.

the four patients had left-ventricular mass measurements less than 100 grams. Thus, the small heart on roentgenogram does not appear to be due primarily to a reduction of pericardial fat but rather is due to a reduction in left-ventricular mass. There has been a prevalent, though not well-documented, belief that the heart is spared the major untoward effects of marasmus. Abel and associates confirmed that, during prolonged states of protein-calorie malnutrition in beagle dogs, marked myocardial atrophy occurs [9]. Nutter and colleagues studied the effect of protein-calorie malnutrition on cardiac structure and biochemistry in young, male Long-Evans rats. Chronic undernutrition produced marked cardiac cachexia of the marasmic type and cardiac atrophy (heart weight, 57% of control). No one has studied in detail the effects of refeeding on left-ventricular mass measurements in animals or individual patients.

Although the reduction in left-ventricular mass in patients with anorexia nervosa does not appear to affect them clinically, what will be important in the future is the question of what will happen to their left-ventricular mass as these patients improve their caloric intake and gain weight through treatment. These findings may have special significance in regard to chronic malnourished patients with marasmus throughout the world and indeed may have long-term importance for myocardial function in patients with anorexia nervosa as they get older.

Exercise Tests

Figure 8-7 describes the heart-rate response, at various cardiac work loads, in patients with anorexia nervosa compared with normal responses, as previously determined by James [4], for patients with a square surface area greater than 1.2. A slightly elevated heart-rate response is seen in patients with anorexia nervosa, with an obvious overall reduction in total work performance in most patients. Figure 8-8 demonstrates the systolic blood pressure during exercise. In general, there is a slightly blunted systolic response when compared to normal. Diastolic blood-pressure response was normal. No arrhythmias were noted either during exercise or in the immediate postexercise periods. Figure 8-9 describes the maximum working capacity in the ten female patients with anorexia nervosa and demonstrates a significant reduction in overall working capacity for eight of

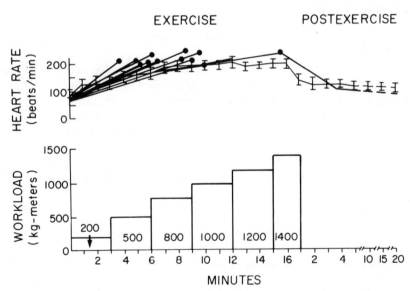

Figure 8-7. Heart-rate response during exercise in patients with anorexia nervosa.

The normal value is the horizontal line with vertical lines running through it. The patients' performance is represented in lines connecting the closed dark circles. The lower panel demonstrates the work load in kilopound meters per minute (KPM) during 3-minute intervals.

Source: Moodie, D.S. and Salcedo, E. Cardiac function in adolescents and young adults with anorexia nervosa. *J. Adolescent Health Care* 2:3(1982). Reprinted with permission.

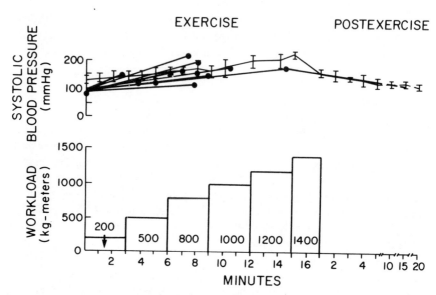

Figure 8-8. Systolic blood-pressure response during exercise in patients with anorexia nervosa.

the ten patients. The two male patients with anorexia nervosa also had marked overall reduction in working capacity.

Our findings would suggest that, despite the fact that anorexia nervosa patients often begin as exercise fanatics, by the time they have lost a significant amount of weight their overall exercise performance is reduced, secondary to a loss of muscle mass. We did not, however, find signficant abnormalities in heart rate and blood-pressure reponse during exercise in anorexia patients. No arrhythmias were noted during the exercise test or immediately following exercise. Thus, it does appear that anorexia nervosa patients are at risk for sudden cardiac compromise during exercise, but they do have a reduction in overall exercise performance secondary to a loss of muscle mass.

Table 8-5
Results of Holter Monitoring in Ten Patients

Sinus Rhythm	Number of Patients
Sinus with intermittent nodal rhythm	2
Sinus with occasional premature atrial contractions	1
Sinus with period of atrioventricular dissociation	1

Note: Monitoring was continuous for 24 hours.

Holter Monitoring

Table 8-5 describes the results in the ten patients who underwent 24-hour continuous electrocardiographic recording. All ten patients were in sinus rhythm. No significant ventricular ectopy was noted at any time in any of the patients during continuous recording. Again, our patients were all in normal sinus rhythm at rest, and none had hypokalemia. In the anorectic patient with vomiting and hypokalemia, Holter monitor recordings should be used to record the number of premature ventricular contractions that occur and to define the reponse to medical antiarrhythmic therapy if necessary.

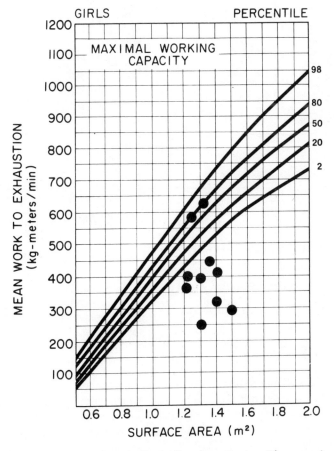

Figure 8-9. Maximum work capacity in female patients with anorexia nervosa.

Source: Moodie, D.S. and Salcedo, E. Cardiac function in adolescents and young adults with anorexia nervosa. *J. Adolescent Health Care* 2:3(1982). Reprinted with permission.

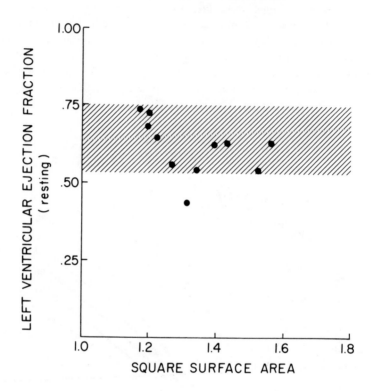

Figure 8-10. Resting left-ventricular ejection fraction in patients with anorexia
nervosa.

Shaded areas are normal values, ranging from 55% to 75%.

Source: Moodie, D.S. and Salcedo, E. Cardiac function in adolescents and young adults
with anorexia nervosa. *J. Adolescent Health Care* 2:3(1982). Reprinted with permission.

Radionuclide Studies

Figure 8-10 shows the results of the resting left-ventricular ejection fraction in
11 of the 12 patients with anorexia nervosa. All patients except one had normal
resting ventricular function; the one patient whose resting ventricular function
was abnormal showed only mild abnormality. Nutter and colleagues demonstrated that, in the presence of marked marasmic malnutrition, there was normal
or enhanced myocardial contractility and left-ventricular function [10]. Abel
and associates, however, demonstrated a consistent decrease in left-ventricular
compliance in their animal model, when compared with normals, and they sug-

gested that protein-calorie malnutrition seriously interferes with normal left-ventricular function in experimental animals by reducing compliance as a result of starvation edema and by reducing myocardial contractility associated with atrophy of the myofibers [9]. Abel and Paul also demonstrated that the adverse effects of semistarvation on left-ventricular function do not seem to be completely reversed by short-term refeeding [11]. Our findings in clincial patients agree with those of Nutter and disagree with those of Abel in that we found normal resting left-ventricular function in all our anorectic patients except one, and that patient's study was only mildly abnormal.

Summary and Conclusions

Cardiac function in adolescent and young adult patients with anorexia nervosa appears to be normal in most instances. Electrocardiograms and 24-hour Holter monitor recordings demonstrate normal sinus rhythm in most patients. The exception to this rule is the anorectic patient who has hypokalemia, most often secondary to chronic vomiting. Such a patient may present with a potassium level well below 2.0 mEq/L and may have ventricular irritability, with consequent premature ventricular contractions, bradycardia, and flattening of the ST segments. Such patients certainly are at risk for acute, severe arrhythmias, particularly ventricular fibrillation. They must be monitored very carefully with electrocardiograms or 24-hour Holter monitoring, and their serum potassium levels should be normalized via intravenous infusion of potassium-containing solutions.

The heart in patients with anorexia nervosa is small, secondary to a reduction in left-ventricular mass. Internal cardiac dimensions are normal, but the mass of the heart is reduced—as is consistent with animal studies. This may not have marked clinical significance, except that we do not know what long-term marasmic malnutrition will do to a heart that has continued reduction of its mass. One could certainly speculate that myocardial function would eventually be compromised if myocardial mass remained reduced.

The exercise performance in anorectic patients, after they have lost 25% of their body weight, is significantly reduced. In general, their heart rate and systolic and diastolic blood-pressure responses to exercise were normal, and we were not able to detect arrhythmias in the exercise or postexercise periods. Thus, despite the fact that these young individuals often initiate their anorexia as exercise fanatics, their exercise performance eventually will become reduced. We believe this reduction in overall exercise performance is secondary to a loss of total body-muscle mass.

Resting left-ventricular function as assessed by radionuclide studies appears to be normal in most patients with anorexia nervosa. Obviously, patients who have metabolic abnormalities, particularly hypokalemia, may have some ventricular dysfunction. In those patients who have anorexia for an extended period of time—with consequent reduction of left-ventricular mass—the left ventricle may eventually become affected. In the adolescent and young adult patients with anorexia nervosa, however, ventricular function studies appear to be normal.

The physician dealing with anorectic patients faces an immense challenge. In general, cardiac function appears to be normal in most of these patients, and detailed cardiac evaluation is usually not necessary. Metabolic derangements may severely affect cardiac function, however, and may be the cause of sudden death in some of these patients. When a physician is faced with such a patient, careful monitoring of cardiac status is critical. With more long-term follow-up in these patients, we hope to be better able to define any progressive abnormalities in cardiac function.

References

1. Task Force on Nomenclature and Statistics of the American Psychiatric Association. Progress report on the preparation of DSM-III. St. Louis: University of Missouri Press, 1976.

2. Gottdiener, J.S., Gross, H.A., Henry, W.L., Borer, J.S., and Ebert, M.H. Effects of self-induced starvation on cardiac size and function in anorexia nervosa. *Circulation* 58:425-433, 1978.

3. Steiger, E., Kovach, K.M., Gross, M., et al. Nutritional studies in anorexia nervosa. Unpublished data.

4. James, F.W. Effects of physical stress on adolescents with normal or abnormal cardiovascular function. *Postgrad. Med.* 56:53-60, 1974.

5. Strauss, H.W., Zaret, B.E., Hurley, P.L., Natarajan, T.K., and Pitt, B. Cinetographic method for measuring left ventricular ejection fraction in man without cardiac catheterization. *Am. J. Cardiol.* 28:575, 1971.

6. Eaton, L.W., Maughan, W.L., Shaukas, A.A., et al. Cross sectional echocardiography I: Analysis of mathematical models for quantifying mass of the left ventricle in dogs. *Circulation* 60:1104-1113, 1979.

7. Thurston, J., and Marks, P. Electrocardiographic abnormalities in patients with anorexia nervosa. *Br. Heart J.* 36:719-723, 1974.

8. Henry, W.L., Ware, O., Gardin, J.M., et al. Echocardiographic measurements in normal subjects. *Circulation* 57:278-285, 1978.

9. Abel, R.M., Grimes, J.R., Alonso, M., et al. Adverse hemodynamic and ultrastructural changes in dog hearts subjected to protein calorie malnutrition. *Am. Heart J.* 97:733-744, 1979.

10. Nutter, D.O., Murray, T.C., Heymsfield, S.B., et al. The effect of chronic protein calorie undernutrition in the rat on myocardial function and cardiac function. *Circ. Res.* 45:144-152, 1978.

11. Abel, R.M., and Paul, J. Failure of short term nutritional convalescence to reverse the adverse hemodynamic effects of protein calorie malnutrition in dogs. *JPEN* 3:211-214, 1979.

Failure to Thrive

John B. Reinhart, M.D.

In the first edition of his textbook *Diseases in Infancy in Childhood* in 1899, L. Emmett Holt wrote the following under the heading "Malnutrition in Infants":

> The history in severe cases is strikingly uniform. The following is a story most frequently told. At birth the baby was plump and well nourished and continued to thrive for a month or six weeks while the mother was nursing him; at the end of that period circumstances made weaning necessary. From that time on the child ceased to thrive. He began to lose weight and strength, at first slowly and then rapidly, in spite of the fact that every known infant food was tried. As a last resort, the child wasted to a skeleton and was brought to the hospital.

In the 1933 edition, under the new editorship and authorship of his son, L. Emmett Holt, Jr., and Ruston McIntosh, the same paragraph appeared, but under the heading "Etiology." It ended:

> Finally it must be admitted that it is not always possible to find why certain infants fail to thrive. Such instances are regarded as due to some congenital weakness of constitution, a concept which is still far from satisfactory. A considerable number of premature infants fall into this group.

This was probably the first use of the term *failure to thrive*, which has persisted in pediatric and child psychiatric literature since that time [1].

Other pediatricians, such as Harry Bakwin [2] addressed this issue, but it was René Spitz who described the clinical syndrome of babies who thrive under their mothers' care but fail to thrive when deprived of this mothering [3, 4]. If their mothers were not restored to them, they persisted in this failure to thrive, not only physically but also psychologically and socially. In 1947, Talbot and colleagues described a similar phenomenon [5], and in 1959, Widdowson published a classic paper, "Mental Contentment and Physical Growth," describing the relationship of the environment—in the psychological and social sense—to the child's ability to thrive and do well [6].

In 1967, in their paper on measurements of growth hormone, Powell, Brasel, and Blizzard described children who, when initially seen, had short stature and lack of growth hormone. Later, after being placed in more suitable environment, these children grew and were producing or releasing growth hormone in normal quantities [7].

Although the syndrome of failure to thrive may be due to a variety of organic conditions, it is well recognized that this condition is primarily caused by psychosocial factors in perhaps 50% of afflicted children. After infancy, this syndrome disappears and blends into growth failure in the preschool years or later years, which is known as maternal deprivation or psychosocial dwarfism. This term implies that parenting of these children is less than adequate to support growth in the physical as well as the social, intellectual, and motor spheres. Indeed, there is evidence that delayed physical development in adolescence might also be related to psychological and social factors.

In pediatric-hospital practice, failure to thrive is the most frequent syndrome seen on an infant ward. Failure to thrive should be considered a point in the continuum of abuse, sexual molestation, and neglect. Estimates are that one in every hundred children in America is so affected.

The criteria for the diagnosis of failure to thrive are as follows:

1. Weight should be below the third percentile at admission, and the infant should respond with significant gain after appropriate environmental stimulation and feedings are begun. Height might not be so severely affected, but this is probably a function of the length of time of deprivation.

2. Usually these infants are also retarded developmentally, and primary mental retardation may be suspected. The head size is usually normal. As with weight gain, these children respond with increased motor and psychosocial development with even the ordinary nursing attention given in a good pediatric hospital.

3. There should be no evidence of any systemic organic abnormality. Renal, cardiac, central nervous system, or gastrointestinal and metabolic abnormalities should be considered, but, as stated earlier, 50% of children admitted to the hospital proved to be without organic disease.

4. The history of child care should support the clinical diagnosis of neglect. The most important part of the workup will be the history of the child's parenting and the parents' past history of being cared for themselves. Such history taking should be the first part of the pediatric management and should precede any laboratory investigations. Evidence of parent-child dysfunction should be expected, and frequent history of deprivation and ineffective parenting of the parents themselves is usually found. Family stresses—financial, social, sexual, and otherwise—are usual.

The mechanisms of growth failure are still not completely understood; however, the failure-to-thrive syndrome may be explained as undereating on the part of the infant or underfeeding on the part of the parent, which are secondary phenomena to the dysfunction in the mother-child unit. Brain growth has been thought to be seriously and permanently affected if growth failure is prolonged in the first year of life. I have, however, observed a patient who had severe growth failure in the first eight months of life but who, at age 50, is of normal height, weight, and intelligence [8].

Case Report 1

The patient was born January 4, 1922, and weighed 6 lb 10 oz at birth. Her mother, a 38-year-old nurse, had had one previous pregnancy, which terminated at six months (following a fall down the stairs and an episode of severe bleeding) with the delivery of a stillborn male infant. The maternal grandmother had also had severe vaginal bleeding following the birth of the patient's mother, her fifth and last child, at the age of 46. The maternal grandfather had been 52 at the time.

Following the patient's birth, the mother also had severe bleeding. She was unable to care for her infant for six to eight weeks, and the baby was cared for by a woman whom the patient still thinks of unhappily. When the mother again began to care for her baby, she was unable to get her to eat or gain weight, and in August 1922, at the age of 7 months, the patient weighed 6 lb 8 oz. She was taken to Philadelphia to see a physician (H. Brooker Mills, M.D.). The patient still had the original formula prescription and directions for feeding from the physician, and her mother had kept accurate nursing notes of the patient's appetite, bowel function, and weekly weights from the time of the consultation in Philadelphia in August 1922 until mid-January 1923. These records had been saved by the patient because her mother had told her of her serious illness—how she had almost died—and had predicted that the record would be valuable to her. This record had been stored away and recently was brought to my attention. Table 9-1 shows the patient's weight gain from age 7 to 12.3 months. (Only monthly weights are given, although weekly records were kept.)

The patient also had a picture of herself at age 23 months, in December 1923, sitting in a chair holding a rattle; she appeared to be a chubby, bright-eyed baby. She went on to complete grade school and high school, obtained both bachelor's and master's degrees, and is active in her profession. She has had no learning disabilities, no serious illness, and no problems with her weight or appetite.

This patient has a documented history of severe failure to thrive, with both physical and psychological recovery. It is possible that mother-child interaction

Table 9-1
Patient's Weight Record, Case Report 1

Date	Age		Weight		
8/7/22	7	mo	6 lb	8 oz
9/10/22	8	mo	9 lb	4 oz
10/8/22	9	mo	11 lb	8 oz
11/12/22	10	mo	14 lb	0 oz
12/10/22	11	mo	15 lb	14 oz
1/14/23	12.3 mo		18 lb	4 oz

in this case was different from that of failure-to-thrive infants on whom we and others have reported. The mother of this infant, though anxious, was involved, kept trying, and did not lose hope. With the consultation and probable encouragement of the Philadelphia pediatrician, she became more relaxed and less anxious and was then able to help her infant accept and absorb feedings, gain weight, and recover. The more typical failure-to-thrive infant has more severe psychological dysfunction, which would seem more likely to be the cause for the subsequent retardation and learning disability than protein or other nutritional deficit.

Mechanisms of a Failure to Grow

Animal experiments suggest that there is a critical point in development when the size of an animal, resulting from a previous plane of nutrition, determines its appetite thereafter and ends its rate of growth and dimension at maturity. The earlier in the life of the animal undernutrition is imposed, the more serious and permanent its effects will be. It is supposed that there is an organization of centers in the hypothalamus during this critical period; after the critical period, there is the possibility of appetite, conscious or unconscious, to insure that intake of nutrients is only slightly more than enough to meet current expenditures on growth and other activities of the body. Neuroendocrine function is not yet clear. (Neuroendocrine function is the relationship between the cortex, the hypothalamus, and the pituitary and the release of specific hormones—in this case human growth hormone, which is required continuously through childhood and adolescence in order to attain normal adult stature.) The mechanisms are complex; deficiencies may be simply in the amount of growth hormone available or may extend to the release of other pituitary hormones as well. Hereditary, isolated growth-hormone deficiency is rare in comparison to idiopathic hypopituitarism. Growth hormone itself does not act directly on growing cartilage but causes the liver to secrete another hormone, somatomedin, which has to do with cartilage growth. Other factors, such as growth-hormone-inhibiting hormone or somatostatin, may be important. These hormones, which are released and may be inhibited, may offer other avenues to future treatment, in addition to diet and improvement in psychological and social environments. It is interesting, however, that cases have been reported in which exogenous human growth hormone had failed to stimulate growth in children who, after a change in environment, began to grow satisfactorily, manufacturing or releasing their own hormone.

Regarding the psychodynamics in failure-to-thrive cases, again the pieces are still being pulled together. As in all patterns of interaction, both the child and his caretaker play a part in the interaction. Some infants fail to respond as well as others. Some infants refuse to suck and are difficult to care for; studies such as those of Thomas, Chess, and Birch, [9] have identified these infants as congenital activity types. Just as children vary in their capacity to respond, parents also vary in their capacity to stimulate and care for infants. When the difficult child has to live with the difficult parent, a difficult situation can be expected. Subclinical cases of failure to thrive can occur even in the best of parenting situations. Keen observers of mother-infant interaction have described infants as young as eight weeks old who became depressed upon the withdrawal of a mother's attention [10]. In one case, a baby gained only 9 oz in a three-week period after his mother had weaned him because she had to care for her older child, who was ill. The infant was described by a nurse as "extremely pale and listless, his fontanelle was depressed, his skin inelastic and his expression lethargic. His conjunctiva color was better than his general appearance would have suggested. He looked cold. I touched him again to make sure his skin was a normal temperature." A nurse described the treatment, which involved the mother giving the infant intense stimulation through many modalities, and the baby responded promptly. It is likely that, had this baby been placed in the hospital for observation and tests at this critical stage, his condition would have deteriorated. This child was in the earliest stages of what we call the failure-to-thrive syndrome. As in cases of infant abuse, prematurity has been noted in many studies of failure to thrive; the problem may be related to the difficulty in bonding created by the premature birth.

In the hospital, infants with environmental failure to thrive have been distinguished from normal infants and from those with organic failure to thrive by their more positive responses to objects and to distant social approaches. They do not respond so positively, however, to close interpersonal interaction, such as holding and touching, and it may be that this behavior precedes the development of the syndrome.

The interaction of children with their families is not always one of gross neglect; it may be subtle. A case history will illustrate [11].

Case Report 2

Kay and Tom, healthy twins, were born in April 1954. Their growth curves were parallel until early in their second year, when Kay stopped growing physically and showed developmental delay in both motor and language skills.

Kay was refused admission to school at age 6 because of her short stature and slow mental development. She weighed 22 lb and was 34 in. tall at 7 years, both far below the third percentile for her age but at the fiftieth percentile for a 2-year-old. Her psychological-test score (Binet L-M) was 65.

By chance, she was admitted to special-education classes, where sensitive teachers suspected Kay had more potential than she showed. In nine months of school, Kay grew 5 inches and gained 18 pounds and her Binet score climbed to

93. She became an active, cooperative child, and her appetite and thirst, initially excessive, returned to normal in her first few months of school. At age 14 she reached the tenth percentile for height and weight—the same level as that of her twin brother. She was performing well in school at her grade level—two years below her brother's—and reading tests showed that she performed at her grade level, whereas her brother performed two years beyond his level. She began to menstruate at age 14 and in all other respects was a normal 14-year-old girl.

In retrospect, her growth failure was related to her mother's depression following the maternal grandmother's death and the fact that the paternal grandparents helped out during the time of the maternal grandmother's death and the mother's spontaneous abortion by taking Kay to their home. It seemed there was an alienation between mother and daughter, and her parents experienced a growing sense of hopelessness regarding Kay as she ceased growing.

Once Kay got to school, she began to grow and learn; her emotional environment improved, and the somatopsychic operation reversed. This little girl, as well as her parents, apparently felt helpless and hopeless for the years between age 1 and age 7, and school—an intervention—helped to restore a sense of optimism. In our experience, however, this is not the usual case.

Families of Failure-to-Thrive Children

Studies of the families of children who fail to thrive indicate that the mothers are generally depressed, angry, helpless, and desperate and have poor self-esteem [12]. As seems to be true in cases of child abuse, these parents have had poor nurturing themselves. Psychiatric studies of the parents are few, but one study of 12 mothers found that 10 of them were suffering from character disorders, while only 2 were diagnosed as psychoneurotic [13]. This study made an extremely important point—that such a diagnosis will greatly influence intervention strategy. Parents with character disorders have limited capacity to perceive and assess their environment, the needs of their children, and their adverse affective state. They also have limited capacity for relationship, they think literally and concretely, and they are not good candidates for the usual problem-solving psychotherapy approaches. These parents are more likely to respond to action-intervention; they need parenting themselves, in an anaclitic relationship, and will need a lengthy treatment program. In some cases, when parents suffer from severe character disorders, so that all attempts to relate to them are unsuccessful, a change in the child's environment will be necessary. In our hospital, we have identified three types of families. The first type is the young and immature mother who responds to support and intervention attempts. This group does well on follow-up. The second group is multiproblem, deprived families, with crowded housing and scarce food. Children from such families also respond in the hospital setting but generally relapse when they return home. The third group is the angry parents, who view their children as bad and who resemble the parents we have seen who abused their children. These families also have a poor prognosis. Our follow-up studies have produced essentially the same results as those of Sheridan [14], done 25 years ago.

Treatment

Hospitalization may be required initially, not only for the protection of the infant but to treat nutritional deficits, anemia, and vitamin deficiencies. Since there is an overlap of neglect and abuse, this must also be kept in mind. Hospitalization serves to separate the infant from an anxious, if not hostile, environment; it affords relief to the parents and gives the physician time to make the necessary investigations, particularly of the families and their ability to parent. Treatment must be thought of in terms of the family. Parents are not born with the ability to parent, and some do not learn and cannot be helped. Fortunately, many families can be helped, but a wide range of supportive services will be needed.

If deprivation has not been severe or prolonged, the children will respond quickly. Children whose deficits are severe will be more difficult to help, however, and long-term daily psychotherapeutic efforts may be needed. In general, the children's cognitive learning will improve much more quickly than deficits in personality development and the ability to relate to others.

Termination of parental rights may sometimes be necessary. Although we are able to consider transplants for unsatisfactory kidneys and other organs, we have yet to consider family transplants seriously. Although divorce is accepted for poor marriages, the divorce of a child from his parents for the same reasons is not as easily accepted.

The failure-to-thrive syndrome may be considered on a continuum, ranging from the relatively healthy child with a situational problem to a child whose family involvement is meager and sometimes even abusive. The prognosis seems to depend on the time of life during which deprivation and failure-to-thrive syndrome exists and the degree of psychopathology of the child-environment interaction. Follow-up studies by Spitz [15], Craviotto [16], and Elmer [17] have shown severe psychosocial and physical-growth retardation secondary to maternal deprivation or lack of dietary intake. Our own follow-up studies of failure-to-thrive infants reveal that children from the multiproblem, angry families have an exceedingly poor prognosis if the children remain in those families. We saw no healthy children by age 10 years of this group of failure to thrive. Followup studies are difficult to evaluate; it seems impossible to separate under-nutrition completely from associated environmental influences since they are part of the same entity.

The child's potential for catching up in physical growth is great, particularly if the deprivation occurs after the period of rapid growth in the first six months of life. The prognosis for intellectual and emotional growth, however, particularly the latter, is guarded. It would seem that, as Ainsworth said, "The effects on personality development of deprivation early in life, though not completely irreversible, are more resistant to complete reversability in more cases than are the intellectual functions." [18] .

References

1. Smith, C.A., and Berenberg, W. The concept of failure to thrive. *Pediatrics* 46:661-662, 1970.

2. Bakwin, H. Loneliness in infants. *Am. J. Dis. Child.* 63:30, 1942.

3. Spitz, R. (1945) Hospitalism. *Psychoanalytic Study of the Child* 1:53-74, 1945.

4. Spitz, R. (1946) Hospitalism. *Psychoanalytic Study of the Child* 2:113-117, 1946.

5. Talbot, N.B., et al. Dwarfism in healthy children. *New Engl. J. Med.* 236:783-793, 1947.

6. Widdowson, E.M. Mental contentment and physical growth. *Lancet* 1:1316, 1959.

7. Powell, G.F., Brasel, J.A., and Blizzard, R.M. Emotional deprivation and growth retardation. *New England J. Med.* 276:1171-1283, 1967.

8. Reinhart, J.B. Failure to thrive: A 50 year follow-up. *J. Pediatr.* 81: 6:1218-1219, 1972.

9. Thomas, A., Chess, S., and Birch, H.G. *Temperament and Behavior Disorders in Children.* New York: University Press, 1968.

10. Taylor, R.W. Depression and recovery at nine weeks of age: Introduction and summary by Mollie S. Smart, *J. Am. Academy of Child Psychiatry* 12:3:506-509, 1973.

11. Reinhart, J.B., and Drash, A.L. Psycho-social dwarfism: Environmentally induced recovery. *Psychosom. Med.* 31:2:165-167, 1969.

12. Reinhart, J.B. Failure to thrive. In J.D. Noshphitz (Ed.), *Basic Handbook of Child Psychiatry,* New York: Basic Books, 1979.

13. Fischoff, J. Failure to thrive. In J.D. Noshphitz (Ed.), *Basic Handbook of Child Psychiatry,* New York: Basic Books, 1979.

14. Sheridan, M.D. The intelligence of 100 neglectful mothers. *British Medical Journal* 1:91-93, 1956.

15. Spitz, R.A. Hospitalism: A follow up report. *Psychoanalytic Study of the Child* 2:113-117, 1946.

16. Craviotto, J. and Delicardie, E. Environmental correlates of severe clinical malnutrition and language development in survivors from kwashiorkor or

marasmus nutrition. *The Nervous System and Behavior,* p. 73–95. Scientific Publication No. 251, Pan American Health Organization, 1972.

17, Elmer, E. Failure to thrive—the role of the mother. *Pediatrics* 25:717–725, 1960.

18. Ainsworth, M. *The Effects of Maternal Deprivation.* Public Health Paper 14, World Health Organization, Geneva, 1962.

10

The Assessment of Nutritional Status in Anorexia Nervosa

K. Miller Kovach, M.S., R.D.

The Nutritional-Status Profile of Anorexia Nervosa

Nutritional assessment is a valuable tool during the diagnostic phase of anorexia nervosa. Indeed, the vast majority of patients with anorexia nervosa exhibit a characteristic nutritional-status profile with respect to overall body composition, visceral protein function, and cell-mediated immunocompetence (table 10-1).

Total body mass, as assessed by percentage of usual or predicted weight and percentage of ideal body weight, is generally severely depleted. The measurement of a severe depletion for percentage of ideal body weight takes precedence over percentage of usual or predicted weight except when the patient has lost a large amount of body mass within a short period of time (that is, greater than four or five pounds per week). In this case the percentage of usual or predicted weight is more indicative of current nutritional status.

Patients with anorexia nervosa typically exhibit a generalized lack of adipose tissue, as assessed by the triceps skinfold. Indeed, approximately 75% to 80% of anorectic patients show tissue values below the fifth percentile for their age and sex, and another 10% to 15% are in the depleted range. A triceps skinfold value above the fiftieth percentile is unlikely in anorexia nervosa.

Like adipose stores, muscle mass is significantly below normal limits in these

Table 10-1
Typical Nutritional-Status Profile in Patients with Anorexia Nervosa

Anthropometric data	
Usual or predicted weight	severely depleted
Ideal body weight	severely depleted
Triceps skinfold	severely depleted
Arm-muscle circumference	severely depleted
Biochemical data	
Creatinine height index	severely depleted
Serum albumin level	normal
Serum transferrin level	normal to mildly depleted
Total lymphocyte count	normal
Delayed-hypersensitivity skin tests	normal to depleted

patients. More than 80% of the patients have arm-muscle circumferences below the fifth percentile, and 90% have measurements at or below the fifteenth percentile. Values exceeding the fiftieth percentile are very rare. The results for creatinine height index parallel those of arm-muscle circumference, with approximately 90% of the patients having abnormally low values.

Although a generalized wasting of total body mass is characteristic of anorexia nervosa, individual variances are observed in the fat-to-lean ratio. One patient may show a severe depletion of adipose stores and a moderate depletion of somatic protein, while another may exhibit the exact opposite. These relatively minor differences are presumed to be a function of the premorbid nutritional status or the disease course. Indeed, the amount of weight loss, the way pounds are shed, and the extent of physical activity are just a few of the individual variances found in anorexia nervosa.

The visceral protein is generally within normal limits in patients with anorexia nervosa. Serum albumin values are intact, with fewer than 19% of the patients having depleted levels and the remainder showing measurements exceeding 3.5 gm/100 ml. Mean serum transferrin levels in patients with anorexia nervosa, like serum albumin levels, are in the normal range. Approximately 25% of the values will indicate either mild or moderate depletion. This is attributed to the relatively short half-life of the protein [1, 2]. Nutritional assessments are frequently done simultaneously with other medical diagnostic procedures, which may require restriction of food intake for a few days prior to the blood sample being drawn. This, in turn, results in an abnormally low value. For a true assessment of visceral protein depletion, both hypoalbuminemia and hypotransferrinemia are needed.

The vast majority of patients with anorexia nervosa have intact cell-mediated immune function. Mean values for total lymphocyte count are well within normal limits. Approximately 15% of patients tested show evidence of some depletion for this parameter and one-third of these are in the severe-depletion range.

Results of delayed-hypersensitivity skin testing closely resemble those for total lymphocyte count. When tested, about 75% of patients with anorexia nervosa respond normally to the antigens. Of the remaining 25%, 20% exhibit relative anergy and only 5% are anergic. As with the visceral protein compartment both parameters should be in the depleted range for an assessment of immune incompetence to be made.

In summary, the protein-calorie malnutrition observed in the majority of patients with anorexia nervosa is characterized by generalized muscle wasting and a lack of subcutaneous fat. The visceral protein compartment and cell-mediated immune system remain at normal or near-normal measured values. This nutritional-status profile is characteristic of marasmic malnutrition, a state in which the somatic and adipose stores have effectively preserved visceral status.

The Role of Nutritional Assessment in Treatment

During the diagnostic phase of anorexia nervosa, the nutritional assessment can be one component in evaluating treatment options. Results from the procedure permit an objective, cost-effective decision to be made regarding the type and degree of nutritional support needed by the patient.

Evidence of either impaired cell-mediated immunocompetence or inadequate visceral protein levels can be considered indicative of severe protein-calorie malnutrition and a high nutritional risk. Patients exhibiting such depletions should be hospitalized, and an aggressive nutrition-support program should be started.

Most patients with anorexia nervosa have normal visceral protein levels and cell-mediated immunocompetence. These cases can be managed adequately with a structured feeding program that insures weight gain. If the patient fails to gain weight over time or loses more than three to five pounds from the weight at the time of diagnosis, it is recommended that the nutritional assessment be repeated to ascertain if changes have occurred in the degree of nutritional risk.

Nasogastric tube feeding is the nutrition-support system of choice. The amount of tube feeding given should be calculated to provide enough kilocalories to permit a weight gain of approximately two pounds per week. Numerous commercial products that are nutritionally complete and isotonic are available at a reasonable price. Following the initiation of tube feedings, nutritional assessments should be repeated every 10 to 14 days until visceral protein levels (particularly transferrin) and cell-mediated immune function are normalized. Once this has occurred, the patient can begin an oral feeding program.

Hyperalimentation, or total parenteral nutrition, is an extremely expensive form of nutrition support that has little place in the treatment of anorexia nervosa. Its use should be restricted to those rare cases when a medical emergency, such as high fever or trauma, induces an obligatory hypermetabolic state or when the patient is assessed as at a high nutritional risk and such enteral forms of support as tube feedings are not tolerated.

Once the diagnosis of anorexia nervosa has been established, the results of the nutritional assessment become the basis for a nutrition-support program to meet the needs of the patient with respect to goal weight, calories, protein, and other major nutrients. Potentially, an improved clinical course and decreased time of treatment may result.

The Assessment Procedure

The nutritional-assessment protocol for anorexia nervosa currently used at the Cleveland Clinic Foundation includes 11 numerical parameters, a food-intake record, and a brief physical examination for clinical manifestations of mal-nutrition. The procedure is part of the diagnostic work-up on all patients with suspected anorexia nervosa. The tests and interpretation of the findings are per-formed by a registered dietitian who is specifically trained in nutritional assess-ment. The numerical parameters assessed are height, current and minimal weight, percentage of ideal body weight, percentage usual or predicted weight, triceps skinfold, mid-arm muscle circumference, creatinine height index, serum albumin, serum transferrin, total lymphocyte count, and delayed-hypersensitivity skin tests to common-recall antigens.

Height assessment is necessary for calculating ideal body weight and also aids in determining the presence and degree of linear-growth retardation, which is sometimes observed with anorexia nervosa. The measurement is obtained directly at the time of evaluation, from the medical record, or subjectively from the patient.

Current weight and minimal weight are the second parameters assessed. Current weight is used as the numerator in calculating percentage of ideal body weight. Minimal weight, as a function of percentage of usual or predicted weight, is needed to fulfill the net-weight-loss criterion for the diagnosis of anorexia nervosa [3]. Sources for the current and minimal weight are the same as those for height.

The percentage of ideal body weight determines the degree of underweight (or overweight) exhibited by the patient in comparison to a reference standard. For patients 18 years of age or older, ideal body weight is obtained by using standard reference tables of desired weight for height [4]. Ideal body weight for patients under 18 years of age is from standardized pediatric growth grids [5]. Percentage of ideal body weight is then calculated as (current weight ÷ ideal body weight) X 100.

If the patient is under 18 years of age and exhibits evidence of linear-growth retardation, percentage of predicted weight is used. Predicted weight is obtained by evaluating past growth records to ascertain the premorbid weight-for-height percentile [5]. Through projection to the current age in the same percentile, percentage of predicted weight is calculated as (present weight ÷ predicted weight) X 100.

Triceps skinfold is an indirect indicator of body fatness and, therefore, nonprotein energy reserves. It involves the measurement, with accurate skin-fold calipers, of a double layer of skin and subcutaneous fat at the midpoint of the upper arm, over the triceps. The reference standards and procedure de-scribed by Frisancho are used, because the values were obtained from the American population [6]. The procedure is simple. With the patient standing, the distance between the olecranon and acromial processes of the relaxed, hanging right arm is measured and the midpoint marked. From the back of the arm, a full fatfold is grasped at the marked midpoint and lifted cleanly from the underlying muscle tissue. The calipers are then applied to the fatfold approximately 1 cm below the fingers. After equilibration, the fatfold measurement is read from the meter on the calipers. The procedure is done three times, and measurements are averaged to obtain the final value.

Arm-muscle circumference provides an estimate of lean body mass, also referred to as the somatic protein compartment. It is calculated from the arm circumference and triceps skinfold. As in the body fatness measurement, the reference standards and procedure outlined by Frisancho are employed [6]. Arm circumference is measured by encircling the upper arm at the marked midpoint with a nonstretchable insertion tape measure. Like triceps skinfold measurement, the measurement is taken three times, and the mean figure is used as the final value. Arm-muscle circumference (cm) is then calculated as arm circumference (cm) - [triceps skinfold (mm) × 0.314].

Creatinine height index, like arm-muscle circumference, is an indirect method of assessing somatic protein stores. Creatinine is a normal waste product of muscle metabolism and is excreted in the urine. The amount of creatinine produced is a function of the amount of muscle present. Therefore, as the amount of lean body tissue decreases, so does urinary creatinine excretion. Creatinine height index is determined through analysis of a 24-hour urine specimen for creatinine content. Actual patient creatinine values are then compared to the expected creatinine excretion if the patient were at ideal body weight. These expected values are 18 mg creatinine per kilogram of ideal body weight per day for females and 23 mg creatinine per kilogram of ideal body weight per day for males [7]. Creatinine height index is expressed as the actual-to-ideal ratio.

Serum albumin value is one parameter used to assess serum protein status, also known as the visceral protein compartment. It is directly quantified as part of the routine blood work.

Serum transferrin, like serum albumin, is a hepatically produced protein that is assessed to determine visceral protein function. It is considered a more sensitive indicator of protein-calorie malnutrition than serum albumin [1]. Serum transferrin levels are obtained by one of two methods. The first utilizes immunological methods to quantify the protein directly. In the second method, serum transferrin (mg/100 ml) is estimated by dividing the total iron-binding capacity (μg/100 ml) by 1.45.

The total lymphocyte count is one of two parameters to ascertain immunocompetence. The depressed immune function found in protein-calorie malnutrition is correlated with total lymphocyte counts of less than 2000/cu mm [8]. The parameter is obtained from the differential of a complete blood count by multiplying the percentage of lymphocytes by the number of white blood cells (per cubic millimeter) and then dividing by 100 to yield the total lymphocyte count (per cubic millimeter).

Delayed-hypersensitivity skin testing to common-recall antigens is the final numerical parameter. Like the total lymphocyte count, delayed-hypersensitivity skin tests are used to assess immunocompetence by measuring the patient's resistance to infection. Five common-recall antigens are employed: *Candida albicans,* 1,000 protein nitrogen units (PNU) per milliliter (Hollister-Stier); mumps skin-test antigen, undiluted (Eli Lilly); tuberculin PPD, 5 tuberculin units per 0.1 ml (Parke-Davis); *Trichophyton,* 1000 PNU/ml (Hollister-Stier); and streptokinase-streptodornase (Varidase), 10 units of streptokinase and 2.5 units of streptodornase per 0.1 ml (Lederle). The risks associated with the delayed-hypersensitivity skin-test procedure are slight. If anaphylactic shock were to occur, it generally would be within the initial quarter-hour following the injections; therefore, the patient should not be left alone during this period. In addition, people with a history of allergic reactions to egg, chicken, feathers, or the preservative thimerosal (Merthiolate) should not be given the mumps skin-test antigen, according to the manufacturer's instructions.

In addition to the foregoing objective tests and measurements, dietary and clinical or physical findings are noted. Overt signs of protein-calorie malnutrition and vitamin or mineral deficiencies are looked for while anthropometric measurement and skin testing are being performed. Particular attention is paid to the skin, hair, nails, and eyes. Dietary data are collected, generally in the form of a 24-hour recall, unless the patient has documented bulimia or laxative abuse. This information is used to ascertain specific areas of nutritional deprivation and to corroborate the reported history of weight loss. Alcohol consumption and the use of nutritional supplements are also recorded.

Analyzing the Data

The data from the nutritional assessment are used to evaluate body composition, visceral protein function, and immunocompetence.

The evaluation of body composition involves determining the adequacy of the somatic protein compartment and adipose stores as well as the overall status of total body mass. The parameters used for this evaluation are height, percentage of usual or predicted weight, percentage of ideal body weight, triceps skinfold, arm-muscle circumference, and creatinine height index. Standards for comparison of body-composition parameters with the degree of nutritional depletion are presented in table 10-2.

Linear-growth retardation in the patient with anorexia nervosa suggests a long-standing, relatively mild history of undernutrition. Such cases can easily go undetected. When the reduced height is accompanied by recent weight loss, a severe form of protein-calorie malnutrition is probable [9]. This frequently is observed in an acute exacerbation of anorexia nervosa in chronic patients.

Percentage of usual or predicted weight determines net weight loss. Thus, it provides an overall picture of the degree of depletion [10]. Although a 25% net weight loss is required for the diagnosis of anorexia nervosa [3], it is not unusual for a patient to have regained some of the weight by the time the nutritional assessment is performed. A percentage of usual or predicted weight of less

Table 10-2
Standards for Comparison of Body-Composition Parameters to
Degree of Nutritional Depletion

Parameter	Normal	Depleted	Severely Depleted
Linear-growth retardation	no	yes/no	yes/no
Usual or predicted weight (%)	>85	75 – 85	< 75
Ideal body weight (%)	>90	80 – 90	< 80
Triceps skinfold (percentile)	>15	5 – 15	< 5
Arm-muscle circumference (percentile)	>15	5 – 15	< 5
Creatinine weight index	>.75	.50 – .75	<.50

than 75% is defined as severely depleted, 75% to 85% is defined as depleted, and greater than 85% is considered normal.

Percentage of ideal body weight is used to assess the patient's present weight in relation to what it should be. Standards for percentage of ideal body weight are greater than 90%, 80% to 90%, and less than 80% for normal, depleted, and severely depleted, respectively.

Percentage of ideal body weight differs from percentage of usual or predicted weight in that the patient's premorbid weight may or may not have been a desirable one. For this reason, percentage of usual or predicted weight and percentage of ideal body weight must be assessed in relation to each other to determine the patient's true degree of overall body-mass depletion.

Subcutaneous adipose-tissue depletion minimizes reserve calorie stores and limits the body's capacity to respond to a catabolic stress. Insufficient adiposity, in addition to psychological stress, is probably responsible for the amenorrhea characteristically seen in females with anorexia nervosa [11]. The degree of deficiency for triceps skinfold is determined by estimating the percentile of the patient's value for age and sex from the reference-standard table (table 10-3).

Table 10-3
Triceps Skinfold Percentiles (mm)

Age (yrs)	Male					Female				
	5th	15th	50th	85th	95th	5th	15th	50th	85th	95th
10½–11½	6	7	10	17	25	7	8	12	20	29
11½–12½	5	7	11	19	26	6	9	13	20	25
12½–13½	5	6	10	18	25	7	9	14	23	30
13½–14½	5	6	10	17	22	8	10	15	22	28
14½–15½	4	6	9	19	26	8	11	16	24	30
15½–16½	4	5	9	20	27	8	10	15	23	27
16½–17½	4	5	8	14	20	9	12	16	26	31
17½–24½	4	5	10	18	25	9	12	17	25	31
24½–34½	4	6	11	21	28	9	12	19	29	36

Source: Adapted from A. Grant, Nutritional Assessment Guidelines, 2nd ed. (Berkeley, Calif.: Cutter Medical, 1979), pp. 19-20.

Adipose stores are considered normal if they are above the fifteenth percentile. Measurements falling between the fifth and the fifteenth percentile are considered depleted, and those below the fifth percentile are indicative of a severe depletion.

The somatic protein compartment (muscle mass) is assessed by the arm-muscle circumference and the creatinine height index. The importance of lean body mass should not be underestimated. Adequate muscle function is necessary for such daily activities as work tolerance, deep breathing, and coughing [10]. Furthermore, muscle tissue acts as the protein reserve for amino acids when body needs exeed intake.

The degree of depletion for arm-muscle circumference is assessed by the same procedure outlined for triceps skinfold. Table 10-4 provides the percentile values for the parameter by age and sex.

The creatinine height index, providing an estimate of total body-muscle mass, is dependent on normal renal function and complete urine collection. It is not uncommon for patients with anorexia nervosa to have abnormally low 24-hour urinary excretions, frequently less than 1,000 cc. The effect, if any, that this has on the determination of the creatinine height index is unknown. Somatic protein is considered normal if the creatinine height index exceeds 0.75. A creatinine height value of 0.50 to 0.75 indicates depleted somatic protein, and a value less than 0.50 means severe depletion.

Serum albumin and serum transferrin values are used to assess visceral protein function. The visceral protein compartment encompasses those body proteins that are not related to muscle tissue. Its status determines the body's ability to cope with physical stress, including wound healing and immune response [10]. In times of metabolic need, muscle tissue is broken down to provide the amino acids required for visceral protein synthesis.

Table 10-4
Arm Muscle Circumference Percentiles (cm)

Age (yr)	Male						Female				
	5th	15th	50th	85th	95th		5th	15th	50th	85th	95th
10½–11½	15.0	15.8	17.4	19.4	21.1		14.0	15.2	17.1	19.5	20.9
11½–12½	15.3	16.3	18.1	20.7	22.1		15.0	16.1	17.9	20.0	21.2
12½–13½	15.9	16.9	19.5	22.4	24.2		15.5	16.5	18.5	20.6	22.5
13½–14½	16.7	18.2	21.1	23.4	26.5		16.6	17.5	19.3	22.1	23.4
14½–15½	17.3	18.5	22.0	25.2	27.1		16.3	17.3	19.5	22.0	23.2
15½–16½	18.6	20.5	22.9	26.0	28.1		17.1	17.8	20.0	22.7	26.0
16½–17½	20.6	21.7	24.5	27.1	29.0		17.1	17.7	19.6	22.3	24.1
17½–24½	21.7	23.2	25.8	28.6	30.5		17.0	18.3	20.5	22.9	25.3
24½–34½	22.0	24.1	27.0	29.5	31.5		17.7	18.9	21.3	24.5	27.2

Source: Adapted from A. Grant, Nutritional Assessment Guidelines, 2nd ed. (Berkeley, Calif.: Cutter Medical, 1979). pp. 19-20.

Standards for assessing serum albumin and serum transferrin are presented in table 10-5. Serum albumin values of 3.5 to 5.0 gm/100 ml are normal. Values that exceed 5.0 gm/100 ml are due to dehydration [12] and are sometimes seen in patients with anorexia nervosa who practice self-induced vomiting or laxative or diuretic abuse. The depleted range of 3.0 to 3.4 gm/100 ml is not associated with clinical manifestations. Measurements indicative of severe depletion—less than 3.0 gm/100 ml—result in edema of the feet and ankles. Hypoalbuminemia is a late manifestation in the clinical course of starvation [13].

Serum transferrin is the protein that transports iron from the liver. Its half-life is 8 to 10.5 days, or approximately 50% that of serum albumin [1, 2]. Transferrin is considered a better indicator of current visceral protein status because it reflects dietary intake for the week preceding the blood test.

Standards to assess the adequacy of serum transferrin are the same whether the value is determined directly or through calculation from the total iron-binding-capacity measurement. Normal values are 190 mg/100 ml or above. Measurements between 100 mg/100 ml and 189 mg/100 ml indicate depletion, and values less than 100 mg/100 ml indicate severe depletion.

The evaluation of immunocompetence completes the nutritional-assessment profile. Protein-calorie malnutrition impairs the T-cell, or thymus-dependent, immune system [14]. The parameters used to assess this cell-mediated immunity are total lymphocyte count and delayed-hypersensitivity skin testing to common-recall antigens. Impaired immune function assessed by these measures is associated with an inadequate visceral protein compartment and can change from normal to severely depleted in as little as seven days [1]. Standards for determining the adequacy of these parameters are presented in table 10-5.

The total lymphocyte count provides a quick, indirect method for evaluating cell-mediated immune function, because approximately 75% of circulating lymphocytes are T-cells [15]. Values for total lymphocyte counts of greater than 1,500/cu mm, 1,000 to 1,500/cu mm, and less than 1,000/cu mm correspond with standards for normal, depleted, and severely depleted, respectively.

Table 10-5
Standards for Comparison of Visceral Protein and Immunocompetence Parameters to Degree of Nutritional Depletion

Parameter	Normal	Depleted	Severely Depleted
Visceral protein compartment			
Serum albumin level (gm/100 ml)	≥3.5	3.0–3.4	<3.0
Serum transferrin level (mg/100 ml)	≥190	100–189	<100
Immunocompetence			
Total lymphocyte count per cu mm	≥1500	1000–1500	<1000
Delayed-hypersensitivity skin tests	≥2+	1+	0+

Delayed-hypersensitivity skin testing to common-recall antigens permits an in vivo evaluation of cell-mediated immunity. Standards for the assessment of adequacy are based on the number of positive responses obtained in the 48-hour period following the injections. For the procedure using the five antigens described earlier, a normal response is defined as two or more positive responses. A single response, or relative anergy, indicates depletion, and an absence of reactivity corresponds with severe depletion, or anergy. It has been observed that some patients with anorexia nervosa will remain anergic throughout the testing period and then will exhibit a positive response anytime from 72 hours to one week following the injections. The causes and implications of this are unknown.

Obtaining a past history of the patient's experience with skin testing and previous exposure to the antigens is important. In addition to providing information that might contraindicate the injections, a history gives insight into the probable outcome. Under normal circumstances, a greater than 90% rate of reaction can be expected from a hospitalized population when the prescribed antigens are used [16]. Patients with anorexia nervosa, however, tend to be younger than the average hospitalized patient and therefore might not have as high a degree of exposure to the antigens used. Since reactions cannot occur without previous exposure, the overall rate of response for delayed-hypersensitivity skin testing to common-recall antigens is probably slightly reduced among anorexia nervosa patients. Individual evaluation of age and past history of exposure helps to negate this discrepancy.

References

1. Bistrian, B.R. Nutritional assessment and therapy of protein-calorie malnutrition in the hospital. *J. Am. Diet. Assoc.* 71:393, 1977.

2. Wright, R.A. Nutritional assessment. *JAMA* 244:559, 1980.

3. Spitzer, R.L. (Ed.). *Task Force on Nomenclature and Statistics: Diagnostic and Statistical Manual of Mental Disorders* (3rd ed.). Washington, D.C.: American Psychiatric Association, 1980.

4. Metropolitan Life Insurance Company. *Statistical Bulletin* 40:3, 1969.

5. National Center for Health Statistics. *NCHS Growth Charts, 1976. Monthly Vital Statistics Report.* 25(3) Suppl. (HRA) 76-1120. Rockville, Md: Health Resources Administration, June, 1976.

6. Frisancho, A.E. Triceps skinfold and upper arm muscle size norms for assessment of nutritional status. *Am. J. Clin. Nutr.* 27:1052, 1974.

7. Bistrian, B.R., Blackburn, G.L., Sherman, M., and Scrimshaw, N.S. Therapeutic index of nutritional depletion in hospitalized patients. *Surg. Gynecol. Obstet.* 141:512, 1975.

8. Bistrian, B.R., Blackburn, G.L., Scrimshaw, N.S., et al. Cellular im-

munity in semistarved states in hospitalized adults. *Am. J. Clin. Nutr.* 28: 1148–1155, 1975.

9. Viteri, F.E., and Torum, B. Protein-calorie malnutrition. In R.S.Goodhart, and M.E. Shils (Eds.), *Modern Nutrition in Health and Disease* (6th ed.). Philadelphia: Lea and Febiger, 1980.

10. Kaminski, M.V., and Winborn, A.L. Nutritional assessment guide. Chicago: Midwest Nutrition, Education and Research Foundation, 1978.

11. Frisch, R.E., and McArthur, J.W. Menstrual cycles: Fatness as a determinant of minimum weight for height necessary for their maintenance and/or onset. *Science* 185:949, 1974.

12. Harper, H.A. *Review of Physiological Chemistry* (16th ed.). Los Altos, Calif.: Lange Medical Publications, 1975.

13. Keys, A., Brozek, J., Henschel, A., et al. *The Biology of Human Starvation.* Minneapolis: The University of Minnesota Press, 1950.

14. Law, D.K., Dudrick, S.J., and Abdou, N.I. Immunocompetence of patients with protein-calorie malnutrition: Effects of nutritional repletion. *Ann. Intern. Med.* 79:545, 1973.

15. Lewis, R.T., and Kelin, H. Risk factors in postoperative sepsis: Significance of preoperative lymphocytopenia. *J. Surg. Res.* 26:365–371, 1979.

16. Palmer, D.L., and Reed, W.P. Delayed hypersensitivity skin testing. I. Response rates in a hospitalized population. *J. Infect. Dis.* 130:132, 1974.

11

Attending to Family Issues in Anorexia Nervosa

Grattan Giesey, M.S.S.A. (ACSW)
and
Frederick H. Strieder,
M.S.S.A. (ACSW)

Family Overview

The typical family that seeks a medical institution to treat anorexià nervosa has sought other modes of treatment previously; and the anorectic symptoms typically have been present for one to two years. As a result, the family is entangled and entrenched in a food-oriented system. It is important to recognize the power and seductiveness that lies in the symptoms presented by the anorectic person. Severe weight loss as a result of continued refusal to eat defies logic. In the most severe cases, radical medical intervention is required to save the patient's life. The life-threatening aspect tends to focus most family members' awareness on the patient's eating behaviors. The patient presents herself as helpless and ill, but she bewilders and confounds all attempts to assist her and, in fact, often may covertly or overtly challenge the helper by increasing the severity or frequency of the poor eating behaviors. It is with this paradox that families become engaged in treatment.

The following is a description of a composite typical anorexia nervosa patient and her family. Jane is a 15-year-old girl who lives with her natural parents, who are in their mid-40s. Her siblings are an older brother, aged 26; a sister, aged 20; and a younger brother, aged 10. Her parents brought the patient for an outpatient evaluation because of their concern for her severe weight loss, 25 pounds over the past six months. The patient currently refuses to eat anything but vegetables, and frequently she does not eat at all. She claims that her behavior is acceptable, and, when questioned about her emaciated condition, she indicates that her figure is attractive. Physical complaints include constipation, feeling cold, and amenorrhea. The patient is often obsessed with food issues, as demonstrated by her counting calories, playing bizarrely with food, wanting to cook for others, but at the same time refusing to eat; and she is typically overinvolved with other family members' eating. The patient often engages in excessive exercise but does not appear to be fatigued. These behaviors have been present for one and one-half years; prior to that, her only food concerns were occasional diets. Preoccupation with, frequency, and intensity of the behaviors have increased notably over the past six months. Although there is a history of some family concern for the patient's physiological state, the family states, upon initial inquiry, that their history of physical illness is unremarkable. The patient's academic record is exceptional, but recently she has complained of having difficulty concentrating, and she states that she has had to increase her efforts to maintain her status of excellence. There has been a decrease in social contacts in the last nine months, but the history indicates that she has been socially active but has had no dating experience.

The family, especially the parents, have reacted in several ways. They have supported, cajoled, demanded, and punished the patient in attempts to change her behavior, but to no avail. Even attempts to work with her eating fetishes by supplying particular foods and tolerating bizarre habits have failed, as the patient continues to lose weight. The parents are now bewildered and express a sense of defeat in attempting to deal with their daughter. They indicate recent fighting between themselves as they attempt to work with her. They do not express any other complaints or concerns, however, regarding themselves or other family members.

When a family pursues treatment, it is because their style of accommodating to the anorexia problem has been thwarted, and the delicate balance within the family system has been upset. At the same time, all family members—particularly the patient and her parents—are entangled in eating behaviors and have a history of futile efforts to change these behaviors. According to Minuchin:

> The systems model postulates that certain types of family organization are closely related to the development and maintenance of psychosomatic syndromes in children, and that the child's psychosomatic symptoms in turn play an important role in maintaining the family homeostasis. Anorexia nervosa is defined not only by the behavior of one family member, but also by the inter-relationship of all family members.[1]

Every family (and each individual) has a style of organizing and managing its actions as an organism. There are repeated patterns of behavior that serve the following functions: regulating responses to internal stimuli, contacting interfacing organisms, and regulating the manner in which feedback is communicated to other organisms. Families with an anorectic person characteristically exhibit patterns of enmeshment, overprotectiveness, rigidity, and lack of conflict resolution. These styles are very similar from one family to another.[2]

Enmeshment can be identified in such families as the boundaries within the family structure are examined. There is a lack of clarity in the differentiation of the roles and tasks of parents and children. Children take on the roles of disciplining their siblings and acting as parents to other children. Parents abdicate the responsibility for setting household rules, or one parent colludes with the patient against the other. Dyadic interchanges often are interrupted by a third party, which confuses interactions. Family members expect others to know their thoughts without having expressed them or constantly act on what they assume the others are thinking.

Overprotectiveness is characterized by excessive concern and reaction to another's distress. A child's complaint elicits the parents' listing of solutions to the problem. Family members often secretly set plans for the other members to help them avoid stress. When a family member verbalizes a concern, the response will be to provide advice quickly or to find some way to excuse the situation and thus decrease tension.

Rigidity is measured by the degree to which a family is or is not able to adapt to an opportunity for change. Rigid families have established rules and patterns of interaction that they maintain in spite of influences from their environment or developmental changes that are occurring within the family. Any movement toward change is seen as a violation of the established family rules. Issues of individuation, independence, and separation threaten the family's established modes of interaction. Symptoms maintain the adolescent's childlike dependence on the family, and family members, in turn, encourage this dependence by focusing on symptoms rather than encouraging the interactional changes that are necessary for the child to become emancipated. Frequently, the symptoms of an anorectic patient regulate this rigidity.

Enmeshment, overprotectiveness, and rigidity contribute, in turn, to a family's inability to negotiate conflict situations. Sequences of interaction evolve that tend to deflect and subdue any attempts to highlight or manage disagreement in the family, and the family becomes trapped.

Other characteristics of families of anorectic patients are pseudomutuality and pseudohostility.[3] Pseudohostility is apparent in the continued haranguing style of interaction among family members to provoke apparently healthy behavior from the anorectic person. (This would seem to be in the best interests of everyone, but it fails consistently.) Pseudomutuality is seen when family members seem to agree that there are no difficulties except the medical anorexia problem. An accurate picture of family relations comes with examination of the styles and sequences of interaction rather than from the family's verbal descriptions of itself. In addition, the use of Minuchin's categories regarding family interaction, mentioned earlier, identifies and clarifies dysfunctional sequences of behavior.

The similarities among anorexia nervosa patients and their families have been pointed out in order to clarify common areas of diagnosis and interventions. Equally important is the recognition of differences in such families. The history of the illness is critical for assessment; we have found that, the longer the symptoms have been active, the greater the entrenchment. Conversely, the more recent the onset of symptoms, the greater the capacity of the patient and the family to respond to treatment prescriptions.

The Diagnostic Assessment and the Treatment Plan

The diagnostic assessment and the treatment plan are inseparable parts of the same process. For clarity, however, they will be dealt with as two distinct components of the initial contact with the family.

The following outline provides a useful guide to the interaction that is essential to the assessment process:

I. Family demographic data
   A. Names and ages of all family members
   B. Employment or current educational level of family members
   C. Activities in and outside the home
   D. Social interaction
II. Presenting problem (as perceived by each member in turn)
   A. Presenting symptoms and their duration
   B. Physical and biological contributors, factors, and predispositions noted in the patient and in the family in general
   C. Current social, educational, and vocational functioning
   D. Financial, sexual, and religious factors, if pertinent
   E. Optimal premorbid functioning
   F. Stressors (for example, significant losses—family death, injury to self or a friend, breakup of a relationship with a boyfriend)
   G. Prior professional help sought
III. Family relationships (often most easily sought by asking, "Who is closest to whom?")
   A. Relationships of parents to children
   B. Relationships of children to parents
   C. Relationships among siblings
   D. Marital relationship
   E. Extended-family relationships (should include both parents' families of origin)
   F. Extrafamilial significant others (should include parents', children's, or whole family's associations who are seen as having a significant impact on the family's functioning)

When possible, all family members should be seen simultaneously for the assessment interview. This enhances various family members' ownership of their perspectives on the problem and assures a relative degree of objectivity in the reporting of their own histories and their efforts to deal with the pathology. The conjoint family interview also sets up clear expectations for family involvement and offers the practitioner the initial opportunity to join with the family and begin to establish a therapeutic relationship.

The gathering of data also provides a forum in which the therapist can engage the entire family and offers an opportunity to observe the family's interactions. It is important to note differences and similarities of both content and style (intensity, affect, and so forth) of various family members' reportage. These can give clues to the accuracy of the data and can provide initial information about the functional structure of the family.

Inasmuch as the identified patient and other family members have specifically requested help for the anorexia symptoms, it is imperative that these be addressed at the outset. Frequently, any effort to assess other elements of patient-family functioning will be met with resistance and often with distrust of the care-giver or treatment facility. Conversely, trust and initial therapeutic engagement of the patient and her family are likely to be enhanced if anorexia-related symptoms are discussed at the outset. This caution is given because it is not unusual for the patient and her family already to have given much of the data involving anorexia symptoms to other members of the treatment team before meeting with the family therapist.

The family treatment plan begins with the diagnostic assessment and is an ongoing, changing process. Family therapy is a critical part of the treatment of anorexia nervosa and should be included in the overall treatment wherever possible. The specific form and direction of this treatment will vary according to the unique issues and interactional structures and processes presented by each case. (Family therapy will be discussed in further detail in the next section of this chapter.)

Because the diagnostic assessment and the treatment plan are inseparable components of the treatment process, the diagnosis must be an ongoing, dynamic continuum. As new information becomes available, the assessment must adjust accordingly. If any change in assessment is significant, the treatment plan must also be altered to accommodate the new or different directions indicated by this information.

Family Therapy

A multifaceted approach to treatment is most beneficial, particularly with hospitalized patients. This approach should include group, individual, family, and milieu therapies. Since the patient is an element in a larger system, and symptoms are not developed or responded to simply in terms of the patient or her relationships, treatment must address all areas. Our point of reference is a systems theory, by which symptoms are seen as a reciprocal-feedback interchange. It is essential to develop and use a theory base that defines and clarifies families as systems. Many family interchanges are confusing, deflecting, and deceptive, and a theory model provides an understanding of what is happening and a subsequent direction for intervention.[4]

Most often, symptomatic behaviors must be the initial focus of treatment, but the ultimate focus of interventions is on the structural-interaction processes in the family. It is not uncommon, over the course of treatment, for other problems to surface, particularly if the patients's eating behavior improves. This often is openly stated or is apparent in interactions. If any process is changed, including anorectic behaviors, stress is placed on the entire system to change. The need for family involvement becomes critical, for these changes address dysfunctional patterns that originate from family problems or multigenerational problems manifested in the present generation.

From the outset, treatment-team members must present family therapy as a helpful part of the overall treatment program. They must join with the family, particularly with the parents, in an effort to help the child. In a multidisciplinary treatment team, all members must present a unified effort toward treatment and must support one another. The decision to include family therapy in a treatment plan must include the patient's capacity to respond and to be involved in an interactive process. If the patient's physical status does not permit this, the timing for beginning family therapy can be altered. The family's ability to engage in conjoint meetings also needs assessment. If family members are unable to alter destructive sequences of behavior, therapy with family subsystems (parents alone, siblings alone) or other methods of treatment must be considered.

Even though symptoms may abate, the anorectic patient will tend to revert to them in times of crisis. Therefore, it is essential that family therapy be continued in order to address the interactional patterns that initially precipitated and maintained the symptoms.

Parental Involvement

Parental involvement in psychiatric hospitalization for adolescents can make a substantial difference in the length and quality of treatment, as well as in the postdischarge maintenance of gains made during hospitalization. Conversely, the lack of parental involvement can be detrimental to treatment in many cases.

Parents who bring their children into the hospital have a wide variety of concerns and misgivings—no matter what the diagnosis may be. They have questions about the course and type of treatment and the competence of the staff, and often they are extremely sensitive to the child's reaction to being hospitalized. Parents who bring their children to the hospital are turning over a large part of their life-role very abruptly. In psychiatric hospitalization, this is especially true, as the parents almost always feel considerably guilty about the possibility that they somehow may have caused the psychological malady.

Another important consideration is that, in most instances, patients must return to their families after discharge. If parents are aware of behavioral changes and are willing to support them, there is a greater probability of successful treatment.

Although these factors apply to all patients in psychiatric hospitalization, they are especially critical in the treatment of patients with anorexia nervosa. Issues of family control, guilt, and symptom maintenance are so integrated into family functioning that successful, lasting treatment may be impossible without family involvement in many cases.

Although the family is not necessarily causal, treatment must focus on the sick child within the family context, rather than simply on the sick child, as has been traditional. Also, children's symptoms can play a major part in maintaining family homeostasis, especially if the symptoms have persisted and have been adapted to over a long period of time.

Parental involvement in the treatment of anorexia nervosa has been offered in a several ways at the Cleveland Clinic, including initial and ongoing supportive contact with particular staff members—a nurse, social worker, or resident or staff doctor. This person, who functions as a liaison between the family and the rest of the treatment team, often is informally chosen by the parents. In this way, parents' concerns, complaints, and confusion can be listened to and clarified when necessary, and pertinent information can be passed on to other staff members.

Weekly group meetings provide a forum for parents of prehospitalized, currently hospitalized, and posthospitalized patients to share experiences and feelings regarding both symptoms and treatment phases. These meetings also afford further opportunity for parents to air their concerns and gather information on treatment questions, since the parents' group is led by members of the adolescent psychiatry staff.

Another important aspect of parental contact is offered when staff members have the opportunity to provide informal counseling during family visits to the hospital; this counseling is primarily directed toward reinforcement of the interaction skills being learned in the formal treatment process. We have found it very useful to provide postdischarge, outpatient treatment in order to allow transition from the controlled, safe hospital environment to the real world of home, school, work, and the resumption of other normal activities. Despite preparatory efforts, this change is abrupt, especially in light of the lengthy hospitalizations of most patients with anorexia nervosa; the followup—usually in the form of continuing family therapy, individual psychotherapy, outpatient group therapy, or supportive contact with the patient and parents—is aimed at the maintenance or increase of positive changes that are made during hospitilization.

Case Management

Although case management is not limited to work with families of anorectic patients, this chapter would be incomplete without a note on case management as it applies to the overall treatment of these patients and their families. Case management may be defined as the coordination of the development of the diagnostic assessment and its subsequent prescribed modes of treatment with the interdisciplinary team, the patient, and the family involvement in treatment. In a medical setting, the physician clearly has the ultimate responsibility, but another team member often has a pivotal position that will best facilitate a coordinating role. It is important that this position be recognized by all staff members to enhance the tasks of the coordinator and to identify one person who can be contacted to provide general information about a patient. This person also attends to any conflict or confusion that might occur during the course of treatment. Since many professionals are involved with the patient's family (doctors, supportive medical staff, nurses, nutritionists, psychologists, social workers, and so forth) issues can arise that need clarification. Often the patient's use of a symptom can mislead treatment-team members or manipulate the treatment system to cause further confusion. We have often seen that the capacity of a treatment team to negotiate its own interaction properly has a direct correlation to the patient's capacity to do the same. A case manager is central to the enhancement of a treatment team's capacity to negotiate and provide a clear, consistent treatment program. In the same fashion, this person can serve as a liaison to parents and can help give focus to their involvement in treatment.

Finally, the case manager can monitor and ameliorate the manner and degree to which the hospital intrudes on the family's life. This task includes preparation for hospitalization, such as orienting the family to the treatment program and insuring appropriate follow-up treatment as part of discharge planning. Although case managers may not directly perform all the tasks described, they attend to the treatment regimes and insure that critical issues are examined.

Notes

1. S. Minuchin, *Psychosomatic Families* (Cambridge, Mass.: Harvard University Press, 1978), pp. 20–21.

2. Ibid., pp. 59–63.

3. V.D. Foley, *An Introduction to Family Therapy* (New York: Grune and Stratton, 1974), pp. 18–25.

4. J. Haley, "Ideas Which Handicap Therapists," in Milton M. Berger (ed.), *Beyond the Double Bind* (New York: Brunner/Mazel, 1978), pp. 65–82.

Bibliography

Foley, V.D. *An Introduction to Family Therapy*. New York: Grune and Stratton, 1974.

Haley, J. *Uncommon Therapy: The Psychiatric Techniques of Milton W. Erickson, M.D.* New York: W. W. Norton and Co., 1973.

——. Ideas which handicap therapists. In Milton M. Berger (Ed.), *Beyond the Double Bind.* New York: Brunner/Mazel, 1978.

——. *Problem Solving Therapy.* San Francisco: Jossey-Bass, 1977.

Minuchin, S. *Psychosomatic Families.* Cambridge, Mass.: Harvard University Press, 1978.

——. *Families and Family Therapy.* Cambridge, Mass.: Harvard University Press, 1974.

Palazzoli, M.S. *Self-Starvation.* New York: Jason Aronson, 1974.

12 An In-Hospital Therapy Program

Meir Gross, M.D.

Selection of a Treatment Program

In dealing with cases of anorexia nervosa, therapists often consider recommending in-hospital treatment for their patients. The choice of hospital may be a question that the therapist or referring physician must resolve. Experience has shown that patients might not benefit from admission to small community hospitals that have no special treatment programs for anorexia nervosa. In such a hospital setting, a patient might tend to take advantage of a lack of collaboration between the primary physician and the other physicians that are called for consultation; for example, the patient might set the primary pediatrician against the psychiatrist who sees the patient for ongoing psychotherapy while the patient is hospitalized in the pediatric department, thus creating a conflict between the two treating physicians. It is well known that anorectic patients often manipulate their environment in their efforts to lose weight. They resist any achievement of the therapy goal that will force them to gain weight. For this reason, the patient should be admitted to a special program that is oriented toward anorexia nervosa and in which the physicians, nurses, psychologists, social workers, and mental-health workers are knowledgeable in the treatment of anorexia. Staff cooperation with the anorexia program director helps avoid any manipulative behavior of the patient. Thus, the common goals of gaining weight, changing attitudes toward food, and developing better coping skills to overcome underlying unconscious conflicts can be reached. It is important, therefore, that the referring physician choose a well-known, established treatment center that has experience in treating this condition.

In most of the medical centers that treat anorexia, treatment is a part of the milieu of a regular adolescent psychiatry program. In other centers, a special section is allocated for the treatment of anorexia nervosa and eating disorders.

Indications for Admission

The primary referring physician must deal with the decision of when to refer a patient to a hospital program. In the experience of most therapists, unless the patient gains at least some weight, the course of psychotherapy will be rough. The patient usually is not responsive to psychological therapy while her weight is in a life-threatening danger zone. Thus, if the patient is seen for psychotherapy on an outpatient basis but continues to lose more than 25% of the original body weight, it is necessary to recommend an in-patient program. Not only might continued weight loss endanger the life of the patient, but the patient might not be responsive to psychotherapy at the lower stages of weight loss. Weight gain is important in increasing the patient's cooperation and strengthening the therapeutic alliance.

Another criterion that should be used in a decision to admit a patient to a hospital program is the ability of the patient to cope with outside life without resorting to vomiting or the overuse of laxatives. When a patient induces vomiting, there is always a danger of potassium loss, and a low potassium level might cause arrhythmias or cardiac arrest. The overuse of laxatives leads to a loss of electrolytes and an imbalance in the electrolytes, which could result in unexpected danger to the patient's well-being.

At times, when there is a power struggle between the patient and her parents at home, it might be important to separate the parents and the patient, even if the weight loss is not yet severe. Admission to an in-hospital treatment program is then indicated. This not only will diffuse the power struggle but will help the parents reevaluate the situation and develop better insight into themselves and their reaction to the problem. It might also help them become motivated to family therapy when it is recommended.

When the patient is being admitted to the hospital, she might try to convince her parents to have her discharged. It is important to help the parents be realistic about the manipulative behavior of the patient and to support them. They might show ambivalence about responding to the patient's request or aligning with the therapeutic team. Parental alignment with the therapeutic team is very important for therapeutic success. If the parents agree to the patients demands to be released from the hospital—supposedly out of concern for the patient—this act might worsen the patient's condition. If this parental alignment with the patient precipitates the patient's death, the parents might not be able to resolve their guilt feelings about the situation. It is important that the therapist meet with the parents to make them aware of the highly manipulative and demanding behavior of the patient and to help them understand and align with the attitudes of the therapeutic team—for the sake and benefit of the patient. It should be made clear to the parents that saying no will benefit the patient and that they should also learn to set up limits and be able to say no to the patient when necessary.

Another indication for admission is a patient's suicidal ideations. It is important that the primary physician or therapist be aware of the suicidal potential of the patient; whenever there is any possibility of a suicidal attempt or gesture, admission to the hospital should be considered as an emergency measure.

Admission of the anorectic patient should also be considered whenever there is associated psychiatric disorder. A patient might have schizophrenia, with secondary anorectic symptoms superimposed on the primary psychotic process. In such cases, it is important that the patient be admitted to the hospital and be treated so that the psychosis will be averted or cured. As the psychotic process abates, the patient's appetite and attitude toward food should improve. It is sometimes important to treat the patient with neuroleptic drugs so that the psychotic process will respond first; only then can the anorexia be addressed. If there is no improvement in the psychotic process, electroshock therapy might be indicated.

In a case of severe psychotic depression, the patient might lose weight because of a lack of appetite. Although the anorectic patient might have an excellent appetite but tends to block it or repress it, the depressed patient is merely losing her appetite, with consequent weight loss. As treatment progresses and the depression is cured, the appetite might improve, and there should not be any problem regarding weight. This type of depression should be recognized, and the patient should be admitted for treatment as soon as possible.

Sometimes a patient gets into a highly obsessive, compulsive behavior, in which she tends to intellectualize. It is extremely difficult to break the cycle of the obsession; the patient might not be responsive to outpatient therapy and so will continue to lose weight. This stage should be recognized, and the patient should be admitted to the hospital to build up weight and to deal with the compulsive behavior before any continuation of the psychotherapeutic process.

Another factor in considering hospitalization is the patient's cooperation and motivation. If the patient is not motivated to start outpatient therapy, it is preferable to admit her to the hospital for participation in an intensive, active program. If the patient refuses and the physical condition is deteriorating, it may be necessary to have a family member commit the patient to the hospital. The family should be aware that, by committing the patient to the hospital, they are doing the right thing and that this measure is necessary to save the patient's life. The deterioration of anorexia to a severely depleted nutritional state should be considered a slow suicide process. The situation should be dealt with before it is too late or before the process of deterioration has become irreversible.

A case to learn from is that of an anorectic 26-year-old woman who cooperated superficially with the therapist on an outpatient basis until confrontation about the severe weight loss was necessary. The patient then said that she did not wish to continue with the therapist and that she would consult with another therapist closer to her home. She asked for a written summary of the treatment prescribed for her so that she could give it to the new therapist. The therapist assumed that she was seeing another therapist, and three months passed before he realized that the patient was manipulating him and had not consulted another therapist. After this three-month period, the patient came to the emergency room. She was found to have a severe infection and within a few hours had toxic shock syndrome. She was transferred to the intensive care unit and given large doses of antibiotics, but, since her immunological system had so deteriorated by that point, she died within a few hours. This unfortunate occurrence could have been avoided if the therapist had been alert to the possible manipulative behavior. It should be emphasized that, in such a case, when the resistance was high and there was lack of cooperation, the therapist might have been suspicious about whether the patient was seeing another therapist. Unfortunately, some patients can manipulate even the most experienced therapist. In this case, the successful manipulation led to death. Hospital admission when the patient wanted to change therapists possibly could have averted the unfortunate consequence.

Occasionally, the treating physician might want to admit the anorectic patient to the hospital once the diagnosis is confirmed or even suspected. The patient can then be evaluated more thoroughly, including ruling out any organic problems. Moreover, most therapists agree that, if the therapy starts in the early stages of the illness, the prognosis is better. Hospital admission of the anorectic patient to start more intensive therapy in a milieu setting undoubtedly will improve the prognosis.

Types of Therapy in the Hospital

The program described here is that used for treating anorexia nervosa at the Cleveland Clinic Foundation. Different therapeutic modalities are used, but the main factor for success is the milieu setting, in which patients are attended to 24 hours a day by a special team that is knowledgeable and experienced in treating anorexia nervosa. One type of treatment is individual, insight-oriented psychotherapy, and supportive therapy is used when insight-oriented therapy is not indicated. Behavioral therapy is widely used as a system of positive reinforcements, with contingencies for increasing weight. Group therapy includes a regular, dynamic group attended also by patients with other illness and a specific group therapy for anorectic patients only. Family therapy, biofeedback therapy, and hypnotherapy, all used within the treatment program, are described in other chapters of this book. Assertiveness training is given to patients who might benefit from it. Psychopharmacotherapy, using various medications, is also used when the treating physician considers it necessary.

The question might arise about the best method for treating anorexia nervosa. Different treatment modalities are considered superior at various centers, and the impression often given is that better therapeutic results are being reported. This could be a source of confusion for both doctors and patients. It is important to emphasize, therefore, that when the various statistics are controlled, the treatment modalities used in different centers appear to have the same rate of success—about 80% of the cases treated.

Individual Therapy

Bruch emphasized that psychodynamically oriented therapy, especially the psychoanalytic type of psychotherapy, is not effective in the treatment of anorexia nervosa [1]. This form of therapy is not effective in inducing weight gain or in changing abnormal behaviors, including the patient's attitudes toward food and health. It is the experience of most therapists who treat anorexia nervosa that immediate, complete emphasis should be placed on problems dealing with the outside world rather than a narcissistic concentration on the body. Insight-oriented therapy that focuses on the narcissistic needs of the patient might increase the dependency of the patient on the therapist and might not achieve the goal of therapy, which is to prepare the patient for more mature, self-reliant, and independent abilities to cope with adult life.

In discussing psychotherapy, the two types of anorectic patients described by Garfinkel, Moldofsky, and Garner should be considered [2]. One type is the starver, who reduces the amount of food eaten. The other type is the binge-vomiter, or the bulimic patient. Sometimes starvers change the nature of their disease and, after a period of few months or less, turn to binging and self-induced vomiting. The starver is characteristically inhibited and repressive and might be very resistant to the therapy in a rather passive way, though superficially cooperative. If this type of patient is treated early enough, the prognosis is good and the rate of recovery is considered fairly good. Bulimic patients are more extroverted, however, and often have other behavioral problems, such as drug addiction, alcoholism, or kleptomania. Treatment of this type of patient is more difficult. The therapeutic goals should be directed toward changes in the habits and behaviors that are more resistant to change. Sometimes the therapy for drug and alcohol abuse should be handled primarily by another therapist who is experienced in these kinds of problems. Help of such groups as Alcoholics Anonymous might be suggested as well. Since the bulimic patient is the more chronic type, the prognosis is less favorable.

Insight-Oriented Therapy

In individual, insight-oriented therapy it is important to emphasize to the patient that gain of the necessary weight is only part of the goal for therapy and that it is more important to deal with the underlying issues or conflicts that produced the anorexia. The anorectic symptoms should be presented as a pathological type of coping skill. Healthier coping skills should be developed during the therapy. The type of insight gained in the therapy should enable the patient to see herself objectively so that body-image distortion is recognized and better solutions for dealing with stresses, problems, and difficulties can be chosen. The role of the therapist is to reflect to the patient the types of difficulties the patient is going through and to point to various possible solutions the patient can choose according to her needs. It is the patient who decides on the best solution, because she is the one who best knows her problems. Many times the therapist is in a position to suggest two or three good solutions for the patient to choose among. These suggestions or solutions are all good for the patient; whichever the patient chooses, she will recover. The type of insight given to the patient enables her to reach self-awareness, since she selected the final solution.

Supportive Therapy

This type of therapy is more direct and involves confrontation with reality. It is reality-oriented therapy that focuses on the patient's interpersonal relationships, needs for control, and difficulties in becoming self-reliant, independent, or mature. Gradually, the idea is presented to the patient that becoming more responsible and assuming a more adult role is the goal of therapy. The emphasis is on more direct suggestion. Healthy defense mechanisms are emphasized and reinforced so that the patient will be able to use them effectively. In comparison with insight-oriented therapy, the therapist is trying not to change any of the defense mechanisms but rather to reinforce the healthy ones and extinguish or reduce the use of the pathological ones. In this type of supportive, reality-oriented therapy, the focus is away from the narcissistic concentration of the patient on her eating and her body. The patient is encouraged to interact and develop interpersonal relationships with other patients and staff members, and any gains are praised and reinforced. Any tendency toward withdrawal behavior or narcissistic preoccupation is discouraged. Many times, anorectic patients talk mainly about foods and calories and try to get the therapist involved in this topic. In supportive therapy, the role of the therapist is to confront the patient with this tendency and to help her get away from self-centered issues by diverting attention to the outside world and how to cope with it.

Since many patients insist on getting more advice regarding diet, issues concerning food are dealt with by a special dietitian who is assigned to the patient. Meetings with the dietitian help the patient realize that she can restrict the daily amount of calories so that she can maintain her weight once the weight goal is reached. This gives the patient assurance that she will not lose control by becoming overweight. The dietetic consulation is part of the supportive therapy that is helping the patient gain more trust and control in her ability to maintain her weight within certain limits once the weight is normal. It reduces the patient's need to have control by not eating, by vomiting, or by using purgatives.

Some of the suggestions given during the supportive therapy are directed toward change in the obsessive-compulsive habits of the anorectic patients and their tendency to perfectionism. The anorectic patients often set goals too high for themselves, in addition to the high goals that are expected by the parents. Ability to compromise and be more flexible is encouraged. It is emphasized that nobody is perfect and that a tendency toward perfectionism might lead to frustration. Attempts at making last-minute changes in daily schedules are encouraged. A suggestion that the patient allow herself to be a little lazy at times is also offered and experimented with. This allows the patient to realize that she can tolerate situations that are less than perfect, can be less anxious, and can be more flexible in her attitudes. The patient comes to realize that things are not only white or black, but that there are gray areas in between.

Another issue that is dealt with during the supportive therapy is the tendency of the anorectic patient to separate feelings from thoughts. This tendency is presented to the patient, and attempts at expressing true underlying feelings are emphasized, rather than the tendency to intellectualize and rationalize behaviors. Whenever the anorectic patient is able to experience the world on the feeling level instead of the intellectual level, it is a good prognostic sign. It indicates that the patient is dealing with the real issues that created the need for the anorexia, and there is a good possibility that the patient is ready to give up the need for anorectic symptoms, face the stresses of growing up, and give up the anorexia.

Medications in the Treatment of Anorexia Nervosa

Medications can be combined with other types of psychotherapy. Drugs are used more often with inpatients, but could also be used for outpatients when an attempt is being made to treat the patient on an ambulatory basis or when the patient is being discharged from the hospital. A few types of medications are being used.

Neuroleptic Drugs

The most commonly used neuroleptic drugs are chlorpromazien and perphenazine. The choice of medication is made according to the physician's familiarity with the medication and with its side effects. At the Cleveland Clinic, we prefer not to use chlorpromazine because of the side effect of orthostatic hypotension. Anorectic patients usually have low blood pressure, and chlorpromazine might cause fainting, as a result of the development of hypotension, when the patient is getting off the bed or changing positions too fast. Thioridazine hydrochloride (Mellaril) does not have this side effect as often as chlorpromazine, and it also has an antidepressant effect. Therefore, it could be a better choice than chlorpromazine. Our first choice at Cleveland Clinic is perphenazine, often combined with amitriptyline, a tricylic antidepressant. We prefer this combination because of its antiemetic and antidepressant effects. The action of the neuroleptic drugs is particularly through the dopaminergic system in the brain. The theory is that the neuroleptic drugs tend to block the dopamine in the synapses of the brain cells. Since dopamine is an inhibitor of prolactin release, the prolactin level may increase during treatment with neuroleptic drugs.

Attention should be given to the side effects of the neuroleptic drugs; generally, these are similar in most of neuroleptics, but there may be some differences. One potential side effect is sensitivity to this type of drug, including rash. If that occurs, the medication should be changed to a different neuroleptic drug or discontinued. Anorectic patients sometimes become constipated, and neuroleptic drugs could increase the tendency toward constipation. These drugs also might obscure development of the paralytic type of bowel obstruction (ileus). The physician should be aware of this possibility, since it could result in severe complications or even death. If fever develops as a reaction to the medication, the possibility of an underlying infection should be investigated. If it is believed that the fever is caused by the neuroleptic drug, the medication should be discontinued. Neuroleptic drugs are depressants of the central nervous system, and a combination of such drugs as barbiturates and analgesics or narcotics could increase this effect. Therefore, caution is advised in the combined use of such medications. Special attention also should be given to the anticholinergic side effect of neuroleptic drugs. If they are combined with any other medication that has anticholinergic side effect, such complications as hesitation in urination, blurred vision, severe constipation, and dry mouth might be so bothersome to the patient that the drugs should be withdrawn.

Neuroleptic drugs could cause abnormalities in the results of liver function tests. Since abnormalities in liver function occur because of severe malnutrition in severe cases of anorexia nervosa, caution should be used in the decision to use a neuroleptic drug.

One of the common side effects of high levels of neuroleptic drug use is the development of extrapyramidal signs, which might simulate Parkinson disease. A tight feeling in the throat, slurred speech, and difficulty in swallowing might develop. These side effects can increase the anorexia, and special attention should be given these patients, since weight loss might be increased. Akathisia and ataxia also might occur. These medications should be used carefully in patients with a history of seizures, since they tend to lower the threshold for convulsions and to trigger convulsions. Moreover, anorectic patients sometimes have seizures during the first stages of weight gain because of a tendency to accumulate fluids in the initial phase of recovery. This might happen more often if tricyclic antidepressants are combined with a neuroleptic drug. If seizures occur unexpectedly, the medication should be stopped and the use of such minor tranquilizers as the benzodiazepines (Librium or Valium) might be considered for their anticonvulsant effect.

Neuroleptic medications can be used for only a few weeks to help the patient accept the therapy and deal with the difficulties of weight gain more easily and calmly. Giving up the anorectic symptoms and being exposed to the underlying depression is a crisis situation for the patient, and use of neuroleptic medications might ease this stress. Once the patient starts to cooperate and gains weight willingly, there is no need for continued use of neuroleptic drugs. If these medications are given for too long, there is danger of development of tardive dyskinesia, involving protrusion of the tongue and involuntary movements in both the tongue and the lips. This could create a severe problem, since there is a question about the reversibility of this condition. Consequently, the length of time that neuroleptic drugs are used should be carefully monitored. We usually don't recommend that these drugs be used for more than a few weeks or one or two months. Perphenazine can be given in tablet form, by injection, or in a concentrated-liquid form. The usual dosage is 2 mg to 4 mg two or three times a day. If the perphenazine is being combined with amitriptyline, smaller dosages should be given, usually not more than 2 mg three or four times a day. Amitryptiline also has a sedative effect, and higher doses of perphenazine combined with amitriptyline could induce lethargy and sleepiness in many patients. A concentrated form can be used in patients who are not cooperative in taking the medication. The medicine should be taken before meals, since it will be easier for the patient to eat with less resistance if she is more calm during mealtimes. If thioridazine (Mellaril) is used, the dosage should be from 10 mg to 25 mg three or four times a day. It usually is not necessary to prescribe more than 100 mg a day, since the anorectic patients are underweight. If chlorpromazine is used, dosages for inpatients should be from 25 mg to 50 mg three or four times per day. If it is being given to outpatients, the dosage usually should be lower, from 10 mg to 25 mg three or four times a day before meals.

Antidepressant Drugs

The antidepressants most commonly used are the tricyclic drugs, especially amitriptyline, usually combined with the neuroleptic drug perphenazine. Another tricyclic antidepressant is imipramine hydrochloride. The antidepressants are needed in cases of anorexia nervosa resulting from underlying depression. This depression is evident in some cases but is masked by the anorectic symptoms in most patients with anorexia nervosa. Patients often will use denial, suppression, and repression and will ignore their underlying depression. Many times, when patients do not want to be in touch with their depression, they will develop the symptoms of anorexia nervosa, thereby avoiding the underlying feeling of depression. The highly obsessive, compulsive behavior, with a strict regimen of eating or not eating, is a mechanism by which the anorectic patient diverts her attention from an underlying depression. It is therefore extremely important to look for this depression in the psychiatric evaluation. If there is evidence of endogenous depression in the family, it is likely that the patient will benefit from antidepressant drugs. It is advisable to find out what medication helped other members of the family when they were depressed and to give the same antidepressant drug to the patient. This decision—based on a family drug history—to give the same medication that helped other members of the family might save time in finding the appropriate tricyclic antidepressant, avoiding the trial-and-error method of giving different types of medication until the best one for the patient is found. It is important to inform the patient that one to three weeks of treatment with the tricyclic medication might be necessary before there are any therapeutic effects.

The mechanism of action of the tricyclic drugs is not yet definitely known. They do not stimulate the central nervous system directly, as amphetamines do. The hypothesis is that they block the uptake of norepinephrine in the synapses of the nerve cells at the nerve endings. Consequently, more epinephrine is available in the synapses.

Since patients with the bulimic type of anorexia nervosa sometimes tend to abuse alcohol as part of the binging behavior, it must be emphasized that this type of patient should be warned against the use of alcohol in combination with antidepressants. The combination can enhance the effect of the alcohol and can cause accidental overdose of both the tricyclic antidepressants and the alcohol. Patients who are taking tricylic antidepressants may get drunk more quickly, even with a smaller amount of alcohol, and they could be involved in accidents, especially while driving. Patients should also be warned about the effect of the tricyclic medication on mental performance and physical abilities. Thus, for outpatients, it might be best to prescribe these medications at bedtime.

Since tricyclic antidepressants can have a sedative effect, combination with other tranquilizers should be prescribed with caution. The common side effects of the tricyclic drugs are dry mouth and blurred vision, resulting from disturbances of accommodation. Patients might suffer from severe constipation and even from paralytic ileus if the drugs are given in very high doses. When higher doses of the drugs are given, patients might also complain about delay in micturition, or even urine retention which can be very disturbing. Side effects might also occur in the cardiovascular system, the major one being orthostatic hypotension. Patients might complain that they feel dizzy, especially when they get out of bed abruptly, and they might even have fainting episodes. High doses of tricyclic medication can cause cardiac arrhythmias, and an electrocardiogram could be necessary if high doses are indicated. Depression of bone marrow can be suspected if pharyngitis or tonsillitis develops. It is necessary to check the blood count—especially the white cell count—including the differential count to make sure that the neutrophils are not reduced.

It should be emphasized that anorexia nervosa sometimes is only secondary to underlying depression, as mentioned earlier. The differential diagnosis is done by taking a good history. In addition to loss of appetite, the depressed patient usually has other physiological signs of depression—such as insomnia, lack of energy, slow bowel movements, or constipation—and feelings of guilt associated with the depression. The anorectic patient, however, is usually overactive, with a great deal of energy for different types of activities, including excessive exercise. The anorectic patient actually has a good appetite but tries to block it, ignore it, or convert it to different feelings, such as bloating or fullness. In cases of primary depression with secondary anorexia nervosa, it is important to prescribe the tricyclic medications. Once the patient benefits from the treatment, appetite will improve and there could be a weight gain. In such cases, treatment should be directed mainly toward the depression. Once it is alleviated, anorexia is unlikely to be involved further.

Other Medications

Another medication that might be used in treating anorexia nervosa is cyproheptadine, an antihistamine drug. It is occasionally helpful in reducing anxiety and inducing weight gain in some patients, but it has not proved to be as successful as the neuroleptic or antidepressant drugs. Insulin has also been used in the past, with the expectation that it will cause some hypoglycemia, which will stimulate the appetite. This type of treatment is useless, however, since there is no lack of appetite in anorexia nervosa. Induction of hypoglycemia by injection of insulin might cause more harm than good, and it is not necessary in the therapy for anorexia nervosa.

Electroconvulsant Therapy

Electroconvulsant therapy can be used in treating anorexia nervosa, but it is reserved for patients in whom depression is the major factor. If the anorexia is only secondary to a severe endogenous depression, and if the patient will not respond to tricyclic medications or monoamine oxidase inhibitors, then electroconvulsant therapy could be considered. Once the patient responds to this type of treatment, the appetite improves and there is no loss of weight, because the depression is being cured. Electroconvulsant treatment usually is not as helpful for primary anorexia nervosa. It should be used only for the primary affective disorders or occasionally as a life-saving measure in severe cases of anorexia nervosa, when the physician suspects masked underlying depression—and only after other methods of therapy have been unsuccessful.

References

1. Bruch, H. *Eating Disorders: Obesity, Anorexia Nervosa and the Person Within.* New York: Basic Books, 1973.

2. Garfinkel, E.P., Moldofsky, H., and Garner, M.D. The heterogeneity of anorexia nervosa, bulimia as a distinct subgroup. *Arch. Gen. Psychiatry* 37: 1036–1040, 1980.

13

A Comprehensive Milieu Program for Treatment of Anorexia Nervosa

Barbara A. Reece, R.N.
and *Meir Gross, M.D.*

Successful treatment of a patient with anorexia nervosa requires a comprehensive in-hospital program that creates an optimal milieu. To begin successful treatment within the milieu, the patient must acknowledge that there is a problem and must truly want help for her own sake—not because a significant other wants it.

At the time of admission to the hospital, a complete medical work-up is done to rule out any possible physical abnormalities. If the patient is severely emaciated, our first concern is to stabilize her medically. Depending on individual circumstances, supplementing the intake is essential. There are several methods of achieving this. The most direct and complex method is total parental nutrition, also known as hyperalimentation. By this method, complete nutrition is provided entirely by the intravenous route. A solution of protein hydrolysate, glucose, electrolytes, minerals, and vitamins is infused at a constant rate through an indwelling catheter that is surgically placed in a major vessel, such as the subclavian vein. (Chapter 17 deals with this method in detail.) Another method of introducing nutrition involves inserting a nasogastric tube and administering tube feedings. Intravenous therapy is also used to replace body fluids. The most noninvasive, nonthreatening means of supplementing the patient's intake is with oral nutritional supplements (Ensure, Sustacal, and the like). All these methods of hydrating and nourishing the anorectic patient must be carefully monitored, and the patient must be weaned slowly, since dependence on the method of weight gain is common. Nutritional supplements are treated as medications and are charted as such; patients are required to drink them in the presence of the medication nurse.

It would be easy to ignore the psychological factors and force the patient to gain weight, against all protestations, by forced feeding and rigid controls, but this form of treatment has been seen to increase the rate of recidivism. Overall, we must recognize that the anorectic patient's mode of relatedness or establishing contact with others involves pathological behaviors and manipulations of her environment and relationships. The matrix of emotional responses and behaviors between the therapeutic team and the patient will somehow mimic that of their home environment. Therapists' honest awareness of their own feelings and responses is vital to maintaining a relationship that is therapeutic for the patient. We must use particular caution in dealing with anorectic patients if we find ourselves having personal difficulties with compliance or rigidity regarding food or weight.

It would be antitherapeutic in the early stages of the treatment to deny patients their behaviors or defenses or to force them to make adjustments that they are psychologically unable to tolerate—unless this is indicated by impending physical crisis. Denying or discounting the patients' feelings only serves to increase their resistance. We must accept their feelings while also exploring with the patients alternate or other observable feelings. We can provide objective feedback to help increase their awareness of the consequences of their feelings and actions while allowing them choices within safe limits. Our focus is on the patient as a person, not on eating habits or weight—unless such a focus is indicated by critical physiological factors. If we concentrate on issues of weight or food, we will only be playing the patients' game—allowing them to avoid dealing with the underlying causes of their disorder. They certainly need to discuss their symptoms, which is what weight and eating behaviors are considered, but this need should be provided for specifically, by limiting such discussion to meetings with the dietitian or a specific staff person. Thus, we can let them ventilate their feelings without allowing weight to pervade all their relationships.

It must be recognized that the anorectic patient is dealing with unconscious conflicts in areas of development that are crucial for all adolescents [1], conflicts that adult anorectic patients have yet to resolve. There is a great deal of regression involved in the disorder, and the patients are still struggling with impulses surrounding basic drives—particularly issues of independence, self-esteem, and the resolution of strong and ambivalent feelings toward significant others. We can expect that each of these conflicts will be acted out in the hospital setting, and this can serve as a guide for our understanding of patients' behavior.

The conflict of independence versus dependence is a major developmental issue for all adolescents. Testing limits and having the opportunity to make choices—whether failing or succeeding in them—are requisites for healthy adaptation. This is the conflict that probably will be acted out most consistently in patients' behaviors; it can be seen in their bargaining, negotiating, or manipulating.

Self-esteem, also vital to a healthy psychological adjustment, is an outgrowth of the successful striving for independence and identity. Adolescents learn much about who they are from the responses of others, and this issue often will be present in our interactions with the patients.

For these patients, the difficulty with acceptance of self is closely related to the last conflict mentioned—resolution of their strong yet ambivalent feelings toward significant others in their lives. This is a particularly difficult conflict, as these patients characteristically are rigid in their thinking and, as mentioned earlier, tend to view the world and themselves in extremes. In moments of intense conflict, on a very primal or childish level, they may have wished for the death of a parent or other significant person or fantasized some great harm coming to him. They also hold an idealized view of the parent, however, and they are unable to reconcile the two visions.

As a result of these conflicts, negative impulses or thoughts may arise that the patients feel a great need to control. As a result, patients generally exhibit very high levels of anxiety, which often becomes unbearable. Their behaviors must be viewed as the response to these often overwhelming stresses and primarily as a means of anxiety reduction. This is particularly true of ritualistic behaviors and denial of symptoms or feelings. Regardless of the cause, the stresses or anxieties related to food or eating produce a psychological state within the patients that drives or motivates them to attempt reestablishment of emotional homeostasis. This is what we are observing in their ritualistic behaviors, their strong denial of the reality of their situation, and their resistance to treatment, particularly in the early stages of hospitalization.

A large part of ongoing therapy for our patients is their participation in the milieu or ward community. As defined by the concept of milieu therapy, the staff gains valuable diagnostic information and opportunities for therapeutic intervention as the patients unconsciously act out their developmental conflicts daily within the milieu community. This community includes all personnel and physical facilities that are part of the patients' daily living on the ward, ranging from the various technicians, maintenance personnel, and peers to the nursing staff and physicians. The milieu approximates real-life situations in which the patients identify the roles played by significant others in their lives. The milieu provides a need for structure in order to compensate for executive ego deficits of the patients [2].

Four basic tools are used in the milieu to assure participation and promote a sense of community and personal responsibility: (1) The patient guide outlines activities and responsibilities of the patients. (2) The patient constitution incorporates the philosophy of the milieu and provides concrete guidelines for dealing with ward issues. The constitution also makes provision for the next two tools of milieu. (3) Ward government is a meeting that is held every weekday, and attendance is required of all patients and as much of the nursing staff as possible. The primary function of ward government is basic information sharing about appointments, activities, and so forth. The meeting also provides a clearinghouse for various ward issues and patient conflicts as they arise. (4) The judicial committee is composed of members of the patient body, with a staff advisor. This committee acts as the governing body of the milieu. It provides for resolution of conflicts on the ward—encouraging peer feedback and a degree of self-governing by all the patients. According to the guidelines of the constitution, the judicial committee can impose restrictions, suspend privileges, and otherwise help make patients accountable for their behaviors on the ward, with approval from the staff. Weekly meetings are held to review attendance at ward government and to see that various patient committees are doing their work. Ward conflicts are dealt with when necessary. The purpose of patient-responsibility levels is twofold: it fosters interdependence among the members of the ward community, and it helps people deal with the reality that a person's life and freedom frequently are affected by the decisions of others.

The anorectic patients is competent at manipulating staff when communications between them are even slightly unclear regarding limits, privileges, or treatment regimen. In working with these patients, there is great potential for staff frustration or anger, as the patient sometimes fails to respond to the best efforts and intentions. Clear communication and consistency are thus important aspects of patient care.

To facilitate the communication process, we use the team approach to patient care. The team is composed of the staff physician; the primary therapist, who is either a resident physician or a nurse; the nursing staff, including the patient-care assistants and the unit secretary; social service personnel; teachers from our school program; and a mental-health worker, who organizes the activity program. Designation of clear-cut roles significantly decreases the amount of successful manipulation by the patient and distributes stress among more staff members.

The team approach is a useful tool in forming a significant relationship between staff and patient. Establishing a safe, trusting relationship is important for the treatment, so that the patient feels comfortable enough to share valuable information. This allows other team members to take a confrontive role if necessary.

A subset of this team is the mini-team, which is composed of the staff physician, primary therapist, medical back-up (resident physician), social worker, school teacher, creative therapist, and any other person who has regular contact with the patient. The mini-team meets at least three times during the patient's hospitalization. The first meeting is held within ten days of admission. At this time, a review of the medical work-up, presenting symptoms, a brief history, and observations of the patient since admission are presented by the primary therapist. The case is reviewed by the team, and a treatment plan is formulated and presented to the patient. The second mini-team meeting is held about midway through the hospitalization. The treatment plan is reviewed and updated as necessary. Then, about one week before discharge, a final meeting is held to review the entire course of hospitalization and plan for any necessary outpatient follow-up.

Holding rounds for the staff is one way of keeping the team informed on each patient's progress. Grand rounds, held twice a week, is the format in which staff members from all disciplines can share vital information, such as pertinent medical findings, updates on family therapy, and the day-to-day reports of the patient's progress on the ward from the nursing standpoint. This time is also used by the teaching staff to report results of any testing and the patient's adaptation to our school program. Our mini-rounds are a briefer form of grand rounds, held three times a week to present the day-to-day data on the patient.

When a patient is admitted, the family undergoes a social-service assessment. Once this is complete, the social worker brings a recommendation to the mini-team as to whether or not family therapy is feasible (See chapter 11 for a discussion of family issues.)

The anorectic patients on our ward attend three types of group meetings. (1) In the regular-unit group meeting, the anorectic patients deal with issues of concern to other patients, some of whom are not anorectic. (2) In the anorexia group, the patients can find others to identify with, people who can understand and accept their symptoms. Once this process is accomplished, they are able to move on to deal with the issues behind the symptoms. (3) The anorectic patients are also involved in our assertiveness-training program. Generally, anorectic patients are nonassertive. They tend to be rather passive and submissive in their interactions with others, sublimating the resentment and anger they feel when their needs are not met. As a result, they covertly hurt themselves and others (passive-aggressive behavior) in order to get what they need and feel more in control. It is essential that anorectic patients learn more effective means of communicating their needs and feelings to others. Assertiveness training helps them replace passive-aggressive behavior with more open, honest, direct, nonmanipulative, and nondecaying means of interacting.

Behavior Therapy: The Weight Contract

How do we respond to the patients' weight changes therapeutically? It is a common expectation of the patients that the team will cure them. The only time we assume responsibility for a patient's eating activity is when there is a real danger to the patient's medical condition or physical damage. Otherwise, the return to a healthy weight must be voluntary and educative. A tool to refocus the responsibility for change is the weight contract, which spells out what is expected of the patient regarding weight gain and how the staff will respond if the patient does not gain the prescribed amount of weight daily. Our margin of safety from physical crisis is provided by setting a clear minimum weight at which we will intervene, thereby not violating basic issues of trust with the patient. The responsibility for weight gain is placed on the patient. The contract is drawn up by the team, and the patient gives her input, thus changing the behavior contract to fit her needs.

Basically, the contract is based on the principle of operant conditioning, with positive reinforcement. The reinforcement is usually a reward given for the patient's ability to gain enough weight by her own effort, above the minimal weight expected. Usually, the patients are expected to gain, on the average, a quarter of a pound per day. A graph is drawn showing the line above which any weight gain will be over this minimal average. The patient is weighed every morning in a hospital gown. If the patient's weight gain stays above the line, she is rewarded with special activities, such as recreational therapy, or special privileges, such as visitation or passes to go on the hospital grounds or outside the hospital. So long as the patient's weight gain is above the line, she can apply for raises in the level of privileges specified in the milieu regulations. If the patient's weight gain is below the line—the average daily gain being under a quarter of a pound per day—she is told that she must stay in bed, as specified by the contract. Staying in bed enables the patient to conserve calories, so that it will become easier for her to gain the expected weight. A dietetic consultation is provided to the patient on admission and whenever requested by the patient in order to help her achieve the weight goal and stay above the line on the way to the goal.

The contract is drawn up by the team only after an observation period of at least ten days, so that the team members get to know the patient well enough to plan the best rewards. In this way, the patient will be better motivated to gain the expected weight. Moreover, before the contract is constructed, it is necessary to estimate the weight goal that the patient is expected to reach. This weight goal is determined according to a special nutritional evaluation (described in chapter 10). Once the patient has achieved the weight goal, she is expected to stay over the goal at least ten days, as one of the requirements for discharge from the hospital.

Behavior therapy as a treatment modality in anorexia nervosa was used successfully by Halmi, Powers, and Cunningham [3]; Leitenberg, Agras, and Thomson [4]; Bhanji and Thompson [5]; Agras and associates [6]; and others. It is a promising method for treating anorexia nervosa in a pediatric or psychiatric department in a hospital setting. If behavior therapy is used in such a way that the responsibility of the weight gain is entrusted to the patient, a direct power struggle between the staff and the patient about eating is avoided. It enables the treatment team to avoid the kind of power struggle that had gone on previously between the patient and the parents at home. Consequently, the patient will not develop any negative transference toward the staff, and any resistance is minimized.

It is important that behavior therapy not be used without the patient's agreement and written consent. Otherwise, the therapy itself can become a source of power struggle, without any beneficial results and possibly with the negative results of severe depression and even suicide by a patient who is pushed too far by enforcement of the weight contract. These perils have been mentioned by Bruch [7].

Patients in therapy soon begin to examine their behaviors to see how they can affect weight changes. They learn the fallacy of their magical thinking and the real relationship between food and weight. In dealing with food and weight under such specific guidelines, patients are much less able to involve these issues in interpersonal relationships, and they subsequently begin to change the basic structure of their interactions with their environment. The treatment of these anorectic patients demands a comprehensive approach in order to custom-tailor an operational plan.

References

1. Shatti, M., McCue, A., Ice, J.F., and Schwab, J.J. The development of an acute short-term inpatient child psychiatric setting: A pediatric-psychiatric model. *Am. J. Psychiatry* 136:427-429, 1979.

2. Rubin, S.R. The community meeting: A comparative study. *Am. J. Psychiatry* 136: 708-711, 1979.

3. Halmi, K.A., Powers, P., and Cunningham, S. Treatment of anorexia nervosa with behavior modification. *Arch. Gen. Psychiatry* 32:93-96, 1975.

4. Leitenberg, H., Agras, W.S., and Thomson, L.E. A sequential analysis of the effect of selective positive reinforcement in modifying anorexia nervosa. *Behav. Res. Ther.* 6:211-218, 1968.

5. Bhanji, S., and Thompson, J. Operant conditioning in the treatment of anorexia nervosa: A review and retrospective study of eleven cases. *Br. J. Psychiatry* 124:166-172, 1972.

6. Agras, W.S., Barlow, D.H., Chapin, H.N., Abel, G.G., and Leitenberg, H. Behavior modification of anorexia nervosa. *Arch. Gen. Psychiatry* 30:279-286, 1974.

7. Bruch, H. Perils of behavior modification in treatment of anorexia nervosa. *JAMA* 230:1419-1422, 1974.

14 Group Therapy for Anorexia Nervosa Patients

Enrique Huerta, M.D.

The use of group psychotherapy in medicine, first reported by Pratt in 1906, was designed to help patients with tuberculosis deal with their physical and emotional reactions to illness. A human tendency to seek others with similar problems is certainly not new and is well documented throughout the history of mankind. From the smallest group to the largest societies, people look for comfort, security, and directions in their alliances. The masses seek leadership to obtain both concrete goals, such as land and wealth, and the most abstract goals, such as freedom and eternal life. We are aware of the tendency of children with behavioral, learning, and physical difficulties to drift toward children with similar problems. They make such comments as, "My best friend understands me because he is hyperkinetic, too." Parents discuss common concerns about their children with their neighbors, and hospitals and clinics witness the spontaneous gathering of parents to discuss children with more unusual problems. Time for discussing these problems in waiting rooms and hospital lounges is limited, so they exchange phone numbers, communicate by letters, and have informal gatherings in their homes. These informal gatherings sometimes develop into formal societies, with specific common goals.

For the past 12 years, while working in large medical-referral centers, I have observed the interactions of hospitalized patients. Several times anorectic patients represented half the population of the adolescent psychiatric units. We have not only been intrigued by their interactions but also stimulated to find ways to capitalize on their group dynamics to promote health. It is interesting that, during heterogeneous group sessions (including patients with other problems), anorectic patients tend to form their own subgroup and either dominate the group process or remain passive and detached from the group. A similar phenomenon occurs in the parents' group meetings, in which the parents of the anorectic patients tend to assume a leadership role.

Three years ago, we started a specialty therapy group for anorectic patients who were receiving treatment in the hospital or as outpatients. Because of the large numbers of patients—and to keep the number less than ten patients per group—separate inpatient and outpatient grous were established. I will discuss here our experience with the outpatient group—the group's characteristics, curative factors, findings, and conclusions.

Group Characteristics

More than 100 anorectic patients participated in the outpatient group during the
first two years. The group, defined as open-ended, meets for an hour and a half
each week. New patients join and old patients drop out at different times
throughout the year. The trend is for new patients to participate regularly and
continuously for the first 8 to 12 weeks and then continue on a bimonthly or
monthly basis. Patients who have recovered occasionally return to share their
progress. They elicit reactions of hope and envy as they solidify their freedom
from anorectic symptoms and their interpersonal transactions. Patients who have
not completely recovered return for another therapy course when their symptoms recur in response to a particularly stressful situation.

The group is composed primarily of female participants, with an occasional
male participant; the age range is 12 to 37 years. Approximately half the group
population consists of starvers, and the other half goes through binge-vomiting
cycles (bulimics). Although about one-fifth of the group is or has been married,
only a few have children (most use contraceptive methods). The patients are
concomitantly involved in other types of outpatient therapy (individual, family,
and pharmacotherapy). According to Yalom, the following statements apply to
this group:

> Homogeneous groups of task-oriented high structure, impersonal individ-
> uals as effective human relations groups which produce change in the
> members. Apparently these groups offer a combination of support and
> challenge. The members supported by their perceived similarity and
> challenged by the task of the group, which demands that they interact
> more intensively and intimately than is their wont. The groups tend to
> be highly cohesive. . . . In general, the atmosphere of the group is pre-
> dictable from their composition. [1]

Curative Factors

The curative factors discussed by Yalom are certainly applicable to this group
[1]. Group sessions set the tone for a free exchange of information among the
members. After being introduced to the group, a new member generally listens
quietly to what other new members say. Nonverbal cues—smiles and nods—reveal
the switch from initial apprehension to rapid identification with the group. It
usually does not take much prompting for new group members to verbalize their
concerns. They often apologize for talking too much, taking everybody's time,
and the like. They also express their surprise at the ease with which they can
speak up in the group, when many of them characteristically have difficulties
speaking in a group situation. Occasionally, new members will be able to release

a great deal of affect—especially sadness, with tears—but this is not the rule. The patients are ambivalent about acknowledging the seriousness of the manifestations of the illness, but support from the group may be useful not only in facilitating their discussion of their concerns but also in revealing the striking lack of concern for their physical condition and their gross body-image distortions [2]. They seem surprised to hear that other members of the group, who are obviously emaciated, express great concern about their fatness. The breaking down of the denial can often be observed as the patients, in tears, express their unhappiness and loneliness. They seem encouraged by acknowledging that other group members have experienced or are experiencing similar situations [3]. Some confessions also take place at this time; for example, a patient might say, "Doctor, I lied to you before when I told you that I was not vomiting, I make myself vomit several times a day but nobody else knows about it, it's so embarrassing." They quickly identify their common denominators, such as decreased tolerance to cold, dryness of hair and skin, bluish discoloration of lips and fingers, and inability to have any free time because of the urge to be busy at all times, whether reading or working. On one occasion, a young woman stated that she ironed her clothes over and over until she was totally exhausted.

Group members discuss their obsession with thoughts of food, eating, and weight and how it seems to occupy most of their waking time and even their sleeping time, in dreams. This obsession correlates with gradually increasing alienation from peers, who first attempt to feed the patient; for example, one of the young girls said that when she went to the school cafeteria, several students started throwing food at her, yelling "Eat!" Following an initial stage of concern by her peers, there seems to be a gradual distancing and outright avoidance of the patient. Some of the patients are aware of the personality changes they have undergone in the early stages of the disorder, such as increased irritability and social withdrawal. Other patients indicate that, although they did not notice the changes, they remember that others have commented about them. Some patients seemed surprised to find that many of the other patients are good people and that most of them are good-looking, especially those who are recovering and are at a healthy nutritional state. Just as the common denominators are discussed, so do the differences become evident. Some patients are in the category of "best little girl in the world"—pseudo-mature, overly neat, straight-A student, never rebellious, eager to please, and always must be "number 1." Other patients are not compulsively neat and show more evidence of flexibility and spontaneity. Other differences pertain to the presence or absence of current symptoms, such as binging, self-induced vomiting, feelings of depression, and use of laxatives and diuretics to reduce weight. In my experience with this group, members tend to confront each other very gently, usually obtaining an honest response. The level of personal defensiveness seems to be greatly decreased within the context of the group. Old members seem to have a knack for asking key questions, with diagnostic and prognostic significance as well as therapeutic value. Sometimes, after only a few minutes of interaction with a new member, one of the patients will say, "I don't think she has it; maybe something else but not anorexia."

As a new patient becomes identified with the group, she asks specific questions about the duration of the problem for other group members, the treatment or treatments received and currently receiving, and the progress of each individual. Patients who come to the clinic with much apprehension about treatment soon become reassured when they find that, although there are some fairly standard treatment modalities, each patient is treated as an individual. It is evident that the group process helps the patients make the transition from perceiving as enemies people who show interest in their health and challenge their self-damaging behaviors (parents, physicians, friends) to considering them allies. This is a crucial step in recovery. Many patients are reassured by the acknowledgment that, although they are regaining their physical health, significant conflicts will not be taken care of automatically: "I'm tired of hearing, just eat and everything will be O.K. again."

Especially for those who have had the disorder for several years, there seems to be a ray of hope as they talk with patients who have been able to make noticeable progress under similar circumstances. Individual strengths become evident within the group, and there is much positive reinforcement for behavior indicative of improving health. Members alternate assuming the leadership role and at other times taking more passive roles. New patients show much interest in finding out about specifics about the hospital program, the daily routine, the behavioral contract, daily weight, restrictions, physical activities, and meals. They want to know about what was accomplished during hospitalization and also about adjustment from hospital to home and school. The question of relapse produces much anxiety, since many patients want to deny this possibility but are confronted with the fact that some patients have required many hospitalizations. In contrast, some patients indicate that they have made a great deal of progress as outpatients, whereby their primary treatment consisted of group therapy and they "did not have to be hospitalized."

"I don't know *how* to eat" (or *what, when, how much*) is a fairly common theme discussed in group meetings, although most of the patients have had at least dietary consultation and several are followed actively by the dietitian. Patients discuss feeling at a loss in interpreting their internal signals (including feelings of hunger or satiety), which they cannot trust. They are afraid that if they start eating they will not know when to stop. They think of a number of schemes to keep from eating, expressing a sense of guilt and defeat whenever they give into their hunger or the pressures from others for them to eat. General principles about the importance of a well-balanced diet—initially divided into several meals scattered throughout the day, and then gradually increasing the number of calories consumed per day to gain weight gradually—are part of the educational process. It is interesting that the patient cannot get away with innumerable excuses, because she will be confronted quickly by other group members who understand the anorexia game. Patients talk about their attempts to avoid fats in their diet and to concentrate primarily on consuming proteins because they want to avoid the buildup of fat. A common concern is expressed: "As I gain weight, will it be mostly fat or muscle, and will it go to the right or wrong places?" We recommend moderate exercising as the patient gains weight, not only to promote healthy body rebuilding but also to facilitate realistic revisions in body image. There is much sharing of education on a patient-to-patient level concerning general questions, such as needing not only a healthy weight in order to restart menstrual periods but also a minimum amount of body fat. (Menstrual irregularities are also common in athletes whose body-fat content falls below a critical level.) When patients approach a healthy weight, they start noticing the opposite sex again. Some of our patients who underwent self-imposed starvation during prepuberty maintained short stature for a period of time; after gaining weight, however, some of them experienced a growth spurt. The patients compare notes about what is helping various group members to regain their health. Although, at the beginning most patients tend to think that their improvement is due primarily to external factors—such as their nutrition, the dietitian, or their parents—it seems that, as they become healthier, they assume more responsibility for the progress that is made and they attempt to communicate their belief: "Nobody can make you well until you decide that you want to get well." It is interesting that medications do not get much credit in the group, in contrast to family therapy, assertiveness training, biofeedback, and self-hypnosis, which obtain much praise. When medications are discussed, it is often in terms of the bothersome side effects. This seems to be in contrast with information obtained in individual therapy and also from observations of family members and other observers, who frequently report the positive changes related to medication.

Discussion of hospital experience seems to encourage some patients to remain outside the hospital and provides further motivation for successful outpatient treatment. Other patients, however, are reassured that being in the hospital may not be as bad as they thought and actually become prepared, so that when they enter the hospital they have at least some idea of what is expected of them and what they can realistically expect of treatment [4]. Inpatients often talk about their longing for the sheltered environment provided by the hospital: "I didn't have to worry about making decisions" and "Whenever I was upset I could find somebody to talk with." On the whole, they seem to use this regression as a temporary step before making important moves toward progress. Some, however, view this regression as too extreme and threatening, leading to total dependency and loss of control. This latter group is the exception to the rule.

The group often resembles a family structure, with parents and siblings represented. Patterns of communication are tested and modified many times by gradual approximation to the desired goal. Direct communications, conflict resolution, and overall assertive behaviors are positively reinforced by the group. It is striking to hear some patients offer the most sensitive and accurate advice to other patients. The other patients may take that advice seriously, follow it, and then report positive results, but the patient who provided the advice may not value her own advice enough to apply it to herself. This may be the first step in her acceptance that what she has to say is of value and that she can become her own best friend rather than worst enemy. As these patients feel more comfortable in dealing with their feelings of anger, fear, anxiety, sadness, and loneliness, they show evidence of increasing self-confidence and strength, manifested by spontaneity and assertiveness.

The group measures progress not only by weight gain and improvement in physical appearance but also by an increase in physical strength, tolerance to cold weather, appearance and texture of skin and hair, and, later, resumption of menstrual periods—which are proudly announced to the group. Group members place even more importance on the subjective changes of improved mood, decreased irritability, more comfortable interpersonal relationships with peers and family members, more realistic body image, decreased preoccupation with food, eating, and weight—with a shift of attention toward defining a clear sense of identity—making moves toward assuming more responsibility for oneself, and increased willingness to make commitments appropriate to the particular developmental stage.

The curative factors may be summarized as follows:

1. *Imparting of information by group members and therapists.* This includes discussion of premorbid personality structure and the anorectic signs and symptoms, with concomitant physiological, psychological, and interpersonal changes. The rationales for treatment modalities are also discussed, as well as their application and suitability for a given individual. Patients become excellent diagnosticians and prognosticians.

2. *Installation of hope and fear as patients are confronted directly by both healthier and sicker people.* Patients see or hear about other group members who have already improved in the group and are particularly impressed by those who have improved without having to be hospitalized. They are ambivalently impressed by the severely cachectic individual, often saying, "I don't want to live like that."

3. *Universality.* Anorectic patients' sense of uniqueness is often heightened by their social isolation ("Nobody understands me"). From very early sessions, this disconfirmation of their feelings of uniqueness is a very powerful source of relief for them as well as an incentive to define their uniqueness in terms of healthy and adaptive qualities.

4. *Altruism.* Patients want to help each other. They derive self-esteem from their ability to be useful to other group members. They no longer need to fight the world and protect their anorexia. As a group, they fight the newly perceived common enemy—their anorexia.

5. *Corrective recapitulation of the primary family group.* As the group resembles a family, with male and female therapists as parental figures, maladaptive, growth-inhibiting relationships are not permitted to become rigid, and the closed, structured system that characterizes many families is prevented. Rigid behavior is constantly challenged, by exploration of relationships and suggestion of new ways of behavior by the therapist. Even the quiet and passive patient, who becomes a spectator, is able to learn from the more active patients when they have difficulties in common. Patients also imitate other members' behaviors, trying them and later discarding or keeping them.

Impressions

Although the initial purpose of this group was to provide additional support for outpatients, in order to avoid hospitalization whenever possible, additional uses have become rather apparent.

1. The group is a diagnostic tool. Even after thorough evaluation, further and crucial information may be obtained in a single group session. As the patient is able to identify with other group members, she becomes less defensive and more willing to reveal information that she was embarrassed or afraid to admit to the physician. Some of this information may be critical in making an accurate diagnosis and, therefore, a reasonable treatment plan.

2. The group can be preparation for intensive treatment in the hospital. Outpatients who have previously denied the seriousness of their illness and actively resisted any treatment may acknowledge the need for treatment and switch from the position of having a treatment *forced* on them to that of being receptive to the idea of treatment and actively participating in the tailoring and implementation of the treatment plan.

3. The group is extended support for patients recently discharged from the hospital. Group participation serves as a transitional stage in which the patient is able to maintain communication with the hospital while going through the difficult adjustment from life in the hospital to a return to the real world.

4. A large proportion of patients make excellent progress on an outpatient basis, with group psychotherapy as the main therapeutic modality and individual and family sessions taking a secondary role.

5. The group is a refresher course for ex-patients who have been away from treatment. Some patients may return for a few sessions when, because of unexpected stressful situations, they become more aware of and concerned about early signs of relapse. Other patients return for one or two sessions whenever they have the opportunity; for example, some students who are away at college visit the group during their vacations. When these patients are doing well, they serve as healthy models for identification by other group members. It is also reassuring for the students to compare themselves with patients who are actively struggling with anorexia; it provides them with a perspective that reassures them

of the important gains they have made—particularly giving up the anorectic identification.

Conclusion

We are currently analyzing demographic, symptomatic, and treatment variables that may be correlated with short- and long-term responses to single or combined treatment modalities.

Patients who do not do well in the group generally are those with borderline character structure, particularly that associated with the syndrome of bulimia. These patients seem to require several hospitalizations, long-term psychiatric hospitalization, or both, with intensive treatment. Patients with the bulimia syndrome seem to fall into two categories. Some respond well to the group we have described in this chapter. Patients in the other category seem to require a more tightly structured, concrete, goal-oriented group that uses clear-cut behavior-modification techniques. We are currently testing a specific tool that may help us identify these two subgroups from the beginning, in order to get them involved in the most appropriate specific treatment.

With ongoing clinical research, we will be able to improve treatment skills and refine our individualized treatment plan. Because anorexia nervosa provides an excellent model for psychosomatic illnesses, improved methods of treatment should become available for other disorders in which physical and emotional factors interact to perpetuate the illness.

References

1. Yalom, I.D. *The Theory and Practice of Group Psychotherapy.* New York–London: Basic Books, 1970.

2. Bruch, H. *Eating Disorders: Obesity, Anorexia Nervosa and the Person Within.* New York: Basic Books, 1973.

3. Stein, A. Group therapy with psychosomatically ill patients. In H.I. Kaplan, and B.J. Sadok (Eds.),*Comprehensive Group Psychotherapy.* Baltimore: Williams and Wilkins, 1971. Pp. 581–601.

4. Lucas, A.R., Duncan, J.W. and Piens, V. The treatment of anorexia nervosa. *Am. J. Psychiatry* 133:1034–1038, 1976.

15 Hypnotherapy in Anorexia Nervosa

Meir Gross, M.D.

Many treatment modalities have been tried for anorexia nervosa with only limited success. At times a cure is elusive; a patient might have exacerbation of the illness even after a few years during which she is considered cured. Some studies have reported a mortality rate of 14% to 21% [1, 2].

Treatment methods for anorexia nervosa can be elaborate and complicated, because most patients are resistant to treatment and usually refuse to relinquish their need for the illness, since it represents other underlying conflicts. Their usual way of dealing with the illness is denial. It is thus understandable that hypnosis has not been widely used in treating this disorder, because the motivation and cooperation of the patient are important factors in successful hypnotherapy. If the patient resists therapy, the best hypnotherapist might fail even in inducing of a trance, much less in achieving a therapeutic goal. In addition, previous attempts to treat anorexia with hypnosis involved giving patients direct suggestions to eat more—an approach that is sure to fail.

Medline library research in 1980 found no listed journal publications on the use of hypnotherapy for anorexia nervosa. A few books in the last few years, however, did mention some beneficial therapeutic results of treating anorexic patients by hypnosis. Kroger and Fezler presented a method of treating their anorectic patients by combining behavior therapy with hypnosis [3]. They gave their patients posthypnotic suggestions associating food and good appetite with pleasant memories, while helping the patient ventilate feelings of aggression, disgust, and hostility. They also emphasized the fact that a hypnotic relationship can foster a rapport between the anorectic patient and the therapist, which can be used for the benefit of the patient by suggesting better appetite and using images to enhance feelings of hunger or emptiness in the stomach.

Crasilneck and Hall described the use of hypnosis for anorexia nervosa in a similar way [4]. They suggested increasing awareness of hunger feelings and enjoyment of eating, since it is good for the health and welfare of the patient. The suggestion to increase eating is only their first step; they also recommended hypnoanalysis to uncover underlying psychodynamic conflicts that produced the anorectic symptoms. They treated 70 cases of anorexia, with marked improvement in more than half.

Thakur proposed hypnotic suggestions for better meaning in life, for better eating habits—including increased food intake for weight gain—for altering the body image, and for self-assertion in interpersonal relationships [5].

Spiegel and Spiegel see the value of hypnosis for anorexia nervosa in helping both in the diagnostic process and later in treatment. Hypnosis is helpful in sorting out underlying psychiatric disorders, thus increasing the effectiveness of therapy [6].

Patient Selection and Results

I have had the opportunity to evaluate and treat 500 patients during the last five years. Diagnosis was based on Feighner's criteria [7]. Ninety-five percent of these patients were admitted to the Adolescent Psychiatry Unit for treatment. Of the 500 patients, only 50 were treated successfully with hypnosis. The other patients were aware of the availability of hypnotherapy but objected to it. When hypnotherapy was suggested, 12 other patients agreed to it but resisted when induction occurred, claiming that they could not get into a hypnotic trance or that they did not believe they were under hypnosis and therefore could not use this treatment modality. The other patients who resisted hypnotherapy openly expressed fear of hypnosis, but underlying this was the fear of losing control over their ability to lose weight or to keep their weight down. The 10% who were willing and motivated to use hypnosis for therapy were able to use it successfully by gaining weight and improving their coping skills in dealing with everyday responsibilities. The 12 patients who resisted covertly could be considered failures of hypnotherapy, but they were treated successfully by other treatment modalities, such as individual therapy, group therapy, behavior therapy, and medications.

Target Symptoms for Therapy

Before describing cases and the suggestions given during the hypnotic trance, it is important to present the symptoms of a typical anorectic patient, as the removal of these symptoms is the goal of successful hypnotherapy. It is important to dwell on certain symptoms and dynamic emotional issues in order to understand better the goal of the hypnotherapeutic suggestions.

Because of external precipitating events—such as the divorce or separation of parents, a sibling leaving home, going away to college, or not being popular in school—the adolescent girl may start to feel powerless; she cannot change the stressful event or prevent it. Life is not perfect anymore, as it used to be. Feelings of inability to cope and to grow up and face the imperfect adult life creep in, associated with feelings of loneliness, self-doubt, and poor self-esteem, causing the adolescent girl to be preoccupied with her appearance and physical development. Remarks by friends or family members about her being too chubby or having big hips or tummy might motivate her to go on a diet, so that friends or others who are important in her life will appreciate her thin body.

As the girl begins to reduce her weight successfully, she feels proud of her willpower. These girls are perfectionists, and the tendency to block and ignore their feelings of hunger makes them proud, which is reinforced by their success in getting thin. Most patients report that they feel hungry but that these feelings are effectively suppressed, either by ignoring them while busy with a heavy daily schedule or by getting involved in exhausting exercises. The patients usually distort normal feelings of hunger or satiation into feelings of emptiness or fullness. This distortion of feelings is accomplished by conversion mechanisms that are seen in conversion reaction, dissociative reaction, or a trancelike state. Hunger or satiation stop being the primary physiological regulators of food intake. The ability to lose weight successfully compensates for feelings of worthlessness or powerlessness and gives the anorectic patients a sense of control, which overcomes her feelings of incompetence [8]. The need for this control becomes so important to the patients that they are willing to manipulate their environment in order to continue losing weight by several means, including ritualistic behavior about eating, eating slowly, vomiting, or using purgatives. They live in constant fear of losing this control over eating. Awareness of hunger becomes completely confused with abnormal self-evaluation and self-concept, including a distorted body image [9, 10].

Normally developing adolescents learn to respond naturally to their inner cues. Anorectic patients have failed to learn this and tend to block their awareness of impulses, feelings, and needs that originate within themselves. The failure to respond to their inner cues is the core of their psychopathology. They tend to separate feelings from thoughts, and this increases as they develop obsessive-compulsive personality, governed by thoughts that drive them to perfectionism.

This constant driving toward perfectionism and ignoring their own impulses create restless overactivity to a degree of exhaustion and inability to relax. They pursue their activities with a driven, obsessive behavior. They cannot sit still unless they are doing something, and they never have time to enjoy feelings of relaxation.

This level of compulsiveness triggers increased sympathetic body tonus, which is evident in attempts to relax with the help of biofeedback equipment. There is overemphasis on the activities of the sympathetic adrenergic system and suppression of the parasympathetic system, which can have an effect on the gastrointestinal tract. There is lowering of peristalsis, constipation, a feeling of fullness, and suppression of hunger. A decrease in the function of the endocrine system also is seen, including a reduction in sexual drive and function and amenorrhea, which is common in anorexia nervosa.

Based on the foregoing symptoms and clinical psychodynamics, the goal of successful hypnotherapy should be toward alteration in body image and interoperception in patients suffering from anorexia nervosa. The patient's difficulties with internal cues should be recognized, and an attempt should be made to sensitize the patient to better self-awareness. An increase in self-perception during the hypnotic trance could help the patient become aware of her inner hunger and satiety cues and her body's need for relaxation in order to reduce the restless overactivity. The hypnotherapy should improve the patient's sense of ineffectiveness, which will boost the much needed self-esteem. Being better able to recognize sexual needs and desires and to increase external perceptions are other goals of the hypnotherapy. The therapist should avoid giving the patient any direct suggestion to eat more, however, since this suggestion will increase the patient's antagonism and can pull her out of the hypnotic trance.

Hypnotic Suggestions for Presenting Symptoms

Similar suggestions are given for each symptom removal, but the suggestions are changed according to the individual needs of the patient and the degree of resistance presented.

Suggestions for Relaxation

One of the earliest beneficial effects of hypnotherapy on anorectic patients is that it helps them relax, reducing the level of hyperactivity common to these patients. Either through regular sessions with a hypnotherapist or by self-hypnosis, patients are able to calm their overactive neuromuscular systems. Hypnotic relaxation, like the relaxation response described by Beary and Benson [11], is associated with a generalized decrease in the activity of the sympathetic nervous system. The heartbeat and respiration rate are decreased. The electro-encephalogram shows slow alpha-wave activity. Not only does the patient benefit physically from hypnotic relaxation, but it also provides time to stop and think about herself and her goals in life.

The suggestions given to the anorectic patient include seeing herself in a nice scenic place, such as a park or beach. While she is relaxed, it is suggested to her that she be in touch with the sensations from her muscles, her stomach, her breathing, and her heartbeat. Suggestions are also given for a greater awareness of external stimuli, such as smelling the grass and flowers in the park or smelling the special salty smell of the sea. These suggestions are directed toward better self-awareness from internal and external stimuli, while enjoying a sense of relaxation all over the body. This self-awareness will enable the patient to be more in touch with tension of her muscles. Only by relaxing the muscles during the hypnotic trance does the patient become aware of the tension before the relaxation; she then appreciates the relaxation more.

Suggestions for Correcting Body Image

Anorectic patients have badly distorted body images. Hypnosis allows the therapist to suggest more rational body types as desirable goals. To help patients see themselves objectively, they are shown photographs of themselves during therapy. The hypnotic imagery of these photographs makes patients realize how thin they are. A healthier body image is suggested by the hypnotherapist as a future goal. Patients are asked also to draw pictures of themselves, so that the therapist can learn the degree of their body-image distortion. Sometimes a patient will draw a normal body size, but with big hips. That helps the therapist understand that the image distortion is located in only part of the body; during the hypnotic trance, the therapist can concentrate primarily on the distorted body part. Suggestions are given to the patient to touch and feel each part of the body during the trance, including areas of the stomach and heart, but especially the parts of the most distorted image. Sometimes a female patient is asked to choose a healthy, normal-weight woman as a model for identification, and it is suggested that the patient project her image in the same weight as the model figure. Projection into the future is a well-recognized hypnotherapeutic technique that can be used quite effectively in the therapy of anorexia nervosa; it has been found to be very beneficial to patients who suffer from distorted body image.

Defect in Interoceptive Awareness

The anorectic patient usually blocks perception of the sensations of her internal organs. She might feel very hungry but will deny it, completely blocking the perception. The self-denial practiced by anorectic patients tends to interdict normal body sensations such as hunger. Because of this, the girl cannot even perceive a sensation of satiation, and sometimes, when she can no longer block hunger, she will eat huge amounts—an eating binge—with no ability to control it. Induced vomiting becomes an artificial means of control, and the use of laxatives might become an everyday measure for reducing weight. It is clear that these patients have lost their natural mechanisms of eating behavior, which for many normal people and animals is regulated with amazing efficiency and minimal conscious control. Natural, self-regulated eating control is being disrupted in these patients by a variety of psychological and environmental factors, to which women appear to be more vulnerable. The source of the preoccupation with food and diet can be explored under the hypnotic trance, so that food and eating behaviors become normalized to their unconscious, autonomous, and natural level of biological, physiological functioning.

During the hypnotic trance, the patient is advised to concentrate on the feelings of hunger and respond to them by recognizing these feelings as hunger, not as bloat or fullness. She is advised to be sensitive to feelings of satiation when she eats, so that she can eat only in order to satisfy the hunger. Being sensitive and attuned to her inner mechanisms gives the patient a sense of security.

The Sense of Ineffectiveness and the Need for Control

Most anorectic patients lack self-esteem. They are perfectionist in their attitudes, so anything they try to achieve seems unsuccessful and not perfect enough. This is the main reason that most patients who suffer from anorexia nervosa also suffer from depression.

Marion, a 15-year-old girl, was rather active before she started to lose almost 40% of her body weight. She participated successfully in ballet dancing, played the piano, and was an A student. During her evaluation, it was found that her parents were on the verge of separation and were actually only nominally living together. They refused family therapy when it was offered. During individual therapy with Marion, it became evident that she felt at a loss, being unable to change the situation at home. The more ineffective she felt, the more she needed some control over these feelings. Reducing the amount of food she ate helped her gain some control over her parents, who became concerned about her. To forget her problem, she became involved in dancing and musical activities.

Learning self-hypnosis enabled her to gain some sense of control. She realized that she could not change her home situation but that she could pursue her own interests and career. Projection into the future during the hypnotic trance helped her separate herself emotionally from her parents and gain control over her own future rather than over the relationship between her parents. She was able to regain her weight and be more assertive and effective in her attitude, with better self-esteem. She was able to deal with her difficulties rather than running away by being too busy. As therapy progressed, she was able to realize that her overinvolvement in many activities and her tendency to overexcel was a running-away mechanism. She was able to reduce her expectations and learn to enjoy her activities rather than trying to be the best and still feeling inferior.

The hypnotic suggestions given were: "See yourself as you would like to see yourself five and ten years from now. Realize how independent and self-sufficient you can be then, having complete control over your life." These suggestions enabled her to gain control over her future, even though she felt helpless about the present.

Therapeutic Abreaction

Sometimes a traumatic event that is the source of the anorexia becomes obvious during the course of hypnotherapy. Even if it is not obvious by regular therapy, hypnotic age-regression might reveal the event, and abreaction of feelings associated with the trauma could alleviate the anorectic symptoms. Recognizing the traumatic event in childhood and working through the abreacted feelings can lead to a successful resolution of the anorexia.

Sara, a 20-year-old Jewish girl, had lost weight over the previous 7 years. When seen, her weight had decreased 30% from the previous percentile. Two years of psychotherapy had not improved her condition; she continued to lose weight while in therapy. She was brought for hypnotherapy as a last resort. During the evaluation process, she was found to be very hypnotizable and highly motivated to use hypnosis. During hypnotherapy, age regression and abreaction were used, and the patient was able to bring forth a traumatic event that had occurred when she was about 12 1/2 years old.

During a fast on Yom Kippur, she was feeling very hungry and sneaked to the kitchen to eat a slice of bread. Her mother caught her eating, and she was spanked severely and punished. She also was told that God would punish her for eating during Yom Kippur. Since then, her appetite had diminished and anorectic symptoms had developed.

During hypnotherapy, she became aware of this incident and was able to recognize her guilt about eating; her appetite gradually improved. She has had no anorectic symptoms during a 4-year follow-up.

Suggestions given to the patient were: "Now you are watching the movie of your life going backward from the present time to your childhood. If you see anything that was very upsetting to you, raise your right finger. I will stop the movie, and you can tell me about it." If the event is too traumatic, the therapist can remind the patient that "it is only a movie."

Resistance

As mentioned earlier, one of the major difficulties in psychotherapy for an anorectic patient is the overt or covert resistance. Since it takes a motivated patient to benefit successfully from hypnotherapy, it is understandable that hypnosis has not been widely used in therapy for anorexia nervosa. Since, in the beginning of therapy, the patient objects to any pressure to eat more, any direct suggestion to increase appetite or eat more will not be accepted and might even increase the resistance.

A knowledgeable therapist can use any wish for improvement in any area in the patient's life to introduce self-hypnosis. This might make the patient interested in the technique, at which time the therapist can suggest better eating indirectly, in order to improve the patient's performance in her hobby, for example. The therapist can emphasize that, with self-hypnosis, the patient will be able to have complete control and that in heterohypnosis, the operator does not control the subject. With the suggestion of self-hypnosis, the patient might realize that it could be used for self-improvement in other areas. It could also be used as a method of maintaining the weight once the patient has reached the weight goal expected during therapy. In that way, the patient will realize that there is a method that will help avoid becoming overweight.

If hypnotherapy is presented as a tool for the patient to gain control over her weight, it might be accepted. Properly presented, self-hypnosis is then eagerly learned by the patients, regardless of the threat to their personal sovereignty, since it is seen as a means of gaining further control.

A good example is Regina, aged 27, who was referred for consultation because of no progress in psychotherapy for 12 years. The diagnosis was anorexia nervosa. She previously had been seen for therapy by three psychiatrists. No progress was made; in fact, the patient continued to lose weight. She had gone from a weight of 120 lbs at age 15 to 70 lbs at age 27. She was superficially cooperative but never participated meaningfully. She was resistant to anything that might make her fat. She liked to play golf in her spare time. Hypnotherapy was suggested, and its benefit for self-improvement was emphasized, especially in reducing anxiety while playing golf. She became excited about the possibility of being less anxious playing golf and became willing and motivated to learn self-hypnosis. While the patient was under a trance, it was suggested that, in order to hit the ball with more force, she could concentrate on how to make her muscles stronger. She gradually started to gain weight and to be more confident, while giving up the anorectic symptoms. In this case, the suggestion to get better and stronger was given to the patient indirectly. She felt she had complete control over her trance, and by suggesting to herself better performance in playing golf, she indirectly concluded that she would have to eat better in order to become a stronger player.

Summary

Hypnosis can be a very useful tool in therapy for anorexia nervosa if it is used in a nonauthoritarian way. An authoritarian approach, with a direct suggestion to increase the appetite and eat more, is too simplistic and is doomed to failure because of prominent resistance in most patients. This is also the reason that only about 10% of anorectic patients are sufficiently motivated to use hypnosis for therapy and benefit from it.

References

1. Hsu, L.K.G., Crisp, A.H., and Harding, B. Outcome of anorexia nervosa. *Lancet* 1:61-65, 1979.

2. Hsu, L.K.G. Outcome of anorexia nervosa, a review of the literature (1954-1978). *Arch. Gen. Psychiatry* 37:1041-1046, 1980.

3. Kroger, W.S., and Fezler, W.D. *Hypnosis and Behavior Modification: Imagery Conditioning*. Philadelphia: J.B. Lippincott Co., 1976.

4. Crasilneck, H.B., and Hall, J.A. *Clinical Hypnosis: Principles and Applications*. New York: Grune and Stratton, 1975.

5. Thakur, K.S. Treatment of anorexia nervosa with hypnotherapy. In H.T. Wain (Ed.), *Clinical Hypnosis in Medicine*. Chicago: Year Book Medical Publishers, 1980.

6. Spiegel, H., and Spiegel, D. *Trance and Treatment: Clinical Uses of Hypnosis*. New York: Basic Books, 1978.

7. Feighner, J.P., Robins, E., Guze, S.B., et al. Diagnostic criteria for use in psychiatric research. *Arch. Gen. Psychiatry* 26:57-63, 1972.

8. Sours, J.A. Anorexia nervosa: Nosology, diagnosis, developmental patterns and power control dynamics. In G. Caplan and S. Lebovici (Eds.), *Adolescence: Psychosocial Perspectives*. New York: Basic Books, 1969.

9. Bruch, H. Perceptual and conceptual disturbances in anorexia nervosa. *Psychosom. Med.* 24:187-194, 1962.

10. Bruch, H. Hunger and instinct. *J. Nerv. Ment. Dis.* 149:91-114, 1969.

11. Beary, J.E., and Benson, H. A simple psychophysiologic technique which elicits the hypometabolic changes of the relaxation response. *Psychosom. Med.* 36:115-120, 1974.

16 Clinical Biofeedback Therapy in the Treatment of Anorexia Nervosa

Michael G. McKee, Ph.D.
and
Jerome F. Kiffer, M.A.

Clinical biofeedback therapy has direct application to the treatment of three main features of anorexia nervosa: (1) disturbed body image, (2) lack of awareness of inner stimuli, and (3) profound sense of lack of control. Therapy for anorectic patients is effective when it increases the sense of effectiveness, releases inner feelings, and corrects hypothalamic imbalance [1]. Biofeedback therapy focuses on increased awareness of inner stimuli, increasing a sense of control, increasing a sense of personal effectiveness, releasing underlying feelings, and restoring homeostatic balance. It thus has special relevance to treatment of those patients for whom the main issue is a struggle for control and for a sense of autonomy and effectiveness.

The first step in biofeedback treatment of anorexia nervosa is a complex diagnostic process to evaluate the extent to which a stress reaction is represented by the eating disorder. This includes an evaluation of psychophysiological correlates of the stress reaction. Finding that a stress reaction exists and that there are psychophysiological correlates indicating a homeostatic imbalance is not sufficient to suggest that clinical biofeedback therapy will be helpful. Biofeedback therapy is no more a panacea than is any other single modality of treatment in this complex disorder, which probably has multiple causal factors [2]. If a stress reaction is indicated, the treatment would be more than training with biofeedback instruments. Biofeedback therapy involves a therapist and manifold therapeutic processes and is itself enmeshed in an even more complex matrix of therapies for the anorectic population. A single case will illustrate the complexity—a case in which biofeedback first was an ineffective part of the treatment and then became an effective part of the treatment, its efficacy depending on the patient's readiness to apply skills learned in biofeedback therapy to her daily life; this readiness rested on other therapeutic gains.

The patient was a 17-year-old girl with a 5-year history of self-induced vomiting and weight loss. At the initial visit, she weighed 65 pounds, down from 118 pounds 5 years earlier. Psychophysiological assessment with biofeedback equipment indicated homeostatic imbalance, hyperarousal, and, in particular, very cold fingers, but she had the potential to reverse the arousal, to warm her fingers, and to relax herself. She could demonstrate changes in digital palmar temperature of more than 15 F in a 15-minute period.

Did she want to exercise this control? Did she want to be relaxed? Did she want to experience the feelings that might emerge? She did not. After a few sessions in which she demonstrated a great deal of control, but an inability or unwillingness to use the control outside the sessions, she said, "Perhaps we should stop. I'm pretty stubborn. I don't want to do this."

There appeared to be several reasons why this patient did not cooperate with this treatment program. Part of her identity seemed to be that of a sick individual. She particularly delighted in defining herself as a medical mystery, as being so complexly ill that she represented an extreme diagnostic puzzle. This identity gave her status and removed her from the ordinary tasks of adolescence. Self-induced vomiting also gave her control—particularly over her father, who had a major drinking problem and volatile temper and who tyrannized the household. The patient could control him by saying, "Behave yourself, I'm sick." The anorexia also gave her control over school, over pressures for sex, and over not having to become an adult and face the demands of adulthood. Her behavior pattern also let her be extremely self-indulgent, so that she could eat good-tasting or junk foods all day long, simply vomiting them and thus not getting fat. Her illness also made her the center of attention in the family, enabling her to win the competition with her brother for family attention. It also served opposite ends, simultaneously distancing her from the family; she could spend weeks in the hospital without being involved with the family. The self-punishing aspects of the disorder partly represented depression secondary to the loss of significant people in her life, particularly the recent death of her grandparents, with whom she had been very close. The extreme somatic preoccupation, of which anorexia was only part, enabled her to deflect almost all important feelings. Furthermore, the anorexia required that she stay at home when she was out of the hospital, thus being a companion for her mother, who found the father intolerable. It gave the father a rationalization for continued drinking, because he was burdened with a child with such a complex illness. Thus, the needs of several family members were served by the patient's illness.

Getting well did not represent enough of a payoff, and therefore quick change was not possible. Because of the illness's value in the family and in allowing the patient to avoid adult responsibilities, major family therapy and major training in coping skills had to be provided before there was a shift in her anorexia nervosa. Following these therapies, she was able to benefit from learning alternate responses to tension. According to her mother, vomiting developed as an infantile reaction to stress and, apparently being partly a conditioned response, elaborated into anorexia nervosa for the reasons discussed. When the elaborating reasons were dealt with, biofeedback therapy was helpful in directly teaching stress management. The patient was able to use imagery and cognitive rehearsal techniques in the biofeedback session to develop skills in generalizing her ability to relax in everyday situations that formerly would have led to aberrant eating or vomiting behavior. In short, she had better control and could use it for health rather than sickness.

Biofeedback equipment helps an anorectic patient gain healthy control by giving precise information about bodily functioning. A piece of biofeedback equipment is a precise electronic mirror that objectively reflects a physiological process and helps correct the distorted body perceptions of the patient.

A basic use of the biofeedback mirror is to teach relaxation techniques, many of which have been used by clinicians for several decades. The use of relaxation techniques is appropriate for anorectic patients because their activity level is unusually high. They tend to deny fatigue and typically display an inability to relax. Many are obsessive individuals with a high level of compulsiveness. This leads them to engage in behavior that produces excessive levels of autonomic arousal, which can generate psychophysiological stress reactions of various sorts. Since biofeedback therapy has been used for many years to treat psychophysiological reactions such as muscle-contraction headache and hypertension [3], the high frequency of somatic complaints and tensions that accompany anorexia nervosa makes biofeedback intervention a logical treatment approach. The biofeedback mirror shapes, guides, and rewards relaxation training. Biofeedback equipment provides physiological information that indicates the depth of relaxation attained. Biofeedback provides knowledge of the desired outcome and appears to accelerate relaxation training [4]. By being connected to the biofeedback machines by sensors placed on the body, the patient becomes an active participant in the process of relaxation training, and attention is directed to the current situation. In this way, the massive denial often encountered in anorectic patients is diffused. It is difficult to deny tense muscles when there is visual and auditory information showing high levels of muscle tension.

Biofeedback is rarely threatening. Adolescents are usually fascinated by electronic gadgetry, and this fascination is amplified by being an active participant in the session and receiving direct information about bodily functions. Most patients quickly develop a positive transference to the biofeedback instruments, and this positive transference often is extended to the biofeedback therapist. With the transference, and with the experience of deep relaxation, the patient's many defenses lower, often for the first time, and repressed feelings surface into awareness. The current experience of deep relaxation sets the stage for heightened awareness of emotions, feelings, and affect.

Clinical biofeedback therapy is also a way of linking thoughts, feelings, and physiological reactions. When an adolescent girl is talking about her life and claiming that everything is good, for example, but when her digital peripheral temperature plummets while she is discussing her boyfriend, she learns that she has negative feelings that she has not been aware of, feelings that are reflected in physiological reactivity.

From another viewpoint, clinical biofeedback therapy is a way of freeing up blocked memories, conflicts, and feelings. When relaxing very deeply, for example, an anorectic adolescent may experience a mental image of her dead mother and feel a surge of tears and sadness; the therapist can help her understand that her difficulty in swallowing has been attributable to her being literally choked up with unresolved grief over her mother's death.

In learning to relax, a patient must learn to think and act differently. A routine part of biofeedback therapy for anorexia nervosa is teaching management of stressors. If a patient interprets every criticism—no matter how slight—as a personal rejection and an indication of lack of self-worth, if she has to get an A on every school examination to have self-respect, it will be very difficult to apply relaxation techniques to life outside the protected clinical setting unless these issues are addressed.

The foregoing illustrations are from six years of experience providing clinical biofeedback therapy to anorectic inpatients. We provide clinical biofeedback therapy as an adjunctive treatment approach within a comprehensive inpatient program, usually being consulted to provide biofeedback therapy shortly after an individual is admitted to the hospital. The initial biofeedback evaluation lasts approximately 90 minutes, and 1-hour follow-up sessions are held weekly or twice a week in the hospital, with less frequent outpatient follow-up.

We use biofeedback instrumentation to measure three modalities: electromyographic (EMG) activity as an index of muscle activity, which is measured with surface electrodes; peripheral skin temperature, which is measured with heat-sensitive thermistors taped to the fingers or toes; and electrodermal activity, which is recorded by measuring skin conductance with sensors on the fingers or the hand. A psychophysiological assessment is performed during the initial biofeedback evaluation [5, 6]. This psychophysiological assessment involves continuous recording of the three modalities during a baseline period, during conversation about presenting symptoms and background information, during a period when the patient is asked to engage in self-relaxation, during a stress-induction procedure, during the stress-recovery period, and during a feedback-assisted relaxation exercise. In addition, presession and postsession measures of respiration rate, blood pressure, and heart rate are collected. We favor gathering the psychophysiological data from the beginning of the session and progressing into the stress-induction procedure and relaxation exercise. This maintains the continuity of the session in which we are meeting the patient for the first time, explaining the principles of biofeedback training, having her accommodate to the biofeedback setting, and at the same time gathering psychophysiological data.

During a stress-induction procedure, we ask the patient to perform mental arithmetic, such as subtracting 7 serially from 1,000, and observe changes in the psychophysiological data. A recovery period follows, in which we ask the patient to relax. She is then asked to visualize either an upsetting experience or a fearful scene, again followed by a recovery period. The stress-induction procedure provides information regarding the specific pattern of arousal accompanying the patient's reaction to stress. A patient may exhibit a large response to stress in the muscle system, for example, but show little activation in the autonomic nervous system. Another patient may display relaxed musculature but show increased autonomic activation by a decrease in peripheral skin temperature and an increase in skin-conductance level. A patient also may show little reactivity to mental arithmetic but exhibit much reactivity to imaginal stressors. The visualizations that produce reactivity can be used in subsequent training sessions.

The recovery period following stress induction is used to assess the duration of a stress response. The psychophysiological data are analyzed to determine the degree to which the data return to baseline levels. Patients with anxiety or psychophysiological symptoms differ from healthy persons in that they take longer to return to prestress levels once they are exposed to a stressor [7]. Anorectic patients display a marked stress response, with poor poststressor recovery. Their drive toward overachievement and fear of failure appear to fuel generalized arousal during the stress-induction procedure. This arousal continues during the recovery period, and the patients tend to ruminate excessively during that time, being overly concerned about the social desirability of their behavior and planning ways to avoid criticism.

By analyzing the psychophysiological data collected during the assessment, it is usually possible to determine whether a patient is a muscle responder—a person who can operate at high levels of muscle tension and react to stress with increased muscle tension; an autonomic responder—a person who responds to stress primarily by changes in peripheral temperature or electrodermal activity; or both a muscle responder and an autonomic responder.

If a patient displays relatively normal levels in one or two modalities but exhibits much reactivity in a particular modality, it is usually best to start with the modality that exhibits the largest amount of variation. If she displays much lability and variation in all three modalities, it is up to the judgment of the clinician to select the initial modality with which to work. Some patients display an ability to relax deeply during the initial session, with all modalities indicating relatively low levels of arousal and muscle tension. We explain to these patients that they have a fine ability to relax, and we discuss ways in which they can use the skill for healthier functioning. At the initial evaluation, we discuss specific goals that can be achieved in further biofeedback therapy, attempt to contract with the individual to allocate time each day for relaxation, and set psychophysiological-retraining goals and symptom-reduction goals.

One of the unique strengths of clinical biofeedback therapy is that it provides both the clinician and the patient with a great deal of information about the patient's psychophysiological functioning; they can see and hear changes that take place during conversation, induced stress, and relaxation. For anorectic patients this may be the first experience of sitting still long enough to become keenly aware of their bodily processes. They often comment that they are amazed that their level of muscle activity can change so rapidly and readily without awareness. At this point we emphasize the need for them to begin to listen to their bodies, to develop relaxation skills, and to be able to differentiate between high levels of arousal and levels of relaxation.

In the majority of anorectic patients, the psychophysiological assessment reveals extremely low peripheral temperature readings, in the range of 70 F to 80 F. It is not uncommon for the temperature readings to remain low and stable throughout the initial biofeedback session. Low peripheral temperature readings are usually associated with overactivity of the sympathetic nervous system that controls the peripheral blood vessels. It is also recognized that the semistarved, emaciated state of the patient produces a hypometabolic state that contributes to low peripheral temperature, but it is unclear whether overactive sympathetic tonus or the hypometabolic state is the primary contributor to low temperature readings. Intolerance to cold, a classic feature of anorexia nervosa, is probably due to a combination of these factors. Some anorectic patients can achieve large increases in peripheral skin temperature with temperature-feedback training. Others achieve negligible increases, even after as many as ten thermal biofeedback sessions, but will exhibit temperature increases once a suitable weight gain is made. It is extremely difficult to tell whether temperature increases are due to weight gain or to effects of thermal-biofeedback training, since they take place concurrently. Many patients who have returned to near-normal weight, however, will still exhibit low resting level-hand temperatures and will benefit from further thermal-biofeedback training.

Electromyographic readings frequently are elevated in one or more muscle groups, indicating the presence of significant levels of muscle tension. We typically gather EMG measurements from the frontalis, cervical neck, and trapezius muscles. The elevated EMG levels found in anorectic patients are typically as high as, and in some cases higher than, the levels found in muscle-contraction headache patients. Nonanorectic patients report severe pain at these EMG levels, whereas many anorectic patients report a blatant lack of muscle tightness. Electromyographic-feedback-assisted relaxation training helps the patient learn to reduce muscle tension, experience deep muscular relaxation, and differentiate tension from relaxation, thus increasing body awareness and self-regulation.

Electrodermal activity varies in patients with anorexia nervosa. They display either very high electrodermal activity, with large and labile fluctuations, or hypoactive electrodermal responses that tend to be very flat and unreactive to stress or conversation. This either-or situation also is apparent during a test of the orienting response, in which a loud auditory, noxious stimulus is introduced; patients react with either labile or hypoactive electrodermal responses. High levels of electrodermal activity are usually associated with a large amount of autonomic arousal, whereas very low, unreactive electrodermal levels may reflect a high level of intellectualization and suppressed affect.

Follow-up biofeedback sessions first focus on achieving the psychophysiological retraining goals. This involves relaxation training, experimenting with a variety of relaxation exercises so that the patient can select one or more techniques with which she is most comfortable. During relaxation training, the biofeedback equipment monitors several modalities but gives visual and auditory feedback from only one modality at a time. If a patient displays very low peripheral temperature readings, for example, we usually work initially with autogenic relaxation exercises and provide temperature feedback. If she displays extremely high levels of muscle activity, we usually begin with progressive relaxation exercises and provide EMG feedback. Emphasis is placed on experiencing total cognitive and physical relaxation. The biofeedback instruments also help establish criteria for effective relaxation skills. Although there are no precise criteria that can be used for all patients, generally it is desirable for the individual to be able to raise peripheral hand temperature to the 92 F range; to lower frontal, cervical, and trapezius EMG activity to the 1 μV level (recorded on our equipment at the 100 to 200 Hz bandpass using the integral averaging method); and to maintain skin-conductance level in the 10 micromho range.

Follow-up sessions routinely involve teaching abdominal breathing techniques. Trapezius EMG feedback can be helpful in demonstrating the variations in muscle activity that occur with inhalation and exhalation and the difference between thoracic and abdominal breathing. For patients who predominantly experience thoracic or clavicular breathing, use of rectus abdominis EMG feedback is helpful in teaching abdominal breathing.

We ask patients to set aside time daily to practice the relaxation exercises outside the biofeedback sessions. The patients also are given small, hand-held thermometers to measure hand temperature throughout the day, as a way of facilitating awareness of fluctuations in peripheral skin temperature. We also encourage them to use cassette relaxation tapes that we record during a biofeedback session and tailor to the patient's needs. For patients on a behavioral contract for weight gain, the daily use of relaxation exercises is generally written into the contract. We also have found it helpful to work with the patients in a group biofeedback setting, using portable biofeedback instruments in a group setting with other adolescent inpatients. This setting allows the anorectic patients to share difficulties they may be having in using the techniques and to get support from their peers. As described in chapter 14, the group setting appears to lower the patient's level of defensiveness and offers a combination of challenge and support.

The degree of defensiveness and denial frequently can be gauged by the number of biofeedback sessions it takes for patients to truly experience total physical and cognitive relaxation. A hard-core anorectic patient may attend as many as fifteen to twenty biofeedback sessions without experiencing deep relaxation. These patients often are highly resistant to any type of psychotherapeutic intervention. They typically require numerous hospitalizations, often in many different hospitals, and represent the long-term, extremely difficult treatment cases. A coexisting personality disorder or schizoaffective disorder often is present in these long-term anorectic patients.

With most anorectic patients, the high degrees of intellectualization and passivity, along with fears of rejection, produces a superficially overcompliant, cooperative biofeedback patient, who frequently will report positive and sometimes grandiose descriptions of relaxation. This is often in stark contrast to the psychophysiological data that are being displayed and recorded by the biofeedback instruments. The biofeedback data may show high levels of muscle tension and autonomic nervous system activity from the beginning to the end of the session, and yet the patient will say she is experiencing deep relaxation. Clearly, a patient's massive denial can operate within the biofeedback training session, with the patient discounting the fact that muscle activity remains at a high level and giving a glowing self-report of feeling very relaxed muscularly. Confronting the patient with her manipulation and denial usually leads to further defensiveness. At this point, it is most important that the clinician focus on structured, concrete, feedback-assisted relaxation exercises and not be taken in by the patient's intellectualized manipulations.

Once an anorectic patient has developed effective relaxation skills, she will be more likely to experience success in achieving symptom-reduction goals. Symptom-reduction goals vary from patient to patient, depending on the psychophysiological reactions that may be present—such as muscle-contraction headaches, migraine headaches, gastrointestinal pain, or other somatic complaints—but several goals are common to all anorectic patients. These include the goals of decreasing high levels of activity and engaging in more frequent relaxation; increasing a sense of effectiveness by using stress-management strategies, which is especially important in patients with compulsive, ritualistic behavior; increasing awareness of internal sensations, particularly those related to eating patterns; correcting disturbances in body image; and increasing awareness of personal resources, underlying conflicts, and repressed emotions. After a patient has developed effective relaxation skills and a good working relationship with the biofeedback therapist, she often is open to working with a wider variety of approaches to facilitating self-regulation and developing healthy self-control skills. Our approach has been to include stress-management training, insight-oriented psychotherapy, behavior-modification techniques, and cognitive-restructuring approaches.

Stress-management strategies in the biofeedback therapy sessions help the patient develop an increased sense of effectiveness by controlling stress reactions and by modulating the amount of stress experienced. Development of stress-management strategies entails looking at the ways that the patient creates stress through unrealistic expectations and demands, rigid beliefs, and ritualistic and compulsive behaviors.

As the patient begins to attend to bodily sensations and can discriminate levels of tension versus relaxation, we teach stress-management strategies related to eating behavior. For those who restrict their caloric intake and engage in self-starvation, we plan a short period of relaxation before and after meals. Anorectic patients usually can identify behavior patterns before meals, when they begin to feel very tense and become very active. By engaging in a short period of relaxation before mealtime, they break their habitual pattern of ignoring internal hunger sensations. For those who are binge-eaters and consume a large quantity of food, with subsequent feelings of guilt and self-induced vomiting or excessive intake of laxatives, the emphasis is on relaxing during meals as well as before and after meals. These patients benefit from behavior-modification methods that are used in the treatment of obesity, such as chewing food more slowly, putting the fork down after each bite, and generally engaging in slower eating behavior. As control is gained over eating behavior, weight often will change in the desired direction.

In summary, anorexia nervosa has multiple causes, and clinical biofeedback therapy is multimodal in attacking those causes. In a biofeedback session with an anorectic adolescent who is hypervigilant, is a perfectionist, emphasizes control, has multiple, poorly understood familial and intrapsychic conflicts, and has sympathetic overarousal—manifested partly through peripheral vasoconstriction, resulting in peripheral skin temperature in the range of 70 F—clinical biofeedback therapy would be introduced as a means of helping the patient achieve even greater control, thus aligning the therapy with the patient's major need. The desired control is to relax and to raise finger temperature. In the process, however, it is likely that multiple psychotherapeutic and psychophysiological processes would be ongoing. These processes include [8]:

1. Operant conditioning of smooth muscles surrounding arterioles in the fingers, with success in increasing digital temperature (with visual and auditory feedback), representing immediate positive reinforcement.
2. Feedback learning, with the biofeedback equipment representing imposition of an external psychophysiological-feedback loop upon existing internal-feedback loops, directly affecting blood flow to the fingers.
3. Feedback learning, with the biofeedback equipment affecting general arousal through impact on existing feedback loops of the homeostatic adaptive-control systems.
4. Learning the relaxation response through imagery and cognitive exercises.
5. Modifying assumptions, attitudes, and expectations that lead to psychophysiological stress reactions.
6. Enhancing self-awareness in general, including awareness of bodily functioning, by obtaining specific information about bodily functioning and by experimenting with the relationship of physiological functioning to thought patterns and emotional patterns.
7. Resolving conflicts by discussing them with a therapist, thus reducing self-generated stressors that lead to psychophysiological reactions.

8. Responding to hypnotic suggestion of greater well-being while in an altered state of consciousness induced by narrowing of attention and relaxation [9].
9. Faith healing, with belief in the process being a curative agent leading to placebo healing.
10. Changing behaviors in order to reduce stressors, in response to specific counseling of the therapist.
11. Experiencing an increase in self-esteem secondary to warmth, genuineness, and empathy of the therapist, thereby reducing stress.
12. Emulating a relaxed therapist, who is not upset by thinking about and discussing emotion-laden topics.
13. Articulating values and shifting them to enable attitudinal, behavioral, and emotional changes.
14. Cathartic reexperiencing and emotional release that reduces stress.
15. Changing the locus of control so that the patient takes responsibility for her own well-being.

The paradox of clinical biofeedback treatment of anorexia nervosa is the use of impersonal electronic machines to promote health in patients who already tend to be concrete and hyperintellectual in processing information and have a mechanistic view of the world. Biofeedback engages patients where they are stuck—an overemphasis on control of the external environment and an inattentiveness to internal stimuli. Biofeedback provides an experiential model for restoring a balance between internal and external interactions by graphically depicting the mind-body interaction. The experiential model also allows the patient to experience total cognitive and physical relaxation and thus to unravel her tangled thoughts and feelings.

References

1. Bruch, H. *The Golden Cage: The Enigma of Anorexia Nervosa.* Cambridge, Mass.: Harvard University Press, 1977.

2. Bemis, K.M. Current approaches to the etiology and treatment of anorexia nervosa. *Psychol. Bull.* 85:593-617, 1978.

3. Pelletier, K.R. *Mind as Healer, Mind as Slayer.* New York: Delacorte Press, 1977.

4. Reinking, R.H., and Kohl, M.L. Effects of various forms of relaxation training on physiological and self-report measures of relaxation. *J. Consult. Clin. Psychol.* 33(1):39-48, 1978.

5. Fuller, G. Current status of biofeedback in clinical practice. *Am. Psychol.* 33(1):39-48, 1978.

6. Gaarder, K.R., and Montgomery, P.S. *Clinical Biofeedback: A Procedural Manual.* Baltimore: Williams and Wilkins, 1977.

7. Malmo, R.B. *On Emotions, Needs, and Our Archaic Brain.* New York: Holt, Rinehart and Winston, 1975.

8. McKee, M.G. Using biofeedback and self-control techniques to prevent heart attacks. *Psychiatr. Ann.* 8:10, 92–99, 1978.

9. McKee, M.G. Spontaneous hypnotic states induced during biofeedback training. In M. Pajntar, E. Roskar, and M. Lavric (Eds.), *Hypnosis in Psychotherapy and Psychosomatic Medicine.* Ljubljana, Yugoslavia: University Press (Univerzitetna Tiskarma), 1980. Pg. 347–351.

17 Total Parenteral Nutrition in Anorexia Nervosa

Richard Chiulli, M.D.,
Margaret Grover, R.N.,
and
Ezra Steiger, M.D.

The field of total parenteral nutrition (TPN) has made dramatic progress over the past 15 years. A once-experimental procedure for providing nutrition by intravenous infusions is now a commonplace modality available in many hospitals. Insertion of a central catheter, initiation and maintenance of intravenous hyperalimentation, and management of complications have been well described in the TPN literature [1].

Anorexia nervosa is an important but infrequent indication for TPN. Because of the anorectic patient's inadequate oral intake and consequent negative nitrogen balance and weight loss, this type of patient would seem to be an ideal candidate to benefit from TPN. The procedure is seldom used on such patients, however, because of patient refusal and the psychosocial aspects of the disease, which complicate TPN usage. Indeed, the anorectic patient should be considered a candidate for TPN only when parenteral nutrition is deemed critical for the patient's survival.

Because of their obsessional fear of weight gain, patients have been known to manipulate intravenous lines, risking air embolus and bleeding, in an attempt to avoid getting fat. Parenteral hyperalimentation is therefore reserved for patients with severe weight loss, when noninvasive methods have failed.

TPN allows the severely depleted patient to regain weight and stamina and prevent death from malnutrition. This chapter presents a practical approach to the use of total parenteral nutrition in the severely malnourished hospitalized patient.

Nutritional Requirements for TPN

The fundamental requirements for good nutrition include: (1) an adequate supply of amino acids that can be used to manufacture proteins, (2) a source of calories sufficient to support protein anabolism, and (3) a host of additives such as fatty acids, electrolytes, minerals, vitamins, and trace elements needed by the body to prevent deficiency states and allow for normal physiological functioning. The exact requirements for an individual vary considerably with the patient's sex, height, weight, initial nutritional status, activity level, and metabolic rate. However, nutritional requirements for hospitalized patients can usually be readily provided with standard guidelines.

Most patients require between 0.8 and 2.0 grams of protein or amino acids per kilogram per day to maintain adequate nutrition [2]. A typical 70 kg man needs 56 to 140 grams of protein or amino acids per day depending on the underlying disease process.

A more accurate method of establishing protein requirement can be determined by nitrogen balance studies. In theory, protein anabolism is possible only when exogenously administered nitrogen (in the form of protein or amino acids) exceeds nitrogen losses in the urine and feces. Urinary nitrogen losses which account for approximately 70% to 90% of total nitrogen loss can be easily calculated. A 24-hour volume of urine is sent to the laboratory for urea nitrogen determination. This is like asking for a BUN on the urine sample and warning the laboratory that the urine will have to be diluted to obtain a meaningful reading. The results are reported in milligrams per 100 ml, converted to grams per liter, and then multiplied by the total liters of urine per 24 hours to obtain the total urea nitrogen. Four grams are added to the total to account for fecal nitrogen losses and other nonurea urinary nitrogen losses [3]. The daily nitrogen loss typically falls between 8 and 16 grams. Thus, a patient would require 8 to 16 grams of exogenous nitrogen per day to maintain nitrogen balance and satisfactory nutrition. The number of grams of nitrogen multiplied by 6.25 equals equivalent grams of protein or amino acids. This amounts to approximately 50 to 100 grams of protein per day, which is similar to the calculation based on the patient's weight.

Protein synthesis by the body is a calorie-requiring process. The caloric requirements for TPN can be estimated from the patient's protein requirement. The optimal calorie-to-protein ratio is approximately 24 to 34 calories per gram of protein [4]. A typical 70 kg man requiring 100 grams of protein thus needs at least 2,400 calories to fully utilize the administered protein. The caloric requirement is higher in sepsis and in severe catabolic states, such as trauma and burns. Each degree-Fahrenheit elevation in temperature above normal necessitates a 7% increase in caloric intake to insure optimal utilization of protein [5]. An approximation of the typical patient's caloric requirement is 45 calories per kilogram of ideal body weight per day [6].

A standard liter of TPN solution contains from 25 to 42.5 grams of amino acids and 250 grams of hydrated dextrose, yielding approximately 850 calories. This provides a calorie-to-protein ratio of approximately 20 to 34 calories per gram of protein. A patient requiring 2,500 calories needs a 3,000 ml infusion of standard TPN solution daily (25% dextrose, 2.5% to 4.25% amino acids) to supply both protein and caloric needs. Note that 12 liters of a 5% dextrose solution would be required to administer an equivalent number of calories. The use of 25% dextrose hypertonic nutrient solutions allows for delivery of a patient's caloric requirement within the limits of her fluid tolerance.

Electrolytes are essential additives of TPN. Sodium, potassium, magnesium, and calcium are the important cations given. Sodium is administered as a chloride or acetate salt, depending on the patient's acid-base status. Potassium is given as a chloride or phosphate salt, depending on the patient's phosphate needs. Magnesium is administered as a sulfate salt, and calcium as calcium gluconate. As the patient becomes anabolic, increased amounts of the intracellular electrolytes (potassium, phosphate, and magnesium) are required by the body. Calcium is included to maintain normal calcium levels. Table 17-1 lists the electrolytes ordered for TPN for a regimen that would suit the average anorexia nervosa patient. Such derangements as bowel fistula, acute renal failure, or chronic diarrhea could alter these requirements significantly. Careful monitoring of serum electrolytes is important for a patient receiving TPN, especially during the initial phase of treatment. Suggested guidelines for monitoring TPN patients are given in table 17-2.

Trace elements, vitamins, and essential fatty acids must be included in the TPN regimen to support metabolic pathways and to prevent deficiency states. Trace elements include zinc, copper, selenium, manganese, and chromium. Iodine and iron can be added if the patient requires them clinically. Suggested requirements for trace elements in TPN are given in table 17-3.

Vitamins are included daily in the TPN schedule in the form of a multivitamin additive (M.V.I.-12). Suggested requirements for vitamins in TPN are also given in table 17-3. Both water-soluble and fat-soluble vitamins are administered in this way. Vitamin K is not included in the intravenous additive and must be given separately by intramuscular (IM) injections if necessary.

Essential fatty acids are given in the form of a 10% fat emulsion given by peripheral vein. Commercial fat emulsions are made from soybean oil or saf-

Table 17-1
Typical Additives per Liter of TPN Formula

500 ml	Freamine II 8.5%	
500 ml	Dextrose	50%
Calcium gluconate	4.6	mEq
Magnesium sulfate	8.1	mEq
Potassium chloride	30	mEq
Potassium phosphate	10	mEq
Sodium chloride	50	mEq
M.V.I.-12[a]	10	ml
Heparin	1,000	units
Trace elements[a]	1	ml
Zinc sulfate	3	mg
Regular insulin	as required	

Source: E. Steiger and V. Fazio, Total parenteral nutrition. Cleveland Clinic Publication F510 (Cleveland: Cleveland Clinic Foundation, 1977).
[a]Added to only one liter per day

Table 17-2
Guidelines for Monitoring TPN

---

1. Vital signs and temperature every 4 hours. Notify physician if sudden change in temperature or shaking chills occur
2. Strict intake and output
3. Daily weights
4. Urine dextrose measurements every 6 hours
5. Encourage ambulation
6. Change IV tubing every Sunday, Monday, Wednesday, and Friday
7. Keep IV flow rate within 20% of that ordered
8. Blood sugar and electrolytes every Tuesday, Thursday, and Sunday
9. SMA-12 every Sunday and Thursday
10. Serum magnesium, serum transferrin, complete blood count, and prothrombin time every Tuesday

---

Source: E. Steiger and V. Fazio, Total parenteral nutrition. Cleveland Clinic Publication F510 (Cleveland: Cleveland Clinic Foundation, 1977).

flower oil and provide 27 and 38 grams, respectively, of the essential fatty acid, linoleic acid, per 500 ml bottle. A 500 ml infusion of the 10% fat emulsion is given three times a week to prevent essential fatty acid deficiency.

Nutritional Assessment

The assessment of a patient's nutritional state is a vital aspect of the TPN program. It is used to determine whether malnutrition is present, to establish the severity of malnutrition, and to assess the progress of a patient currently receiving TPN. Nutritional assessment is based on a series of observations and measurements that are designed to give an overall picture of the patient's nutritional status.

The simplest measurements are the patient's height and weight. Drastic changes in body weight are important to document. A 20% loss of body weight is associated with increased mortality when the patient is subjected to acute stresses, such as surgery or trauma. A 40% weight loss is associated with mortality on the basis of malnutrition alone [7]. Weight gain not exceeding half a pound per day is a good indication that a patient is responding well to TPN [3].

The triceps skinfold can be measured easily and correlated with the total body-fat stores of the patient. It is measured with a special caliper in the mid-triceps region, halfway between the acromion and olecranon processes. The measurement can be compared to a standardized chart, and a percentile rank can be obtained for body fat [8].

Lean body mass can be quantified by the creatinine height index. A 24-hour urine specimen is collected for creatinine, and the creatinine height index equals 24-hour creatinine (mg) divided by height (cm). The creatinine height index is

Table 17-3
Vitamins and Trace Elements in TPN

	1980 RDA *(oral)*	*AMA Guideline* *(IV)*
Vitamin C	60 mg	100 mg
Thiamin	1.2 mg	3.0 mg
Riboflavin	1.4 mg	3.6 mg
Niacin	16 mg	40 mg
Pyridoxine	2.2 mg	4.0 mg
Folacin	400 μg	400 μg
Vitamin B_{12}	3.0 μg	5.0 μg
Biotin	100–200 μg	60 μg
Pantothenic Acid	4–7 mg	15 mg
Vitamin A	5000 IU	3300 IU
Vitamin D	200 IU	200 IU
Vitamin E	10–20 IU	10 IU
Vitamin K	70–140 IU	–
Zinc	15 mg	2.5–4.0 mg
Copper	2–3 mg	.5–1.5 mg
Manganese	2.5–5 mg	.15–.8 mg
Chromium	.05–.2 mg	.01–.015 mg
Selenium	.05–.2 mg	–

RDA = recommended daily allowance

Sources: AMA Department of Food and Nutrition, Guidelines for essential trace element preparations for parenteral use, *JAMA* 241(19):2051–2054, 1979; G. Nichoalds, H. Meng, and M. Caldwell, Vitamin requirements in patients receiving TPN, *Arch. Surg.* 112(9):1061–1064, 1977.

then compared to standardized tables, and a percentile rank is assigned for lean body mass. A patient with less than 60% of the expected lean body mass is considered to be significantly malnourished [9, 10].

Skin testing with antigens that evoke delayed hypersensitivity (PPD, mumps, *Candida*, *Trichophyton*, streptokinase, streptodornase) correlates well with nutritional status. Anergy implies a severely malnourished state, with decreased host resistance. The mortality for the anergic patient undergoing major surgical procedures is prohibitively high. Skin tests can be repeated following several weeks of TPN. A change from anergy to reactivity indicates good nutritional response to TPN and a return to normal host resistance [11, 12].

Serum albumin and serum transferrin levels are also indicators of malnutrition. Albumin levels less than 2.7 gm/100 cc and transferrin levels less than 150 mg/100 cc indicate significant malnutrition. The half-life of transferrin is only 5 days; albumin has a half-life of 20 days. Therefore, transferrin is more responsive to changes in nutrition. Both measurements are useful clinically, however.

Total lymphocyte count can be calculated directly from a complete blood count and differential. Total lymphocyte count is determined by leukocyte count multiplied by lymphocyte percentage, divided by 100. A lymphocyte count of less than 1,200 calculated in this manner is associated with significant mal-nutrition [3].

The nutritional assessment is not based on a single determination, but rather is an overall picture of the various factors involved. Occasionally, a patient will appear deceptively well on clinical examination but will have indications of significant malnutrition on laboratory examination. A complete evaluation of nutritional status will guide the clinician in efficient use of TPN. Chapter 10 discusses the diagnosis of malnutrition in more detail.

TPN Solutions

The basic TPN solution is a mixture of amino acids and glucose. A liter of solution is composed of 500 ml of 50% dextrose and 500 ml of 8.5% amino acids. The resulting solution has 25% dextrose concentration, which delivers .85 kcal/ml, and 4.25% L-crystalline amino acids containing both essential and nonessential amino acids in physiological proportion. The high dextrose concentration allows administration of a large caloric load with rather small quantities of fluid. There are two technical drawbacks to the high glucose concentration. First, the hypertonic solution is severely irritating to peripheral veins and must be given by a large-bore central venous catheter. Second, the solution is an excellent culture medium for bacteria and fungi. It must be mixed under strict aseptic technique and refrigerated while awaiting use. The time between mixing and infusion should be minimized to avoid potential bacterial growth [13].

To prevent marked hyperglycemia, the TPN infusion is started at one liter per day and gradually increased over 24 to 48 hours to the full feeding of three liters of TPN fluid per day. If necessary, insulin is added directly to the TPN bottle to maintain blood-glucose concentration of 100–150 mg/100 ml. This eliminates the need for subcutaneous injections and varies the insulin in direct proportion to the glucose load. Some insulin is absorbed in the glucose bottle and IV tubing, but this can be compensated by adding extra insulin [14]. The infusion rate of TPN is kept constant when the full daily load is reached to avoid wide fluctuations in blood sugar. Commercially available infusion pumps are well suited for this purpose. The termination of TPN should be accomplished gradually over one to three days. Terminating TPN too rapidly could result in symptomatic hypoglycemia.

Heparin (1,000 units) is added to each liter of TPN solution to prevent fibrin deposit and catheter clotting. The total dose of heparin is insufficient to interfere with the patient's normal hemostatic mechanisms.

The necessary laboratory evaluations are ordered regularly for proper TPN monitoring. Evaluations of serum electrolytes, liver function, calcium, magnesium, phosphorus, albumin, and transferrin and complete blood counts and coagulation studies are ordered routinely. Daily measurements including weight, urine reductions, vital signs, and fluid balance are needed for full evaluation of the patient's progress (see table 17-2).

Catheter Placement

Insertion of a subclavian venous catheter for intravenous fluid was perfected by Aubiniac, a French surgeon working in Vietnam [15], and has recently become widely used for TPN. Infraclavicular subclavian lines offer long-term central venous access, coupled with good patient comfort and a low complication rate [16, 17]. Central venous cannulation is imperative in TPN infusion because of the hypertonic 25% dextrose solution. Typically, a catheter is inserted into the subclavian vein and positioned so that the tip is in the superior vena cava. The high rate of blood flow in the vena cava allows this hypertonic solution to be diluted rapidly, thus avoiding the thrombosis and phlebitis that would occur in a peripheral vein.

Percutaneous infraclavicular subclavian vein catheterization should be considered a surgical procedure. Faulty catheter placement can lead to serious complications, and therefore the catheter must be carefully inserted by an experienced physician. The suggested technique is as follows.

The patient is placed in the Trendelenburg position, with a roll placed longitudinally under the upper thoracic spine to allow the shoulders to fall posteriorly. Either side may be used, but clavicular fracture or other injuries might make the involved subclavian vein difficult to catheterize. The lower neck and upper chest area of the chosen side is shaved and cleansed with acetone to defat the skin and povidone-iodine solution is applied. Sterile gloves are replaced after the skin preparation. With the patient's head turned to the opposite side, sterile drapes are applied to isolate the area from the midclavicle to the suprasternal notch. Local anesthetic is infiltrated into the skin just inferior to the clavicle, two-thirds of the way from the suprasternal notch and along the anticipated course of the venipuncture. A 14-gauge, 2-inch-long needle is attached to a 5 cc syringe after the plastic catheter is removed. The needle is advanced, beveled side facing down from the skin-wheal site, and passed under the clavicle, with the tip aimed at the anterior margin of the trachea in the suprasternal notch. The syringe barrel and attached needle are kept parallel to the chest wall to prevent puncture of the thoracic cavity. Prompt filling of the syringe with blood confirms that the tip of the needle has entered the vein. With the patient holding his breath, the syringe is removed from the needle hub and the plastic catheter is inserted until it reaches the hub. An IV bag and tubing containing 5% dextrose in water is attached to the catheter hub rapidly. A flashback of blood in the IV tubing when the bag is placed lower than the patient signifies proper placement. Next, the needle is withdrawn and a protective shield is placed over the beveled end. To prevent extrusion of the catheter, a suture is placed through the skin lateral to the catheter and tied around the catheter. The catheter area is then dressed, using aseptic technique (see the next section, on catheter care).

Before infusion of hypertonic fluid is started, the patient should have a chest roentgenogram to demonstrate proper placement of the catheter tip in the superior vena cava and to rule out a pneumothorax.

Catheter Care

Proper care and maintenance of the subclavian line dressing are important defenses against catheter-related sepsis [18]. Ideally, the dressing is changed three times a week by a trained nurse. Tubings are also changed every other day, and the pathway from the bottle to the patient is considered a closed system. Alternate uses for the central line, such as antibiotic administration and central venous pressure measurements are prohibited, as they are potential sources of contamination. With good catheter care, the sepsis rate of TPN can be as low as 1% to 2% [19].

A technique for changing the dressing with the patient lying flat in bed involves the following steps:

1. Remove the old dressing, being careful not to pull on the catheter. Inspect the site for inflammation or drainage.
2. Clean the area twice with acetone. Start at the catheter entrance site and move outward. Never return to the entrance site with the same swab.
3. Clean the area with povidone-iodine solution in the same fashion. Repeat this cleansing process four times.
4. Apply a small amount of povidone-iodine ointment to the catheter entrance site.
5. Apply a small occlusive dressing to the area and tape securely.

Infusion pumps are frequently used with TPN to administer the solution at a constant rate. Most pumps can operate on a battery and can be placed on a rolling IV pole, allowing the patient freedom to ambulate. Patients receiving TPN are not confined to bed rest, and ambulation is encouraged to stimulate anabolism.

Patient Monitoring

After TPN is initiated, specific laboratory studies are obtained, and nursing orders are carried out (see table 17-2). The patient's intake, output, and weight are observed daily for proper fluid management. Urinary dextrose determinations are checked every six hours. Adjustments can be made to the infusion rate or insulin can be added if blood dextrose is above 150 mg/100 ml. Any temperature elevation is closely observed and possible sites of infection explored. If catheter sepsis is suspected, the catheter is changed.

When a patient begins oral intake, the amount of TPN solution infused every day is decreased. A dietitian can help by doing calorie and nutrient counts to determine if oral intake is adequate. The weaning process usually takes four to five days. After TPN solutions are decreased to 500 cc every 12 hours, they may be discontinued.

Complications of TPN

Complications of TPN can be divided into two major categories: catheter-related problems and metabolic derangements.

Catheter insertion can lead to many technical problems, but fortunately most of them are relatively rare. Laceration of the pleura, for example, can cause pneumothorax. A small, asymptomatic pneumothorax can be watched safely with serial examinations and chest roentgenograms, but a chest tube may be needed for a significant pneumothorax. Mishandling of an open catheter can lead to an air embolism [20]. If this occurs, the patient should lie on his left side until symptoms subside, thus allowing air bubbles to displace into the right atrium. A hemothorax or mediastinal hematoma can result from subclavian artery laceration. Pressure over the arterial puncture site for ten minutes will usually stop the bleeding. A chest tube will usually be required for a hemothorax, and thoracotomy may be necessary. Misplaced catheters can enter the internal jugular vein, the opposite subclavian vein, the pleural space, the mediastinum, or the right ventricle [21, 22]. Catheter embolism can result when the catheter tip is sheared off in the intravascular space [23]. Injury to adjacent structures, such as the brachial plexus, phrenic nerve, thoracic duct, or trachea, can occur during needle insertion.

Late catheter complications are secondary to the presence of a foreign body in the intravascular space. The catheter may cause thrombosis of the ipsilateral subclavian vein or even of the superior vena cava, causing superior vena cava syndrome. The catheter may chronically irritate the vein wall and erode into the mediastinum or pleura. A catheter that is misplaced in the right ventricle may cause ventricular irritability or actual ventricular-wall perforation [21, 24]. Such complications, although rare, are potentially fatal.

An indwelling catheter can be a nidus for infection by contaminated TPN solutions or a coexistent bacteremic process. The patient may develop high spiking fevers, leukocytosis, tachycardia, and frequently hypotension. The septic episode will subside rapidly upon catheter removal, and culture of the catheter tip will reveal the causative bacteria or fungus. Often a central catheter is removed during sepsis but an alternate cause of sepsis, such as pyelonephritis or peritonitis, is discovered later. In such cases, another catheter can be inserted and TPN can be resumed.

Potential metabolic complications of TPN are numerous and may include excesses or shortages of almost any ingredient of the TPN orders. The nutrient requirements change from patient to patient, thereby making prevention of complications less predictable. Close monitoring of the patient, both clinically and chemically, generally will uncover problems at an early stage and thus prevent serious complications.

A large inadvertent bolus of TPN solutions, or a continued infusion of TPN in a patient who is unable to handle the glucose load (such as a diabetic patient) may result in nonketotic hyperosmolar coma, requiring immediate cessation of TPN and initiation of therapy, including isotonic saline infusion and regular insulin [2, 25]. A sudden cessation of TPN may induce severe hypoglycemia secondary to elevated endogenous insulin levels. The hypoglycemia may manifest as tremulousness, tachycardia, syncope, or frank convulsions. Intravenous glucose provides immediate correction. Hypophosphatemia may develop in a patient receiving TPN who is not receiving adequate phosphate ion. As anabolic metabolism progresses, increased amounts of phosphate are required, and serum levels drop. Symptoms include paresthesias, weakness, confusion, and an unexplained hemolytic anemia.

Essential-fatty-acid deficiency may develop in patients receiving long-term TPN who do not receive fat emulsion. The syndrome consists of a desquamative skin rash, poor wound healing, thrombocytopenia, and anemia. Addition of 500 ml of a 10% fat emulsion three times a week prevents essential-fatty-acid deficiency.

Zinc deficiency is manifest by poor wound healing, diarrhea, dermatitis, alopecia, and depression. Copper deficiency may present as an unexplained macrocytic anemia refractory to folic acid and vitamin B_{12}. Chromium deficiency presents as a diabetic state and responds to the addition of a small amount of chromium to the TPN.

Conclusion

Total parenteral nutrition is a readily available, useful tool for the management of severely depleted nutritional states. The clinician caring for the patient with anorexia nervosa should be aware of the efficaciousness of TPN for treatment in selected cases. The combination of carefully administered and monitored TPN in conjunction with psychotherapy offers the best chance of recovery for these patients. This procedure is an additional tool for the physician who cares for anorectic patients.

References

1. *Total Parenteral Nutrition: References, Matrices and Bibliography* (8th cum. ed.). Deerfield, Ill.: Travenol Laboratories, 1980.
2. Deitel, M. *Nutrition in Clinical Surgery*. Baltimore: Williams and Wilkins, 1980. Pp. 75-81.
3. Grant, J.P. *Handbook of Total Parenteral Nutrition*. Philadelphia: W.B. Saunders Co., 1980. P. 77.
4. Long, C.L., Crosby, F., Geiger, J.W., and Kinney, J.M. Parenteral nutrition in the septic patient: Nitrogen balance, limiting plasma amino acids, and calorie to nitrogen ratios. *Am. J. Clin. Nutr.* 29:380-391, 1976.
5. Kinney, J.M. Energy requirements for parenteral nutrition. In J.E. Fischer (Ed.), *Total Parenteral Nutrition*. Boston: Little, Brown and Co., 1976.
6. Fischer, J.E. Parenteral and enteral nutrition. *DM* 24(9): 1-86, 1978.
7. Steffee, W.P. Malnutrition in hospitalized patients. *JAMA* 244(23): 2630-2635, 1980.
8. Frisancho, A.R. Triceps skinfold and upper arm muscle size norms for assessment of nutritional status. *Am. J. Clin. Nutr.* 27:1052-1058, 1974.
9. Blackburn, G.L. Nutritional assessment and support during infection. *Am. J. Clin. Nutr.* 30:1493, 1977.
10. Bistrian, B.R., Blackburn, G.L., Sherman, M., and Scrimshaw, N.S. Therapeutic index of nutritional depletion in hospitalized patients. *S.G.O.* 141:512-516, 1975.
11. Copeland, E.M., MacFadyen, B.V., and Dudrick, S.J. Effect of intravenous hyperalimentation on established delayed hypersensitivity in the cancer patient. *Ann. Surg.* 184:60-64, 1976.
12. Meakins, J.L., Pietsch, J.B., Bubenick, O., et al. Delayed hypersensitivity: Indicator of acquired failure of host defenses in sepsis and trauma. *Ann. Surg.* 186:241-250, 1977.
13. Rowlands, D.A., Wilkinson, W.R., and Yoshimura, N.N. Storage stability of mixed hyperalimentation solutions. *Am. J. Hosp. Pharm.* 30:436-438, 1973.
14. Weber, S.S., Wood, W.A., and Jackson, E.A. Availability of insulin from parenteral nutrient solutions. *Am. J. Hosp. Pharm.* 34:353, 1977.
15. Aubiniac, R.L. L'injection intraveineuse sousclaviculaire: Avantages et techniques. *Presse Med.* 60:1456, 1952.
16. Wilmore, D.W., and Dudrick, S.J. Safe long term venous catheterization. *Arch. Surg.* 98:256, 1969.
17. Bernard, R.W., and Stahl, W.M. Subclavian vein catheterizations: A prospective study, I. Non-infectious complications. *Ann. Surg.* 173:184, 1971.
18. Miller, R.C., and Grogan, J.B. Incidence and source of contamination of intravenous nutritional systems. *J. Pediatr. Surg.* 8:185-190, 1973.

19. Sanderson, I., and Deitel, M. Intravenous hyperalimentation without sepsis. S.G.O. 136:577-585, 1973.

20. Mattox, K.L., and Bricker, D.L. Air embolism following subclavian vein catheterization. *Tex. Med.* 66:74, 1970.

21. Brown, C.A., and Kent, A. Perforation of right ventrical by polyethylene catheter. *South. Med. J.* 49:466-467, 1956.

22. O'Reilly, R.J. Aberrant venous catheter position within the left chest. *Contemp. Surg.* 12:29-34, 1978.

23. Burri, C., and Krischak, G. Techniques and complications of administration of TPN. In C. Manni, S.J. Magalini, and E. Scrascia (Eds.), *Total Parenteral Nutrition.* New York: American Elsevier Publishing Co., 1976. Pp. 306-315.

24. Brady, R.E., and Weinberg, P.M. Atrioventricular conduction disturbance during total parenteral nutrition. *J. Pediatr.* 88:113-114, 1976.

25. McCurdy, D.K. Hyperosmolar hyperglycemic nonketotic diabetic coma. *Med. Clin. North Am.* 54:683, 1970.

18 Bulimia

Meir Gross, M.D.

Diane, a 16-year-old white girl, was brought for consultation because of episodes of binging followed by excessive vomiting after almost every meal. The episodes of binging and vomiting were as frequent as three or four times a day. She had been an excellent student, but during the last year her grades had deteriorated, because she was unable to study or concentrate on her school assignments. She started to isolate herself at home, no longer going out with friends. At home she seemed to be very nervous, tense and edgy. Her tolerance of frustration became so low that she could not stand any remarks, criticism, or suggestions from her parents or her brothers and sisters. During the last year she had managed to reduce her weight by about ten pounds, but her face did not look thinner because some swelling had appeared under both her ears.

When seen for consultation, Diane was very resentful of being forced to come for psychiatric evaluation. She claimed that there was nothing wrong with her and that her vomiting was a way to watch her weight, since she could not fast for long. She had discovered that vomiting could be a solution to her fear of gaining too much weight. She pointed out that one of her sisters and her mother were overweight and said she would not want to become like them. She claimed she did not need treatment, and if it were not for the pressure from her parents, she would not have come for the consultation. As the inteview continued, however, it became evident that she might be willing to get help if she could find a solution for her weight problems. If she could find a way not to gain too much weight, she claimed, she would be willing to become involved in therapy. She admitted that the binging and vomiting were consuming too much time. She thought about food all day, and it interfered with her ability to concentrate on her studies or anything else. Since she had to binge and vomit all the time, she preferred not to go out with friends after dinner, because she needed the time for the vomiting and was afraid that her friends would find out about it. She admitted to feeling very low about herself, even though she was a good student. She did not feel smart enough and did not believe she could accomplish much in her life. She was very concerned about her appearance and always made sure that her clothes were in accord with the latest fashion. Trying to come up to the expectations of her peers made her feel very frustrated and sometimes very depressed. In order to deal with these feelings, she consumed large amounts of alcohol, occasionally getting drunk. In the past, she had tried to lose weight by using amphetamines and over-the-counter diet pills. More recently, in addition to vomiting, she had started to take large amounts of laxatives to be sure that nothing stayed in her stomach.

Diane is one of numerous young women—and fewer men—who use vomiting as a way to control their weight. Unfortunately, it became a very popular weight-control method on college campuses, and many young women and teenagers began to use vomiting in order to avoid weight gain while still enabling them to enjoy eating. Many of these people had tried to use fasting as a weight-control measure but could not persist because of their voracious appetites. Once they discovered the possibility of vomiting, they could give in to their hunger and consume large quantities of foods, feeling sure that they could get rid of it. Such behavior is usually secretive, but it is much more common than was previously known. It is believed that up to 80% of female college students use vomiting at least once in their lives to avoid gaining excessive weight or because they feel guilty for eating too much food. This phenomenon has become more and more common in the last few years. The medical term for it is *bulimia*, which is defined as an abnormal craving for food that results in excessive binging, followed by self-induced vomiting after the gorging episodes. The food that is consumed is usually of high caloric content with high levels of carbohydrates. Usually it is consumed so fast that the person can hardly chew it properly. After the gorging episode, the person might feel guilty or fearful of becoming obese. There also is a feeling of being too full, causing abdominal pains. The solution to the problem is disgorging the contents of the stomach through the mouth by irritating the pharynx with the finger or by artificial means. In many cases, the vomiting reflex is developed to the point that pressure on the stomach or activation of the gag reflex might be sufficient to produce the vomiting. Once the stomach is empty, there is decreased abdominal distention and pain, allowing the person to continue eating or binging.

Bulimia is not a disease; rather, it is a symptom of underlying problems. Most people with bulimia show great concern about their weight and usually make repeated attempts to control it by dieting or use of cathartics, diuretics, or diet pills. Many of these people have frequent weight fluctuations because of alternating binges and fasting. Fasting is very common, but long periods of fasting might increase the hunger, producing another binge episode, which is then followed by self-induced vomiting. These people usually feel that their lives are becoming dominated by food and that their levels of functioning are being reduced to a minimum. Many college students realize that these habits might affect their learning, and many end up dropping out of college. Their frustration might lead to severe depression, which can lead, in turn, to intermittent substance abuse—most frequently with alcohol and occasionally with amphetamines or barbiturates.

The disorder usually begins during adolescence or early adulthood, when there is overconcern about appearance and attractiveness. It is more prevalent in girls who are concerned about their appearance. The symptoms might continue for many years or change intermittently and might alternate between periods of binge eating, with self-induced vomiting, periods of normal eating, and periods of fasting. Usually the binging and vomiting increase when the person is under stress such as before important examinations or following a traumatic event. The disorder becomes a way for the person to handle stress by regressing into herself; that is, she becomes preoccupied with herself rather than cope properly with outside conflicts or stresses.

There is no familial pattern for this disorder, but frequently there is a family history of obesity, and the bulimic person might fear becoming overweight like other family members.

The dire results of bulimia are not only social isolation and inability to concentrate and function academically, but also potentially severe nutritional and physical deficiencies (see table 18-1). Frequent episodes of overeating and vomiting might lead to severe weight loss. If the weight loss is more than 25% of the original body weight, there is usually cessation of menstrual periods. The condition is then classified as a variant of anorexia nervosa, and is sometimes called bulimia nervosa [1], or bulimarexia. It might lead to severe protein and

Table 18-1
Medical Complication of Bulimia

Organ	Complication
GI tract	Pharyngitis
	Esophagitis
	Gastritis
	Hiatal hernia
	Bloody diarrhea from laxative abuse
	Enlargement of parotid glands
Teeth	Decay in teeth and gums
Blood	Severe hypokalemia
	Other electrolyte disturbances
	Severe dehydration
	Hypotension
Heart	Arrythmias
	Cardiac arrest
Genitourinary	Irregularity of menstruation; amenorrhea
	Inability to concentrate urine resulting in general edema
	Polydipsia
	Polyuria
Skin	Bruises and lacerations over the knuckles
	Ecchymoses on face and neck
	Stretch marks due to fluctuations in weight
	Hernia due to increased pressure during vomiting
Eyes	Hemorrhages in conjunctiva
Liver	Abnormality in liver function

calorie malnutrition, which can affect the immunological system of the body. Consequently, the person can succumb to any encountered infection. Even if the weight remains within a reasonable range, excessive vomiting can lead to dehydration and electrolyte disturbances. The most prevalent disturbance is hypokalemia, a low level of serum potassium. In hypokalemia, changes in the heart beat can occur, and, if the potassium level in the blood becomes very low, it can result in cardiac arrest and death. Excessive vomiting also can lead to enlargement of the parotid glands, with swelling on both sides of the face under the ears [2]. Excessive dental-enamel erosion also can result from chronic vomiting, necessitating excessive dental work. Even if there is not cessation of menstrual periods in bulimic women, the frequent fluctuation in weight can produce menstrual disturbances. Excessive vomiting can lead to hemorrhages in the conjunctiva or in other parts of the face. If a finger is used to produce the gag reflex, bruises or lacerations over the knuckles might occur.

The diagnostic criteria for bulimia suggested by the Diagnostic and Statistical Manual of Mental Disorders (DSM-III) of the American Psychiatric Association are as follows [3]:

A.   Recurrent episodes of binge eating (rapid consumption of a large amount of food in a discrete period of time, usually less than two hours).
B.   At least three of the following:
  1.   Consumption of high-caloric, easily ingested food during a binge
  2.   Inconspicuous eating during a binge
  3.   Termination of such eating episodes by abdominal pain, sleep, social interruption, or self-induced vomiting
  4.   Repeated attempts to lose weight by severely restrictive diets, self-induced vomiting, or use of cathartics or diuretics
  5.   Frequent weight fluctuations greater than ten pounds due to alternating binges and fasts.
C.   Awareness that the eating pattern is abnormal and fear of not being able to stop eating voluntarily.
D.   Depressed mood and self-deprecating thought following eating binges.
E.   The bulimic episodes are not due to Anorexia Nervosa or any known physical disorder.

Differential Diagnosis

The differential diagnosis of bulimia to be considered first is anorexia nervosa (see table 18-2). Whereas in anorexia nervosa there is severe weight loss that might lead to life-threatening malnutrition, the weight in bulimia fluctuates but not as extremely as in anorexia. After a long period of fasting, however — for months or even years—anorectic patients might turn to vomiting and binging

Table 18-2
Differential Diagnosis of Bulimia

Illness	Differential symptoms
Anorexia nervosa	Only if weight loss is over 25% of original body weight
Schizophrenia	Delusions associated with food
Brain tumor (Hypothalamic area)	Destruction or overstimulation of the hunger and satiety centers
Epileptic seizures	Affecting the stomach or stimulates vomiting
Severe migrains	Associated with vomiting but not self-induced
Psychogenic vomiting	Not related to binges and no fear of weight gain
Early pregnancy	Voracious appetite with usually early morning nausea. Vomiting not self-induced
Klein Levin syndrome	Ravenous appetite in young males followed by sleep, 3–4 times per year. No vomiting seen

in order to lower their weight. It was estimated by Casper and associates that about 47% of their anorectic patients resorted to bulimia [4]. Garfinkel, Moldofsky, and Garner estimated that close to 50% of their patients did so [5].

Bulimia also should be differentiated from schizophrenia in which the psychotic delusion revolves around eating. In such cases, however, it is clear that the person has unreasonable delusions and that episodes of not eating or eating voraciously are a result of these delusions. Other conditions that might appear similar to bulimia would be a brain tumor or epileptic-equivalent seizures. Functional psychogenic vomiting might appear similar to bulimia but usually involves vomiting episodes in the morning as a result of underlying psychological problems. This condition is seen more often in younger children than in adolescents and is often a result of the chidren's conflicts about going to school or separating from their mothers. Excessive vomiting and voracious appetite are sometimes seen in the early stages of pregnancy; the cause will become evident, however, once the pregnancy is confirmed.

Treatment

Medical work up (see table 18-3) is important in order to take care of any medical complication (table 18-4). There is one treatment modality that shows successful result in treatment of bulimia. Many clinicians believe that, since it might be a symptom of underlying conflicts, the treatment approach should be intensive, individual, insight-oriented therapy to uncover the source of the conflict in the patient's life. This therapy might lead to abreaction of past traumatic events that might have been the source of the illness. Once abreaction of trauma

Table 18-3
Recommended Tests

Test	Rule Out
Blood glucose	Hypoglycemia
Urea nitrogen	Dehydration
Electrolyte	Hypokalemia and electrolytes imbalance
X-rays of upper GI tract	Hiatal hernia and gastric or duodenal ulcer
X-rays of lower GI tract	Crohn disease, colitis
Xylose test and fat absorption	Malabsorption syndrome
EEG	Epilepsy or brain tumor
CT scan of brain	Brain tumor
ECG	Cardiac arrhythmias or hypokalemia

has occurred, there will be no further need for the symptoms, since the underlying conflict or trauma will be resolved. Many times, however, prolonged insight-oriented therapy does not lead to a change in the symptoms of binging and vomiting. In such cases, the therapist might look into other possibilities, such as identifying binging and vomiting as substitutes for feelings that are unrecognized by the patient. Aggressive drive that is not being expressed assertively, for example, might be converted unconsciously into binges—as a means of getting the aggression out by crushing food excessively. If the patient's sex life were investigated, too, it might be discovered that binging and vomiting are substitutes for sexual satisfaction or are a result of fear or sexual conflicts. The role of the therapist is to let the patient relate the entire story that surrounds her

Table 18-4
Treatment Modalities for Bulimia

1. Medical treatment:	Correcting of dehydration and electrolyte imbalance with special attention to hypokalemia
2. Psychotherapy	a. Individual insight oriented (psychoanalytic)
	b. Individual supportive
	c. Group (general including patients with other problems)
	d. Group for eating disorders
	e. Assertive training group
	f. Family therapy
	g. Biofeedback
	h. Hypnosis
	i. Psychopharmachotherapy (medications)
	j. Creative or art therapy
	k. Recreational therapy
	l. Vocational rehabilitation (if necessary)
	m. Behavior therapy

bulimia in a nonjudgmental atmosphere. This can lead the therapist to the underlying conflict, since the patient will be able to free-associate about her problems, giving clues to the symbolic meaning of the symptoms.

Dietary instructions are important so that the patient realizes that she can have better control of her fear of weight gain. She might then be able to maintain a proper diet, without needing to vomit or use laxatives, diuretics, or diet pills. Knowledge of proper dietary needs will provide the patient with a sense of security.

Changing the patient's structured environment may be helpful at times. It was noted that many patients who were admitted to the hospital stopped their binging and vomiting episodes for up to two or three months while they were in the hospital. Many of them were able to continue this therapeutic gain after discharge, but a few reverted to bulimic episodes when they returned home. In these cases, the home environment appears to be too stressful, and it might be advisable to suggest that the patient move away from her parents' house. If the patient is living alone, the therapist could suggest that she change her lifestyle or get involved in other activities, sports, or hobbies that might give more content in her life. Sometimes the episodes of binging and vomiting recur when the patient becomes bored being alone. In such cases, encouragement of social interactions might be beneficial.

Psychiatric evaluation should be done on each bulimic patient in order to find out if there are other psychopathologies. The bulimia might be the presenting symptom for underlying depression or severe anxiety, and such conditions must be addressed in therapy before any success in alleviating the bulimic symptoms can be achieved. In cases underlying psychopathology, treatment might include use of medications if indicated. Antidepressant medications, for example, might help resolve the problem of underlying endogenous depression. Some success has been achieved by the use of tricyclic antidepressants or monoamine oxidase inhibitors for resolving underlying depression and subsequently alleviating the bulimic symptoms. Phenytoin was found to be beneficial in reducing binging episodes [6, 7] but more experience with it is needed. Group therapy is also useful. It provides patients with appropriate feedback by which they are able to see themselves and their problems and realize that others have the same difficulties. The group situation also provides mutual support and communality, allowing patients to feel that they are not alone in this world with such a problem. Self-help groups also are being organized under the auspices of the Society for Anorexia Nervosa and Associated Disorders and the National Anorexic Aid Society. Such groups, which are being formed in several cities of the United States, are patterned along the lines of Alcoholics Anonymous.

Behavioral therapy is being provided in the structured environment of hospital programs, but it is more difficult to apply this method to outpatients. Although behavioral therapy might be successful in changing eating habits, it is important that, when it is used, a great deal of individual support be given to the patient to prevent depression or frustration. New techniques such as bio-feedback and hypnosis are promising. They rely mainly on relaxation, which enables the patient to be more attuned to the needs of her body, thus recognizing her feelings of hunger. Once the patient is able to recognize these feelings and separate them from such other feelings as aggressive drive or sexual drive, the need for binging and vomiting is reduced. Hypnosis also can provide the patient with a tool for gaining better control over her eating habits. Learning self-hypnosis might give the patient a means by which she can increase her willpower, thus controlling her eating habits better. It should be emphasized that hypnosis is being used successfully for losing weight and that it will also help the patient maintain her weight. Self-hypnosis also provides the patient with a sense of security, and consequently the need for vomiting as a measure of control is no longer needed. Hypnosis also is being used successfully to age-regress the patient to previous traumatic events, enabling the therapist to uncover underlying conflicts. Working through these conflicts can help the patient rid herself of the binging and vomiting symptoms altogether.

It is important to emphasize that the success rate is higher in centers in which the bulimia problem is addressed as part of an overall program for eating disorders. Being treated in such a program enables the patient to benefit from the various treatment modalities that are offered. The possibility of better results is increased because the patient can find the best treatment for her problem; that is, the treatment program can be tailored to the specific needs of the individual patient.

A bulimic patient can be considered cured only if there is self-acceptance of her appearance as well as an end to the bulimic symptoms.

References

1. Russell, G. Bulimia nervosa: An ominous variant of anorexia nervosa. *Psychol. Med.* 9:429-448, 1979.

2. Levin, A.P., Folko, J.M., Dixon, K., Gallup, M.E., and Sounders, W. Benign parotid enlargement in bulimia. *Ann. Intern. Med.* 93:827-829, 1980.

3. American Psychiatric Association. *Diagnostic and Statistical Manual of Mental Disorders* (3rd ed.) Washington, D.C.: American Psychiatric Association, 1980.

4. Capser, R.C., Eckert, E.D., Halmi, K.A., Goldberg, S.C., and Davis, J.M. Bulimia. Its incidence and clinical importance in patients with anorexia nervosa. *Arch. Gen. Psychiatry* 37:1030-1035, 1980.

5. Garfinkel, E.P., Moldofsky, H., and Garner, M.D. The heterogeneity of anorexia nervosa: Bulimia as a distinct subgroup. *Arch. Gen. Psychiatry* 37:1036-1040, 1980.

6. Wermuth, B.M., Davis, K.L., Hollister, L.E., et al. Phenytoin treatment of the binge-eating syndrome. *Am. J. Psychiatry* 134:1249-1253, 1977.

7. Green, R.S., and Rau, J.H. Treatment of compulsive eating disturbances with anticonvulsant medication. *Am. J. Psychiatry* 131:428-432, 1974.

19 The Psychology of Anorexia Nervosa

Eugene L. Bliss, M.D.

Generally, five types of patients can be identified as those who lose weight excessively for psychological reasons. The first type are paranoid schizophrenics, who perceive their food to be poisoned. Second are severe depressives, who experience a profound loss of appetite. Both of these types appear rarely and are not considered to be examples of anorexia nervosa. Third, however, are those patients who go on diets and become caught up in the process. Fourth are those who suffer somatic problems, such as dysphagias and gastralgias; these patients usually are considered to be hysterics with conversion symptoms. Finally, there is an ill-defined, small population of unhappy, anxious, and despondent people with psychological miseries, who do not begin with diets but soon follow the anorectic pattern. I offer these categories as provisional distinctions.

Changes in the Syndrome

There have been two dramatic changes in the anorexia nervosa syndrome over the past decade. Thirty years ago, when I first studied cases of anorexia nervosa, they were few—representing a rare and exotic disorder. More recently, however, the numbers have increased remarkably, until such cases are now commonly and frequently encountered. These large increases do not appear to be primarily a function of the expanding population, nor do they seem to be attributable to earlier or more frequent recognition of the disorder. Rather, the increase seems to stem from another recent phenomenon—the fad of dieting. In 1954, Kay and Leigh reported that 61% of investigated cases began with a reducing diet [1]. In 1970, Theander culled from past hospital records a large series of cases, of which 47% began with a diet [2]. In contrast, in my recent series of cases spanning the years 1975 to 1980 ($n = 62$) and a Maudsley series from 1973 to 1975 ($n = 23$), 85% and 87%, respectively, began with a diet [3]. By now, it could well be that some 90% of cases of anorexia are initiated by a diet. What seems

I am indebted to Drs. Dennis Hill and Dennis Leigh at the Institute of Psychiatry and the Maudsley Hospital, London; to Drs. Noel Walsh and Mary Darby at the Sisters of Charity St. Vincent's Hospital, Dublin; to Dr. David Wood at the Farnsborough Hospital, Kent; and to Drs. Hubert Green and Arthur Crisp at the St. George's Hospital Medical School, London. All made records of anorexia nervosa cases available, for which I am most grateful.

to be happening is an enormous increase in dieting in the adolescent and young-adult female population. The concern about obesity and the contemporary conviction that "thin is beautiful" have become a female preoccupation in the affluent Western nations—an obsession that is now infiltrating much of the world. As a result, dieting has become epidemic, creating a huge female population that is at risk for anorexia nervosa.

Incidence

In Sweden, Nylander reported an incidence of one severe case in 150 adolescent girls [4]; in England, Crisp, Palmer, and Kalucy found an incidence of one severe case in 100 girls over age 16 [5]. Both of these studies, as well as that of Huene-mann and associates in the United States [6], found dieting commonplace among adolescent girls, with a peak in the 17- to 18-year-old group; in contrast, dieting is uncommon in the male adolescent population.

If we accept the figure of one severe case in every 100 late-adolescent girls, and assume that, in this population of 100 females, only 50 diet with dedication—an arbitrary and as yet uncertain premise—then we may conclude that 2% of the seriously dieting population in this age range develop the severe syndrome. That raises the critical question of why, from the group at risk, only 2% develop the severe form and perhaps 5% the mild form. What distinguishes the small, susceptible minority from the large majority of the dieting population?

Hypotheses

Based on my clinical experience with anorexia nervosa cases, two possible explanations seemed plausible and were tested.

Spontaneous Self-Hypnosis

Practically all of the afflicted girls develop an intense weight phobia. They become obsessed with the fear that, if they eat normally, eating will become uncontrolled and they will become fat, and being fat takes on various meanings. Many are unhappy adolescents who equate obesity with unhappiness, unattractiveness, a lack of emotional strength and control. In contrast, being thin comes to mean the possibility of happiness, attractiveness, and control. Rarer associations also are found, such as equating fat with sexuality, maturity, or pregnancy and equating thin with asexuality, immaturity, lack of pregnancy, or an ascetic form of self-redemption. The central feature in most cases, however, is the girls' desire to diet in order to be thin and physically attractive. Somehow this powerful idea becomes imbedded in their psyches in a potent form, resulting in a phobic, obsessional concern that dominates behavior.

Recently, I have been investigating in other forms of psychopathy a mental process that can instill potent irrational ideas. In the nineteenth century, there was an enormous interest in hypnosis, although it has since become unfashionable. During that period, however, there was ample evidence from studies by many physicians—including Braid [7], Esdaile [8], Elliotson [9], Janet [10, 11], Bernheim [12], Forel [13], Bramwell [14], Breuer and Freud [15], Prince, [16, 17], and Sidis [18, 19], to mention only a few—that powerful ideas could be introduced into the mind by hypnosis in excellent hypnotic subjects. These ideas or complexes could then influence and direct behavior in irrational ways. Breuer went a step further and noted, in his case of "Anna O.," spontaneous "self-hypnotic" or "hypnoid" states [15, 20].

I have found spontaneous self-hypnotic states in many psychiatric syndromes [21, 22]. Self-hypnosis is a primitive coping mechanism, observable in animals as well as humans, which occurs spontaneously and unconsciously in people with excellent hypnotic capabilities when they are emotionally distraught and psychologically trapped. The question is whether a comparable mechanism is operating in patients with anorexia nervosa. Do these subjects have unusual hypnotic capabilities, and did they go spontaneously into hypnotic states, introducing weight phobias and irrational self-images? The first hypothesis, then, is that these girls should be excellent hypnotic subjects, well above the normal range—a trait presumably in part genetic in origin.

Dedication to a Task

The second hypothesis stems from the observation that most obese persons are poor dieters. Stunkard and McLaren-Hume summarized the dilemma of the obese [23]. They reported that most obese persons will not stay in treatment for obesity. Of those who stay in treatment, most will not lose weight, and of those who do lose weight, most will regain it. In their study, using conventional outpatient treatment, only 25% lost more than 20 pounds and 5% more than 40 pounds. Behavioral therapy has recently added a modest increment of success to these figures, but the overall rate of clinical success with the treatment of obesity remains disappointing.

In contrast, patients with anorexia nervosa are magnificent dieters. Far from being pathetic waifs, they are indomitable, versatile, and successful losers of weight. Not only can they take off weight, but they also can maintain the losses. The question, then, is what other traits besides the weight phobia and the possible hypnotic mechanism allow them to succeed where the obese fail so miserably. It was postulated that patients with anorexia nervosa have facilitating traits that enhance their capabilities to stick to the dieting task with a tenacity of purpose.

Subjects and Methods

The study is based on a lengthy self-report that was completed by 65 patients with anorexia nervosa—62 females and 3 males. The analysis was limited to the 62 females, all of whom demonstrated a substantial loss of weight, resulting from a refusal to eat adequately, in the absence of any known medical disease. Seven patients were tested with the Stanford Hypnotic Susceptibility Scale to ascertain their hypnotic capabilities [24].

Results

Analysis of Weights

Analysis was made of 456 cases of anorexia nervosa from the literature (see table 19-1). The average patient began at a weight of 123 pounds and dropped to 79 pounds—a loss of 44 pounds. An interesting fact is that only 7% of the patients reported in the literature ever weighed more than 150 pounds; in my series, only 13% were ever above this weight. If they began at over 150 pounds, their lowest weight, with rare exceptions, never went below 78 pounds. In contrast, the most severe cases, with weight dropping below 70 pounds—comprising 25% of the cases in the literature and 18% in my series—began at a mean weight of 114 pounds.

Table 19-1
Analysis of Weight, Sex, Age, and Height in Patients with Anorexia Nervosa

	Bliss Series	*Cases Reported in the Literature*
Sex		
Female	95% (*n* = 62)	90–95%
Male	5% (*n* = 3)	5–10%
Mean age of onset	17–18 years	17–18 years
Weight change (average)	From 127 to 80 lbs (*n* = 62)	From 123 to 79 lbs (*n* = 456)
Height		64½ in. (*n* = 90)
Weight		
Began at > 150 lbs	13% (*n* = 62)	7% (*n* = 173)
Began at > 150 lbs and dropped below 78 lbs	3 cases (*n* = 62)	1 case (*n* = 173)
Lowest weight < 70 lbs (mean starting weight, 114 lbs)	18% (*n* = 62)	25% (*n* = 173)

These observations lead to the conclusions that anyone who weighs over 150 pounds is unlikely to develop a severe case of anorexia nervosa and that the most extreme cachexias begin in females who are only slightly overweight or have normal weights. The superobese practically never develop the syndrome. Furthermore, the cachexias below 70 pounds are to be found in only about 20% of the cases. Why substantial obesity and superobesity should provide safeguards remains unanswered.

Age of Onset and Sex

The mean age of onset is 17 to 18 years. The reasons for this remain speculative. Presumably, it is because that age is a period of transition and turmoil—a time of adolescent crises—when peer pressures are powerful, the need to be attractive, thin, and conforming is most insistent, and dieting is most imperative. From 90% to 95% of cases occur in females, which seems to be predominantly a function of the dieting population—almost all female.

Facilitators of a Diet

Over half the patients in my series reported a normal appetite prior to onset of the disorder, although a minority (36%) felt that their appetites had been strong (see table 19-2). An overwhelming urge to eat did not seem to be a dominant force in most cases prior to the diet (13%) and consequently was not initially a powerful countervailing force to a successful diet.

The intensity of the motivation to diet was not measured, but clinical experience with these girls indicates that most are very strongly motivated by a general unhappiness, which is focused on their presumed-grotesque figures.

A striking feature of these patients is their diligence (74%), perfectionism (72%), and persistence (74%). These traits are demonstrated academically, and most anorectic girls are excellent students. The majority of these girls will persist in a task tenaciously when they accept its importance, and they apply this dedication to dieting. Furthermore, they diet sensibly, intuitively discovering behavioral tactics to facilitate the diet by eating low-calorie foods, delaying eating until they are no longer hungry, eating slowly, and the like. In the process of dieting, many lose their appetites (72%) and develop physical distress with eating (87%). Both processes make dieting simpler and inevitable. For many, malnutrition becomes a pleasant state (65%), and it may well be that a moderate underweight has psychological virtues.

Almost all patients are consumed by the fear of obesity—a state they have come to dread (89%). Most are reinforced by the satisfaction of self-control (73%), which gives them a feeling of self-worth and strength that was lacking

Table 19-2

Factors Contributing to Diet (Facilitators)

(1)	*Premorbid appetite*		(5)	*Loss of weight leads to loss*
	Normal	(58%)		*of appetite* (72%)
	Strong	(23%)		Highest weight ($n = 40$) 125 lbs
	Very strong	(13%)		Weight when lost
	Below normal	(6%)		appetite 96 lbs
(2)	*Motivation to diet*			Lowest weight 78 lbs
(3)	*Personality*		(6)	*Eating leads to physical dis-*
	Diligence (excellent student)	(74%)		*tress after lost weight* (87%)
	Perfectionist	(72%)	(7)	*Malnutrition a pleasant state*
	Self-report[a]			Less bulky (74%)
	Persistence	(74%)		Light and free (65%)
	Neatness	(67%)		A pleasant way to live if
	Worry	(62%)		people didn't bother me (61%)
	Self-control	(58%)		Feel energetic (55%)
	Guilt	(53%)		Feel healthy (53%
	Creature of habit	(51%)	(8)	*Phobic obsessional state*
	Impulsiveness	(39%)		When thin afraid to let self
(4)	*Dieting tactics*			eat—would become fat (89%)
	Low-calorie foods	(76%)	(9)	*Advantages being thin*
	Delay eating until hunger			Good feeling of self-control (73%)
	leaves	(55%)		Insurance against obesity (65%)
	Eat slowly	(44%)		People notice you (39%)
	Small bites	(42%)		Control over people (35%)
	Taste food more	(27%)		Reduces sexual problems (31%)
				Feel morally purer (27%)
				Cuts out menses (24%)

[a]Patients were asked to rate themselves on a scale of 1 to 10. Only those who gave themselves a high rating—8 to 10—were included in the calculation of the percentages.

before their diet. Contrary to some opinions, most patients do not view their leanness as a desirable escape from sexual problems or menstruation, and few perceive malnutrition as a means to attain moral purification. In my experience, also, although some patients do die from their cachexia, few if any are motivated to use dieting as a means of suicide. The dieting seems to be motivated and enhanced by other forces, although the end result for a few may be death.

Other Critical Elements

Other critical elements in cases of anorexia nervosa are the following (see table 19-3).

Fear of Obesity (Phobic, Obsessional State). All patients refuse to eat a normal diet, which is the dominant cause of their malnutrition, and the vast majority (85%) begin with a reducing diet. Although 60% were not victimized by a phobia of obesity prior to the diet, almost all (89%) develop this phobia in the process

Table 19-3
Analysis of Critical Elements

(1) *Began with a diet*	(85%)
(2) *Fear obesity (phobic-obsessional state)*	
Refuse to eat normal diet	(100%)
Eating binges	(62%)
Vomiting (self-induced)	(46%)
Laxatives (to lose weight)	(23%)
(3) *Remarkable energy*	
Before lost weight	
More active than most	(36%)
Less active than most	(20%)
After lost weight	
More active	(44%)
Less active	(41%)
(4) *Food phobia*	
Obsessed with getting fat before anorexia	(40%)
Premorbidly not obsessed	(60%)
When thin, phobic about obesity	(89%)
Calorie expert	(59%)
Enjoy cooking for others	(50%)
(5) *Faulty body image—unaware of cachexia*	
Did not feel thin	(69%)

of dieting. The phobia, in turn, is enhanced and facilitated by the elements that previously have been enumerated.

To avoid obesity, they use a variety of strategies to prevent normal alimentation. They all refuse to eat a normal diet. If they do eat, the noxious calories are extruded by vomiting (46%), which often is preceded by eating binges (62%). A minority uses laxatives as a strategy to lose weight—to flush out the calories before they can be absorbed (23%). Some hide and then dispose of their food. All these tactics are contrived as counterphobic measures to maintain leanness and to avoid obesity.

Increased Activity. Since the body is a machine subject to the first law of thermodynamics, there are only two ways to lose weight—diminishing the calories, so that less energy enters the system, or increasing the work and the physical activity emanating from the system. Many patients are very active, and some exercise zealously. One of the questions that arises is whether the patients who have been described as overactive simply are following premorbid patterns or have, in fact, become more active in their malnourished state. The answer appears to vary. Prior to their diets, about one-third of the patients (36%) perceived themselves as more active than most of their friends, whereas 44% became more active during the phase of malnutrition, and 41% became less so. An increase in activity or physical expenditure of calories appears, therefore, to be characteristic of about half the subjects. In some, it seems to be voluntary—as a means to lose weight and to remain very thin—but in others it seems to be spontaneous. It must be noted, however, that many become less active (41%) and that most lose their strength when their weight reaches very low levels.

Faulty Body Image. Much attention has been paid to anorectic patients' distorted self-perceptions. Even when they become very thin, many do not see themselves as thin (69%). Their internal perceptions do not match the external reality, and these cachectic girls continue to feel fat.

I contend that this misperception, though startling, is not unique to anorexia nervosa. Powerful ideas tend to operate in just such an irrational fashion. Phobics characteristically perceive the feared object as both overpowering and immense, despite all evidence to the contrary. An intense fear of water, or public speaking, or anger converts these factors into huge obstacles, far exceeding their real danger. The same phobic process, concentrated on the fear of obesity, appears to be operating in anorectic patients.

Self-Hypnotic Pathology

It was postulated earlier that spontaneous self-hypnosis may play a role in the production of the phobic process of anorexia nervosa. As a corollary, it was deemed likely that these patients would prove to be better-than-normal hypnotic subjects.

I have now examined 12 patients with anorexia nervosa for their hypnotic capabilities. All 12 have proved to be good-to-excellent hypnotic subjects—all having entered a trance state within a few minutes of induction. These findings have been from clinical experiences only, but from previous studies of hypnosis during the last three years, I have matched my judgments against scores on the Stanford Hypnotic Susceptibility Scale and have reason to believe that these clinical judgments tend to be accurate. To insure more objective and more scientifically acceptable data, however, we have begun to test patients with the Stanford Hypnotic Susceptibility Scale. All seven anorectic subjects tested have scored well above the mean (table 19-4). The sample is being increased, but it appears thus far that patients with anorexia nervosa are excellent hypnotic subjects by both clinical and test standards. This is supported by Frankel and Orne's study, which indicated that many phobic patients have higher-than-normal hypnotic capacities [25].

These observations, if confirmed by future studies, suggest that hypnotic susceptibility may play an important role in the evolution of anorexia nervosa. Presumably, the hypnotic capability facilitates the introduction of the phobia; in anorexia nervosa, the phobia is obesity. These hypnotic implants tend to be

Table 19-4
Hypnotic Susceptibility Test Scores

	Anorexia Nervosa Group	Control Group 1[a]	Control Group 2[b]
Number	7	124	17
Scores	12		
	12		
	11		
	11		
	10		
	8		
	8		
Mean and S.E. mean	10.29 ± 64	5.25 ± .29	5.65 ± .80

$p < .001$
Note: The highest score attainable on the Stanford Hypnotic Susceptibility Test is 12.
[a]Sample from A.M. Weitzenhoffer and E.R. Hilgard, *Stanford Hypnotic Susceptibility Test* (Palo Alto, Calif.: Consulting Psychologists Press, 1965).
[b]Sample from F.H. Frankel and M.T. Orne, Hypnotizability and phobic behavior. *Arch. Gen. Psychiatry* 33:1259-1261, 1976.

fixed during periods of emotional turmoil, and this distress is certainly present in most patients during the early stages of anorexia nervosa.

Furthermore, driven, impulsive behaviors—such as stealing, alcoholism, drug addiction, suicide attempts, and self-inflicted injuries—are reported in these patients, more commonly in the bulimic group [26]. All these behaviors are consistent with self-hypnotic pathology, since they are commonly found in patients with other psychiatric disorders who demonstrate this underlying hypnotic mechanism [21, 22].

Physical Changes When Thin

As a result of semistarvation, primarily due to a reduction in fats and carbohydrates, physical changes occur (table 19-5). These changes are widespread, and some—such as amenorrhea, sensitivity to cold, skin and hair alterations, weakness, and edema—are detected by the patients. A surprising finding was the high percentage who reported amenorrhea only after weight was reduced.

Therapy

This analysis of anorexia nervosa emphasizes the phobic nature of the disorder, the dedication of these patients to valued tasks, and the patients' hypnotic

Table 19-5
Physical Changes When Thin

Amenorrhea	
Before lost weight	8%
After lost weight	92%
Sensitivity to cold	92%
Weakness	84%
Dry Skin	66%
Constipation	65%
Loss of hair	55%
Brittleness of hair	52%
Hair on face	32%
Leg edema	27%

capability—which presumably is a major element in the fixation on the phobia of obesity.

Logically, therefore, therapy might be directed toward counterphobic tactics, the use of hypnosis, and the mobilization of the patients' potential for dedication to a desirable task. It would also seem reasonable to assess the extent of their general psychopathology and maladaptation prior to onset of the disorder. Some of these girls were normal adolescents who inadvertently acquired a disabling symptom by initiating reducing diets. They were apparently unfortunate victims of an excellent hypnotic capability, which converted an innocent diet into a phobic process. Others, however, had more generalized neurotic problems before the diet, which would require more extensive therapy than merely symptomatic relief.

I have been experimenting with various tactics, but data are still insufficient to estimate their worth. Realimentation, with weight gain, is clearly necessary and seems to be best achieved by using a series of rewards to motivate the weight gain; penalties also are applied for failure to regain weight.

The gain in weight is a counterphobic tactic that generates anxiety and somatic discomfort and goes counter to the usual lack of appetite. Therefore, reassurance, compliments, and rewards are necessary motivators to overcome these obstacles. The patients must confront the fear, tolerate the short period of physical unpleasantness and poor appetite, and learn to master the process. Since these patients have reduced eating to a shambles, regular meals must be initiated to reinstitute a normal rhythm of eating. A gain in weight is usually but not always attainable. The more formidable obstacle in most cases is the phobia, which often remains even when the patients reach normal weight.

Psychological exercises in both hypnosis and reality can be tried to increase the patient's confidence in her ability to control her appetite. Other means to solve personal problems—rather than concentrating on dieting—can be explored, and regular physical activities can be recommended, but the phobia remains a formidable obstacle.

Eating binges are another troublesome symptom. Even after their weights have returned to acceptable levels, many patients continue to go on eating sprees. There is a temptation to overeat, especially during periods of discontent and emotional distress. The urge becomes overpowering and a binge ensues, only to be followed by vomiting to forestall weight gain. This is usually succeeded by remorse and starvation. Eating is reduced to chaos, living is concentrated on alimentation, and all problems of life are inappropriately managed by the gastro-intestinal tract.

I sometimes admit such patients to the hospital initially to replace these patterns with a regular schedule of eating, at a caloric level that is acceptable and will not lead to obesity. The patient must learn to eat a normal diet. Next, I try hypnotic exercises to teach them how to control the urge to overeat. They must learn that the urge to binge is not irresistible and can be mastered. I also ask the patients hypnotically to associate the urge to binge with the dysphoric feelings of guilt, loss of self-respect, and the financial expense involved rather than the immediate satisfactions of the binge. Finally, I try to prohibit vomiting, so that the binge will be punished automatically. It remains to be seen whether these strategies will be effective.

Conclusion

Anorexia nervosa appears to be primarily a phobia created partly by a spontaneous self-hypnotic process. Anorectic patients are excellent hypnotic subjects who develop a morbid fear of obesity during a period of emotional turmoil when they begin a diet. The fear, in turn, leads to the use of a variety of tactics—such as reduced caloric intake, vomiting, eating binges, ingestion of cathartics, and exercise—to insure malnutrition and to protect against obesity. These patients' perfectionism and commitment to a task seem to facilitate the dieting process. Other irrational features of the disorder, such as a distortion in body image and compulsive stealing, probably are facilitated by the self-hypnotic process.

References

1. Kay, D.W., and Leigh, D. The natural history, treatment and prognosis of anorexia nervosa, based upon a study of 38 patients. *J. Ment. Sci.* 11:411-431, 1954.

2. Theander, S. Anorexia nervosa. *Acta Psychiatr. Scand. [Suppl.]* 214: 1-194, 1970.

3. Bliss, E.L. Unpublished data.

4. Nylander, I. The feeling of being fat and dieting in a school population. *Acta Sociomed. Scand.* 3:17-26, 1971.

5. Crisp, A.H., Palmer, R.L., and Kalucy, R.S. How common is anorexia nervosa. *Br. J. Psychiatry* 128:549-54, 1976.

6. Huenemann, R.L., Shapiro, L.R., Hampton, M.C., and Mitchell, B.E. A longitudinal study of gross body composition and body conformation and their association with food and activity in a teenage population. *Am. J. Clin. Nutr.* 18:325-338, 1966.

7. Braid, J. *Neurypnology; or The Rationale of Nervous Sleep.* London: John Churchill, 1843.

8. Esdaile, J. *Mesmerism in India and Its Practical Application in Surgery and Medicine.* London: Longman, 1846.

9. Elliotson, J. *Numerous Cases of Surgical Operations Without Pain in the Mesmeric State.* London: H. Bailliere, 1843.

10. Janet, P. *L'Automatisme Psychologique.* Paris: Alcan, 1889.

11. Janet, P. *The Major Symptoms of Hysteria.* New York: Macmillan Co., 1907.

12. Bernheim, H. *Suggestive Therapeutics.* New York: G.P. Putnam's Sons, 1902.

13. Forel, A. *Hypnotism or Suggestion and Psychotherapy.* New York: Rebman Co., 1907.

14. Bramwell, J.M. *Hypnotism: Its History, Practice and Theory.* Rev. ed. Philadelphia: Lippincott, 1928.

15. Breuer, J., and Freud, S. *Studies on Hysteria.* New York: Basic Books, 1957.

16. Prince, M. *The Dissociation of a Personality.* New York: Longman's, Green and Co., 1906.

17. Prince, M. *The Unconscious.* New York: Macmillan Co., 1914.

18. Sidis, B. *The Psychology of Suggestion.* New York: D. Appleton and Co., 1898.

19. Sidis, B. *Nervous Ills: Their Cause and Cure.* Boston: Gorham Press, 1922.

20. Freud, S. *An Autobiographical Study.* London: Hogarth Press, 1948.

21. Bliss, E.L. Multiple personalities: A report of 14 cases with implications for schizophrenia and hysteria. *Arch. Gen. Psychiatry* 37:1388-1397, 1980.

22. Bliss, E.L. Hypnosis and hysteria: The entity of spontaneous self-hypnotic disorders. Unpublished manuscript.

23. Stunkard, A.J., and McLaren-Hume, M. The results of treatment of obesity: A review of the literature and report of a series. *Arch. Inter. Med.* 103:79-85, 1959.

24. Weitzenhoffer, A.M., and Hilgard, E.R. *Stanford Hypnotic Susceptibility Scale.* Palo Alto, Calif.: Consulting Psychologists Press, 1965.

25. Frankel, F.H., and Orne, M.T. Hypnotizability and phobic behavior. *Arch. Gen. Psychiatry* 33:1259-1261, 1976.

26. Garfinkel, P.E., Moldofsky, H., and Garner, D.M. The heterogeneity of anorexia nervosa: Bulimia as a distinct subgroup. *Arch. Gen. Psychiatry* 37: 1036-1040, 1980.

Appendix A

Origins and Purposes of the National Anorexic Aid Society

Patricia L. Howe Tilton

A diagnosis of anorexia nervosa or bulimia is not hopeless, but the hopelessness and desperation of those who are suffering from these illnesses or living with someone who has them may be overwhelming.

For people who have anorexia or bulimia, it can be a very lonely, frustrating, and frightening experience. In many families, a love-hate relationship may develop as families struggle with feelings ranging from understanding to resentment.

The National Anorexic Aid Society (NAAS) came into existence in 1977 in response to the growing needs of victims of these disorders and their families to find support and medical treatment in communities across the country. It was founded in Columbus, Ohio, as a nonprofit educational and support organization for people suffering from anorexia nervosa, bulimia, and related eating disorders and for their families.

We are working with medical and mental-health professionals nationally to bring anorexia nervosa and bulimia out into the open, so that they can be discussed, problems can be shared, and the causes, treatment, and hopes for recovery can be explored. Our services are not a substitute for medical and psychological treatment but rather an adjunct to therapy.

When I actively began working with anorexia and bulimia in 1976, I had no idea how many people suffered the disorders. I was familiar only with cases reported by doctors in hospital settings. I thought anorexia was rare, until nationally syndicated columnist Helen Bottel, of King Features, published an article from a distraught father whose daughter was seriously ill with the problem. The mail poured into Helen's Sacramento office, and she asked me to help her answer the letters, since I had suffered from and recovered from anorexia.

The mail we received awakened us to the fact that a support and educational organization could be very beneficial to victims of the disorders and their families, as well as to medical and mental-health professionals and educators.

As a result of our early efforts, NAAS has become an organization of communication, information, education, and research. We provide many services to families, schools, and the medical and mental-health community, including self-help groups for the victims and their families; a state-by-state listing of doctors and hospitals treating the disorders; information and referrals; published literature; and educational programs in the community.

Support Groups

Both anorectic and family support groups are operating in communities across the country. Support for victims of anorexia and bulimia is viewed as peer support. The groups promote trust, acceptance, and understanding, but also create a challenge for each member to grow. Participants are not required to be involved in treatment, but we have been very successful in getting them to physicians for diagnosis and help.

All the women and men attending group meetings share common problems—a preoccupation with food and eating, an obsession for dieting, and an unreasonable fear of being fat. For many who attend the meetings, it is their first contact with someone else who has an eating disorder. Talking with others helps break through their feelings of being different.

Those who participate in the groups must want to help themselves. We do not have any secrets for recovery; what worked for many of us might not work for someone else. We can only offer these people hope that recovery is possible and encourage them to continue. We are also careful not to foster an anorectic or bulimic problem or offer support to the person who wants to hold on to a problem. Instead, we encourage each participant to accept a certain amount of responsibility for herself or himself, including seeking medical treatment and making an effort to get well.

In the three anorectic support groups operating in Columbus, Ohio, recovered anorectic and bulimic victims work with the support groups as facilitators. When a victim contacts NAAS about attending a meeting, personal contact is made before the meeting by a trained and recovered member. This enables us to screen the person and make any necessary medical referrals.

The groups are not appropriate for severely emaciated people requiring hospitalization. We can only work with those who realize that they have a problem and are starting to help themselves. When someone is hospitalized, we assign a recovered member to maintain a one-to-one contact, but the patient or physician must request a hospital visit.

Family support groups are particularly helpful for families who have a newly diagnosed child. Many times the families are frantic, confused, angry, and overwhelmed with feelings of guilt. It is particularly helpful to have parents who have been through a similar experience on hand for support and encouragement during a time of crisis.

The family support groups usually are run by parents or mental-health professionals. Those attending are parents, grandparents, brothers and sisters, spouses, and, occasionally, friends.

Medical Referrals

When NAAS began in 1977, one of the first things we did was identify available medical treatment for eating disorders nationally. Treatment for anorexia nervosa and bulimia is considered a speciality, and many families are at a loss to find medical help in their communities.

We have developed a state-by-state physician-referral list to mail to families and individuals requesting assistance in locating treatment close to home.

Published Literature

One of our foremost goals has been communication, which is facilitated nationally through the NAAS quarterly newsletter, through other publications, and through correspondence with victims and their families.

People who pay an annual membership fee receive newsletters four times a year. Anyone who writes to NAAS for the first time can receive a current newsletter, a letter about NAAS services and membership, and information on anorexia nervosa and bulimia.

Educational Programs

Since the onset of the eating disorders usually occurs in adolescence, after the age of 13 years, public awareness and community education is a very important national need. We hope to provide information to parents, educators, family physicians, pediatricians, school nurses, and clergymen, which will aid in the early recognition, diagnosis, and treatment of the disorders.

A speakers bureau has been set up by NAAS to deal with the many requests we receive from hospitals, social-service organizations, colleges, and junior and senior high schools. Programs are presented by three-person teams, consisting of a physician or mental-health professional, an NAAS representative, and a recovered anorectic or bulimic person.

Summary

Although NAAS does provide services nationally, Columbus is the home base and the center for the majority of our activities. Our program is affiliated with the Bridge Counseling Center in Columbus and works with North Area Mental Health Services, one of seven centers operating within the Franklin County Mental Health Board.

Information on the National Anorexic Aid Society can be obtained by writing to NAAS, P.O. Box 29461, Columbus, Ohio 43229.

Appendix B

Further Information about the National Anorexic Aid Society

Judy Johnson

Frequent Questions Asked by Patients

The following are questions about the National Anorexic Aid Society that are frequently asked by patients:

Q How can the National Anorexic Aid Society help me, the anorectic patient?

A The Society can provide friendship, emotional support, and education by giving anorectic patients a chance to share their problems with others who suffer from the same condition. It is this idea—that common sufferers best understand each other—that perpetuates the support groups of the society. How much it can help you also depends, however, on how much you want help.

Q Exactly who is in the society?

A Anorectic people of all ages and stages are members, including those on the way to recovery, current sufferers, and even those who think they may have begun to "think anorectic" and have been advised by their physician, social worker, or psychiatrist to attend. Although the majority of victims are in their teens and 20s, there seems to be an increasing number of older sufferers, in their 30s and sometimes 40s. One would think that the age difference might tend to cause communication difficulties, but that is not always true. In a time when women are discovering themselves and their potentials more than ever, the support groups are a good place to learn—and there is so much to learn from and about one another! Recovered anorectic patients may also join and, in fact, are encouraged to help with coordination of the groups.

Q Are men allowed to participate?

A A small percentage of the membership is made up of men. Research has shown that only about 2% of all anorectic patients are men. A male point of view is always appreciated, however, because, after all, we are interested in looking at ourselves objectively. Although the society reaches out mostly to women, because of the predominantly female nature of anorexia, male sufferers are in no way excluded from any society activities.

Q   Where and when do these discussion groups meet?

A   Groups meet in homes, hospitals, meeting halls, churches—wherever they can talk informally and feel comfortable. They meet at consistent times, but how often they meet is up to the group members, since each support group maintains a great deal of autonomy and may even split into smaller groups. Contact between members outside meetings also is encouraged, to maintain ties and strengthen bonds that may have only begun to form during group sessions.

Q   What do they talk about?

A   Participants talk about anything that is on their minds, anything that may be causing anxiety. Sometimes there is a planned program, but every group is free to decide its own course. You don't have to tell everything about your anorexia at once. Trust relationships take time and are motivated by a continuing atmosphere of honesty. The conversations do not have to focus on food, diets, treatment modes, or nutrition. If you have very basic questions about anorexia, we will try to answer them for you. No question is dumb or stupid, and every question deserves an honest answer. (Unfortunately, however, some questions about anorexia cannot be answered at this time, even by the best researchers.) Although no one but you can ultimately answer your own questions about life values, direction, and purpose, we believe that sharing, comparing, and caring can have a positive impact on those life-changing decisions that are so important to recovery. The society espouses no particular religion, ethic, or moral system of philosophy.

Q   Is there a lot of emphasis on group sharing?

A   The existing support groups differ, so it is difficult to say whether they all use group encounter as a primary means of communication. The national organization does not necessarily emphasize it all the time, however, and, in fact, may be turning its emphasis toward individual, one-to-one communication methods. It is the network of communication that must be maintained. Years ago, anorectic victims and their families had nowhere to turn for emotional support; at least they now have a telephone number to call.

Q   What if I'm the type of person who can't open up or talk about myself? What if I have problems I don't want everyone to know about, or can't even begin to define myself?

A   That's all right—it just means you could be a good listener. By just listening, you may be able to contribute much more than you think. Everyone has something to share, and there will be a place and a time for opening up when you are ready. No one is forced into anything.

Q How did the society get started, and how big is it?

A Patricia Howe, a journalist with a past history of anorexia, founded the organization. She developed contacts with health professionals all over the country, promoting an interest in developing new treatment modes and research, but keeping the society's main goal of communication and support in the forefront. There are patient and parent support groups in Ohio, New York, Maryland, Tennessee, Michigan, Mississippi, Minnesota, Arizona, and California. In other states, there are scattered contact persons, who can refer anorectic victims to physicians with experience in treating anorexia.

Existing Support Groups

Arizona

Phoenix. Patient support group: Contact Ms. Shelley Vebber, 4444 N. Dromedary, Phoenix, AZ 85018, (602) 959-1605. Family support group: Contact Roger Perry, 2935 E. Sherran Lane, Phoenix, AZ 85016, (602) 955-9404.

California

Burbank. Anorexia support meetings are held every Tuesday at 7:30 p.m. at 1624 West Olive Avenue, Burbank, California. Contact Pat, (213) 769-3195.

Garden Grove. Anorexia support meetings are held at the Seventh Day Adventist Church, 12702 9th Street, Garden Grove, CA 92642. Contact Sandy or Shonna, (714) 527-6728. For further information, contact Dr. Joni Kellogg, Ph.D., Anorexic Self-Help Group, P.O. Box 1313, Garden Grove, CA 92642.

Sacramento. Family support meetings are being held. Contact Mrs. Valorie Phillips, Sacramento Anorexic Self-Help Group, P.O. Box 161641, Sacramento, CA 95816, (916) 383-5123.

San Luis Obispo. An anorexia support group has begun under the direction of Dr. Gene A. Rubel. For further information, contact Dr. Gene A. Rubel, President, Anorexia Nervosa and Related Eating Disorders (ANRED), P.O. Box 1012, Grover City, CA 93433, (805) 773-4303.

Van Nuys. Mrs. Jill Brownstein, 5249 Ranchito Avenue, Van Nuys, CA 91401, (213) 789-6320.

Illinois

Northfield. Anorexia Nervosa and Associated Disorders (ANAD), Vivian Meehan, President, 550 Frontage, Suite 2020, Northfield, IL 60093, (312) 831-3438. (Educational materials are also available.)

Kansas

Wichita. Chris Curless, R.N., 2343 N. Dellrose, Wichita, KS 67208.

Maryland

Annapolis. Dr. Jon Williams, Ph.D., Psychological Services, Inc., 111 Annapolis Street, Annapolis, MD 21401, (301) 263-8255.
Lutherville. Ann Boyer, ACSW, Maryland Anorexia Nervosa Associates, 222 Gateswood Road, Lutherville, MD 21093, (301) 252-7407.

Massachusetts

Lincoln. Mrs. Patricia Warner, ANAS of Massachusetts, Box 213, Lincoln Center, MA 01773.

Michigan

Detroit. Mrs. Peggy Debelak, 15761 Oakfield, Detroit, MI 48227, (313) 837-1663.

Minnesota

Rochester. Patient and parent support groups: Diane Parsons, Self-Help Groups, Box 476, Marian Hall, Rochester, MN 55901, (507) 288-2746.
Willmar. Family support reference: Mrs. Lois Johnston, 1415 W. 13th Street, Willmar, MN 56201.

Mississippi

Hattiesburg. Patient support groups: Mrs. Barbara Fisher, 315 Venetian Way, Hattiesburg, MS 39401, (601) 583-6201, or Pine Belt Mental Health and

Retardation Services, (601) 544-4641. Anorexia support meetings are held the last Tuesday of the month at 7 p.m. at Episcopal Church of the Ascension, Arlington Loop, Hattiesburg, MI 39401.

New Jersey

Teaneck. American Anorexia Nervosa Association, 101 Cedar Lane, Teaneck, NJ 07666.

New York

Long Island. Anorexia support meetings are held weekly and parent support meetings are held monthly at the Pederson-Krag Clinic, Huntington, NY. Contact William Davis, Ph.D., (516) 421-5664 or (212) 724-5353. Dr. Davis is also starting support groups in Manhattan at the Institute For Contemporary Psychotherapy.
New York City. Contact Dr. William Davis, (212) 724-5353.

Ohio

Cincinnati. Parent support meetings are held monthly at the Children's Hospital Medical Center (fifth-floor boardroom), Elland and Bethesda Avenues, Cincinnati, OH 45229. For additional information, contact Michael J. Maloney, M.D., (513) 559-4701. For further information on anorexia support groups, contact Bette Gillman, MSW, (513) 559-4681.
Cleveland. Monthly parent support and anorexia support meetings are held at the Cleveland Clinic, 9500 Euclid Avenue, Cleveland, OH 44106. For further information, contact (parent group) Mrs. Marilyn Cohen or (patient group) Tibi Scheflow, Cleveland Anorexic Aid Society, P.O. Box 21314, Cleveland, OH 44121.
Columbus. Anorexia support meetings are held every other Saturday morning at North Area Mental Health and Retardation Services, 1925 E. Dublin-Granville Road, Columbus, OH 43229. A parent support group meets every other Saturday morning. Contact (patient group) Patricia Howe or (parent group) Mrs. Atha Parnes, Columbus Anorexic Aid Society, P.O. Box 29461, Columbus, OH 43229.

Oregon

Eugene. Lorrie Smith, R.N., 4895 Mahalo, Eugene, OR 97405, (503) 484-0456.

Pennsylvania

Pittsburgh. Parent support meetings are held the second Monday of the month at 8 p.m. at Western Psychiatric Institute and Clinic, 3811 O'Hara Street, Oakland, Pittsburgh, PA 15213. Contact Mrs. Margaret Barati, (412) 881-1593, or Mrs. Phillip J. Cavett, (412) 563-0650.

Tennessee

Knoxville. Parent support meetings are held the last Monday of the month at 7:30 p.m. at the First United Methodist Church, Kingston Pike, Knoxville, TN. Contact Mrs. H.L. Minnich, 8612 Springfield Drive, Knoxville, TN 37919.
Oak Ridge. Parent support meetings are held at 221 W. Tyrone Road, Oak Ridge, TN 37830. Contact Mr. and Mrs. Joseph Pidkowicz, 135 N. Seneca Road, Oak Ridge, TN 37830.

Wisconsin

Milwaukee. Lois Rollman, MSW, Mt. Sinai Medical Center, 950 N. 12th Street, Milwaukee, WI 53233, (414) 289-8150.

Canada

Toronto. Isobel Roncari, Psychosomatic Medicine Unit, Clarke Institute, 250 College Street, Toronto, Ontario, Canada M5T 1R8.

United Kingdom

Diane Bayley, Secretary/Overseas Correspondent, 7 Willow Dene, Bushey Heath, Hertfordshire, England.

Bibliography

Books

The Empty Face, Katharina Havekamp, Richard Marek Publisher, 1978.
Eating Disorders: Obesity, Anorexia Nervosa and the Person Within, Hilde Bruch, M.D., Basic Books, 1973.

The Golden Cage: The Enigma of Anorexia Nervosa, Hilde Bruch, M.D., Harvard University Press, 1977 (recommended for anorectic patients).
Self Starvation, Mara Palazoli, Jason Aronson, 1978.
Psychosomatic Families: Anorexia Nervosa in Context, Salvator Minuchin, M.D., Harvard University Press, 1978.
Anorexia Nervosa, Robert Vigersky, Raven Press, 1977.
Adolescent Psychiatry, Volume 5, Sherman C. Feinstein and Peter Giovacchini, eds., Jason Aronson, 1977.
The Best Little Girl in the World, Steven Levenkron, Contemporary Books, Inc. (recommended for anorectic patients).

Professional Journal Articles

"A Conceptual Model of Psychosomatic Illness in Children," Salvador Minuchin, M.D., Lester Backer, M.D., Leroy Milman, M.D., and Thomas Todd, M.D. *Archives of General Psychiatry,* Vol. 32, August 1975.
"The Enigma of Anorexia Nervosa," Hilde Bruch, M.D. *Medical Times,* Vol. 104, No. 5, May 1976 (pamphlet).
"Anorexia Nervosa: A Review," Hilde Bruch, M.D., and Ross Timesaver *Dietetic Currents,* Vol. 4, No. 2, March-April 1977. Ross Laboratories, Columbus, Ohio.
"Anorexia Nervosa: An Affective Disorder," Dennis Cantwell, M.D., Susan Sturzenberger, Ph.D., Jane Burroughs, MSW, Barbara Salkin, MSW, and Jacquelyn K. Breen, M.D. *Archives of General Psychiatry,* Vol. 34 September 1977.
"On The Course of Anorexia Nervosa," Regina C. Casper, M.D., and John M. Davis, M.D. *American Journal of Psychiatry,* September, 1977.
"Anorexia Nervosa," Alexander Lucas, M.D. *Contemporary Nutrition,* Vol. 3, No. 8, August 1978. General Mills Nutrition Department (pamphlet).
"Diagnosing Anorexia Nervosa in Males," William M. Hogan, M.D., Enrique Huerta, M.D., and Alexander Lucas, M.D. *Psychosomatics,* Vol. 15, Third Quarter 1974.
"Anorexia Nervosa," Hilde Bruch, M.D. *Nutrition Today,* September-October 1978.

Papers

"Catastrophe Theory, Part Two: Anorexia Nervosa," E.C. Zeeman, Mathematics Institute, University of Warwick, Coventry, England, January 1976. (From this came the article "Trance Therapy," *Scientific American,* April 1976.)

"Successful Treatment of Anorexia Nervosa with Imipramine," James White, M.D., University of Texas, Medical Branch, Galveston.

Popular Magazine Articles

"If Your Teenage Daughter Diets, It Could Become A Frightening Illness," Monica Wilson. *London Observer*, February 24, 1974.

"Anorexia Nervosa Is Starvation by Choice," Carolyn See. *Todays Health*, May 1975.

"Anorexia Nervosa—Dying of Thinness," Judith Ramsey. *Ms.*, August 1976.

"The Starving Disease," Nonie Carol Murphy. *Vogue*, November 1976.

"The Gorging Purging Syndrome," Marlene Boskind-Lodahl and Joyce Smith. *Psychology Today*, March 1977.

"Are You Obsessed With Being Thin?" Barbara Coffey. *Glamour*, March 1977.

"Anorexia Nervosa—The Dieting Disease," William A. Nolen, M.D. *McCall's*, June 1977.

"How Unhappy Girls Lose Weight Dangerously," Karen Meehan. *Cosmopolitan*, August 1977.

"The Girl Who Wouldn't Grow Up," Joseph P. Blank. *Readers Digest*, October 1977.

"Obsession—Why Some Girls Starve Themselves," Beverly Solochek. *Seventeen Magazine*, June 1978.

"Medics" (story about Hilde Bruch, M.D.). *People*, June 26, 1978.

Glamour, February 1979 and October 1981.

Appendix C

Professional Resources

Meir Gross, M.D.

The following is a state-by-state list of medical professionals and institutions that provide consultation or treatment for anorexia nervosa. The list was compiled with the help of patients, their parents, and local anorectic aid societies and is intended as an aid to patients and parents in finding professionals in their local areas to help deal with the unique problems of anorexia nervosa. The list will also be useful for physicians who wish to refer their patients to medical centers that have special programs for anorexia and bulimia or to locate professional resources for patients who are leaving their area but need to continue therapy.

This list should not be considered complete or entirely up to date, nor is sponsorship or recommendation of the listed resources intended.

Alabama

Birmingham

Patrick Linton, M.D.
Department of Psychiatry
University Station B
Birmingham, AL 35294
(205) 934-5156

Huntsville

Robert F. Froelich, M.D.
201 Governors Dr. S.W.
Huntsville, AL 35801
(205) 536-5511

Mobile

Claude L. Brown, M.D.
176 Louiselle St.
Mobile, AL 36607

University

Ana Dvoredsky, M.D.
Box 6291
University of Alabama
University, AL 35486
(205) 348-7942

Arizona

Phoenix

Camelback Hospital
5055 N. 34th St.
Phoenix, AZ 85018

Thomas O'Brien, M.D.
St. Luke's Hospital
Phoenix, AZ

Otto L. Pendheim, M.D.
5051 N. 34th St.
Phoenix, AZ 85018
(602) 955-1090

Robert J. Ranucci, M.D.
908 N. 24th St.
Phoenix, AZ 85006
(602) 944-8567

Scottsdale

Raymond Lemberg, Ph.D.
Camelback Hospital Mental
    Health Center
6411 East Thomas Rd.
Scottsdale, AZ 85251

Tucson

Henry W. Brosin, M.D.
Department of Psychiatry
University of Arizona
Tucson, AZ 85724
(602) 882-6337

John C. Lewis, M.D.
899 N. Wilmot Road D-5
Tucson, AZ 85711
(602) 296-8663

Ruth Mayer, M.D.
Department of Psychiatry
University of Arizona
Tucson, AZ 85724
(602) 882-6337

Charles P. Newmann, M.D.
Lisa Stroder, M.D.
Department of Psychiatry
University of Arizona
Tucson, AZ 85724
(602) 882-6337

Arkansas

Little Rock

Fred O. Henker, M.D.
University of Arkansas
4301 W. Markham
Little Rock, AR 72201
(501) 565-7260

California

Beverly Hills

Paul R. Fox, M.D.
Ben Kohn, M.D.
Cedars Sinai Medical Center
450 N. Bedford
Beverly Hills, CA 90210
(213) 651-1575
(213) 274-9670

James P. Rosenblum, M.D.
9615 Brighton Way, #302
Beverly Hills, CA 90210
(213) 276-1668

Carmichael

Robert Treat, M.D.
6620 Coyle Ave., #310
Carmichael, CA 95608
(916) 966-1422

Greenbrae

Paul L. Kingsley, M.D.
1321 S. Eliseo Dr.
Greenbrae, CA 94904
(415) 461-0900

Huntington Beach

James H. White, M.D.
William M. Young, M.D.
17822 Beach Blv., #437
Huntington Beach, CA 92647
(714) 842-9377

Paul E. Wood, M.D.
18821 Delaware St., #106
Huntington Beach, CA 92647
(714) 962-5000

Irvine

Justin D. Call, M.D.
Louis A. Gottschalk, M.D.
Mark Markowitz, M.D.
Donald Summers, M.D.
University of California
Irvine, CA 92717
(714) 634-6023
(714) 833-6415

Los Altos

Stanley Frischman, M.D.
715 Altos Oaks Dr.
Los Altos, CA 94122
(415) 941-7676

Los Angeles

William F. Kiely, M.D.
University of Southern California
1200 N. State St.
Los Angeles, CA 90033
(213) 226-7975

Jerry Martin, M.D.
1001 Gayley Ave., #201

Los Angeles, CA 90024
(213) 660-2450

Marilyn Mehr, Ph.D.
Robert W. Bonar, M.D.
Richard Mackenzie, M.D.
Childrens Hospital of Los Angeles
4650 Sunset Blvd.
Los Angeles, CA 90054
(213) 660-2450

Joel Yager, M.D.
Dennis Cantwell, M.D.
Neuropsychiatric Institute, UCLA
    Center for the Health Sciences
760 Westwood Blvd.
Los Angeles, CA 90024
(213) 825-0057

Menlo Park

Arthur Hardy, M.D.
1010 Doyle St.
Menlo Park, CA 94025
(415) 327-1312

Newport Beach

Barton Blinder, M.D.
400 Newport Center Dr.
Newport Beach, CA 92660
(714) 640-4440

Palo Alto

Stewart Agras, M.D.
George Gulevich, M.D.
Stanford University Medical Center
Palo Alto, CA 94305
(415) 497-7107

Joellen Werne
Stanford University Medical Center
560 Oxford Ave.
Palo Alto, CA 94304
(415) 327-8816

Sacramento

Hugo Biertuempfel, M.D.
601 University Ave., Suite 274
Sacramento, CA 95825
(916) 925-2571

Hal Bovermand, M.D.
Irving Berlin, M.D.
University of California
2315 Stockton Blvd.
Sacramento, CA 95817
(916) 453-3835

Arthur Burton, M.D.
87 Scripps Dr.
Sacramento, CA

Murray Kleinstein, M.D.
Student Health Center
University of California
Sacramento, CA 95616

San Diego

James Ferguson, M.D.
University of California
3427 Fourth Avenue
San Diego, CA 92103
(714) 299-3510

San Francisco

Allen J. Enelow, M.D.
Pacific Medical Center

2340 Clay Street
San Francisco, CA 94115
(415) 563-5500

Ames Fischer, M.D.
Langley Porter Neuropsychiatric
   Institute
401 Parnassus
San Francisco, CA 94143
(415) 681-8080

Harold Sampson, Ph.D.
H. Thomas Stein, M.D.
Mt. Zion Hospital and Medical Center
Sutter Street
San Francisco, CA 94115
(415) 567-2577
(415) 921-1818

Alan Teitelpaum, M.D.
Mt. Zion Hospital
3641 Sacramento St.
San Francisco, CA 94118
(415) 931-5650

San Luis Obispo

Ellen Newell
1400 Stafford St. C15
San Luis Obispo, CA 93401

Colorado

Aurora

Doris Callender, M.D.
1809 Cryotal St.
Aurora, CO 80011

Denver

Thomas Crowley, M.D.
Geoffrey B. Heron, M.D.
Donald A. Johnston, M.D.
University of Colorado
4200 E. 9th Ave.
Denver, CO 80220
(303) 394-7573

Durango

Howard A. Winkler, M.D.
P.O. Box 1549
Durango, CO 81301
(303) 247-0199

Connecticut

Farmington

Mahlon S. Hale, M.D.
Allan Tasman, M.D.
University of Connecticut Health
    Center
Farmington, CT 06032
(203) 674-2000
(203) 674-2890

Hartford

Hartford Retreat
Hartford, CT

Institute of Living
Hartford, CT

Mt. Sinai Hospital
500 Blue Hills Ave.
Hartford, CT

New Haven

Stephen Fleck, M.D.
Yale University
25 Park Street
New Haven, CT 06519
(203) 436-4682

Elaine Glass, MSW
Memorial Unit of the Yale-New Haven
    Hospital
New Haven, CT

Hospital of St. Raphael
1450 Chapel St.
New Haven, CT

Richard Meth, MSW
Jewish Family Services
152 Temple St.
New Haven, CT 06511

D.E. Redmond, Jr., M.D.
Yale University School of Medicine
34 Park St.
New Haven, CT 06510
(203) 789-7333

William Sledge, M.D.
John Strauss, M.D.
Yale Psychiatric Institute
New Haven, CT 06519
(203) 436-4446

Norwalk

Henry Gloetzner, M.D.
71 East Ave.
Norwalk, CT 06851

Joyce Stone, Ph.D.
Catholic Family Services
3 Main St.
Norwalk, CT 06851

Delaware

Wilmington

Edward Bohan, M.D.
1003 Delaware Ave.
Wilmington, DE 19806

Mary Traynor, M.D.
Chief of Psychiatry
St. Frances Hospital
Wilmington, DE 19805

District of Columbia

Martin Ceasar, M.D.
3800 Reservoir Road NW
Washington, DC 20007
(202) 625-0100

Donald Delaney, M.D.
Children's Hospital
Washington, DC

Burton G. Schonfeld, M.D.
5225 Connecticut Ave. NW, Suite 501
Washington, DC 20015
(202) 363-7755

Jeremy Waletsky, M.D.
2020 K Street NW
Washington, DC 20006
(202) 466-6781

Jerry M. Wiender, M.D.
2150 Pennsylvania Ave.

Washington, DC 20037
(202) 676-4072

Florida

Cocoa Beach

L.G. Cross, M.D.
1980 N. Atlantic
Cocoa Beach, FL 32931
(305) 783-3821

Delray Beach

Penny W. Mize
South County Mental Health Center
100 E. Linton Blvd.
Delray Beach, FL 33444
(305) 272-3111

Daytona Beach

Gloria Abad, M.D.
2763 S. Ridgewood Ave.
South Daytona, FL 32019
(904) 767-6384

Miami

Frank E. Bishop, M.D.
H.G. Diaz, M.D.
Raphael Good, M.D.
Marc Silbret, M.D.
Psychiatry—UMED
Box 520875
Miami, FL 33152
(305) 377-3819
(305) 325-6881
(305) 325-6115
(305) 547-6949

Elizabeth Gilmore, M.D.
1150 NW 14th St., Suite 705
Miami, FL 33136
(305) 324-8829

Tallahassee

Royce V. Jackson, M.D.
1630 North Plaza Dr.
Tallahassee, FL 32303
(904) 877-3102

Tampa

Pauline Powers, M.D.
12901 N. 30th St., Box 14
Tampa, FL 33612
(813) 974-2118

Georgia

Atlanta

Donald Keppner, Ph.D.
Midtown Medical Center
789 Peachtree St., NE
Atlanta, GA 30208
(404) 874-4848
(404) 353-0773

Douglas A. Kramer, M.D.
Atlanta Psychiatric Clinic and Center
    for Personal Growth
6363 Roswell Rd., NE
Atlanta, GA 30328
(404) 256-2792

Hawaii

Honolulu

Walter Char, M.D.
1356 Lusitana St.
Honolulu, HI 96813
(808) 548-3420

Illinois

Chicago

Regina Casper, M.D.
1601 W. Taylor
Chicago, IL
(312) 341-8125

Sherman Feinstein, M.D.
Michael Reese Hospital
University of Chicago
Chicago, IL

Highland Park

Highland Park Hospital
718 Glenview
Highland Park, IL 60035

Rockford

Gerald K. Hoffman, M.D.
419 N. Gardiner Ave.
Rockford, IL 61107
(815) 398-4114

Springfield

Helen J. Conran, M.D.
University Medical Building
901 North First St.
Springfield, IL 62705
(217) 528-0245

Terry Travis, M.D.
Southern Illinois University
Box 3926
Springfield, IL 62708
(217) 782-3318

Indiana

Bloomington

Joel H. Griffith, M.D.
2801 N. Walnut St.
Bloomington, IN 47401
(812) 336-4929

Elkhart

O.D. Klassen, M.D.
The Oaklawn Center
2600 Oakland Ave.
Elkhart, IN 46514

Indianapolis

Don Churchill, M.D.
Child Guidance Clinic
Riley Hospital
Indianapolis, IN

Eugene Roach, M.D.
James E. Simmons, M.D.
1101 W. Michigan St.
Indianapolis, IN 46202
(317) 264-8622

Portage

Marion Groves, Ph.D.
72 Shore Dr., Box 719

Portage, IN 46368
(219) 762-6715

South Bend

G.W. Erickson, M.D.
South Bend Clinic
211 N. Eddy at Colfax Ave.
South Bend, IN 46634
(219) 234-8161

Jeff Samelson, Ph.D.
1225 E. Coolspring Ave.
Michigan City, IN 46360
(219) 879-6531

Iowa

Iowa City

Nancy C. Andreason, M.D., Ph.D.
University of Iowa
500 Newton Rd.
Iowa City, IA 52242

Kansas

Lawrence

James Stachoviak, Ph.D.
Psychology Department
University of Kansas
Lawrence, KS 66045

Topeka

Edwin Levy, M.D.
Menninger Clinic

Box 829
Topeka, KS 66601
(913) 234-9566

Wichita

George Dyck, M.D.
1001 N. Minneapolis
Wichita, KS 67214
(316) 268-8821

Kentucky

Lexington

Maxie C. Maultsby
Lexington, KY

Louisville

Nina Kateryniuk, M.D.
2327 Medical Arts Bdg.
Louisville, KY 40205
(502) 451-4960

Our Lady of Peace Hospital
2020 Newburg Rd.
Louisville, KY 40205
(502) 451-3330

Theodore Lynch, M.D.
354 Medical Towers So.
Louisville, KY 40202
(502) 585-3297

Mohammad Shafii, M.D.
200 E. Chestnut
Louisville, KY 40202
(502) 588-6941

Louisiana

New Orleans

Arthur Brudon, M.D.
Thomas Conklin, M.D.
William M. Dean, M.D.
3500 St. Charles Ave.
New Orleans, LA 70115
(504) 899-1335

Peter E. Dorsett, M.D.
Max Sugar, M.D.
1542 Tulane Ave.
New Orleans, LA 70112
(504) 568-6001
(504) 888-7363

Maryland

Annapolis

Jon Williams, Ph.D.
Psychological Services, Inc.
111 Annapolis St.
Annapolis, MD 21401

Baltimore

Arnold E. Andersen, M.D.
Marshal Folstein, M.D.
Ghislaine Godenne, M.D.
Johns Hopkins Hospital
Department of Psychiatry and
    Behavioral Sciences
Phipps 506
601 North Broadway
Baltimore, MD 21205
(301) 955-5541
(301) 338-8277

Virginia Huffer, M.D.
645 W. Redwood St.
Baltimore, MD 21201
(301) 528-6090

Mayer Liebman, M.D.
Sheppard-Enoch Pratt
Box 6915
Baltimore, MD 21204
(301) 823-8200

Bethesda

William C. Carrigan, Ph.D.
7910 Woodmont Ave., Suite #909
Bethesda, MD 20014
(301) 654-1600

Michael Ebert, M.D.
NIMH Clinical Center Bldg.
9000 Rockville Pike
Bethesda, MD 20014
(301) 496-1891

Mark Groban, M.D.
7315 Wisconsin Ave., #929
Bethesda, MD 20014
(301) 657-2700

Howard Gross, M.D.
Walter Kaye, M.D.
NIMH Clinical Center Bldg., Room
   2S.243
9000 Rockville Pike
Bethesda, MD 20014
(301) 496-1871
(301) 496-1891

Gerald M. Levitis, M.D.
5413 W. Cedar Lane, 101C
Bethesda, MD 20014
(301) 823-8200

Chevy Chase

Maryann Turak, M.D.
4701 Willard Ave.
Chevy Chase, MD 20015
(301) 652-5696

Rockville

Howard Gross, M.D.
RM 10B19 HFD-123
5600 Fishers Lane
Rockville, MD 20852
(301) 443-3504

Massachusetts

Amherst

Myron L. Stein, M.D.
233 N. Pleasant St.
Amherst, MA 01002
(413) 256-0201

Boston

The Beth Israel Hospital
Boston, MA

Amelia Blackwell, M.D.
Deborah Waber, Ph.D.
Nancy Rollins, M.D.
Leon Eisenberg, M.D.
Gordon Harper, M.D.
Robert Zimin, M.D.
Children's Hospital
300 Longwood Ave.
Boston, MA 02115
(617) 734-6000

Sanford Cohen, M.D.
80 E. Concord St.
Boston, MA 02118
(617) 247-6453

Ramon Greenberg, M.D.
75 E. Newton St.
Boston, MA 02116
(617) 247-6571

Alan Marks, M.D.
Dr. Madias
Tufts New England Medical Center
Boston Floating Hospital
20 Ash St.
Boston, MA 02110

University Hospital
Harrison Avenue
Boston, MA

Brighton

W. McCarthy, M.D.
280 Washington St.
Brighton, MA

Cambridge

Jessica R. Oesterheld, M.D.
51 Brattle St.
Cambridge, MA 02138
(617) 354-6920

Framingham

Cavin P. Leeman, M.D.
25 Evergreen St.
Framingham, MA 01701
(617) 879-7111

Holliston

Michael Petersen, M.D.
St. Luke-Marselin Institute
120 Goulding So.
Holliston, MA 01746

Stockbridge

R. Ian Story, Ph.D.
Austen Riggs, Inc.
Stockbridge, MA 01262

Michigan

Ann Arbor

George Curtis, M.D.
Elva Poznanski, M.D.
University of Michigan
Ann Arbor, MI 48109
(313) 764-5348
(313) 764-0245

Robert P. Kelch, M.D.
George E. Bacon, M.D.
University Hospital
C.S. Mott Hospital
Ann Arbor, MI 48109
(313) 764-5175

John C. Marshall, M.D.
University Hospital
Kresge II, Room R3044
Ann Arbor, MI 48109
(313) 763-1544

Angela Wallenbrock, M.D.
4116 Jackson Rd.
Ann Arbor, MI 48103
(313) 663-8571
(313) 663-7008

Detroit

Joseph Fischoff, M.D.
Children's Hospital of Michigan
3901 Beaubien Blvd.
Detroit, MI 48201

Farmington Hills

Kenneth E. Pitts, M.D.
27970 Orchard Lake Rd.
Farmington Hills, MI 48024
(313) 851-7881

Grosse Pointe Woods

Calier Worrell, M.D.
20250 Mack Ave.
Grosse Pointe Woods, MI 48236

Minnesota

Golden Valley

Arlene Boutin, M.D.
Corman Psychiatric Clinic
6155 Duluth
Golden Valley, MN 55422
(612) 545-8117

Minneapolis

Elke D. Eckert, M.D.
Bruce K. Seal, M.D.
University of Minnesota
Box 393, Memorial Bldg.
Minneapolis, MN 55455
(612) 373-8858

Rochester

Alexander Lucas, M.D.
Mayo Clinic
Rochester, MN 55901
(507) 282-2511

Mississippi

Hattiesburg

Duane Burgess, M.D.
Hattiesburg Psychiatric Group
Hattiesburg, MS 39401

Jackson

Julius Collum, M.D.
William Johnson, M.D.
Vicki Kulik, M.D.
Glenda Scallorn, M.D.
2500 N. State St.
Jackson, MS 39216
(601) 968-3500

Missouri

Columbia

Parviz Malek Ahmadi, M.D.
803 Stadium Rd.
Columbia, MO 65201
(314) 882-3176

St. Louis

Samuel Guze, M.D.
4940 Audubon Ave.
St. Louis, MO 63110
(314) 454-3875

Felix Larocca, M.D.
Suburban Psychiatric Services
Ballas-Parkway Medical Center
522 N. New Ballas
St. Louis, MO
(314) 567-4178

Charles C. Schober, M.D.
4524 Forest Park Blvd.
St. Louis, MO 63108
(314) 367-6299

Montana

Billings

Eugene Weisner, Ph.D.
Eastern Montana College
Billings, MT

Nebraska

Kearney

Glenn E. Christiansen
South Central Community Mental
   Health
Box 2066
Kearney, NB 68847

Omaha

Jane Dahlke, M.D.
James A. Davis, M.D.
John Donaldson, M.D.
Louis Eaton, M.D.
Oliver Nikolovski, M.D.
602 S. 45th St.

Omaha, NB 68106
(402) 541-4668
(402) 541-4519
(402) 541-4670
(402) 541-4885
(402) 541-4522

New Hampshire

Hanover

Richard B. Ferrill, M.D.
9 Maynard St.
Hanover, NH 03755
(603) 643-4000

New Jersey

Cresskill

Charles Wuhl, M.D.
144 Knickerbocker Rd.
Cresskill, NJ 07626
(201) 683-7377

Glen Rock

Gisela H. Ucko, M.D.
39 Benson Rd.
Glen Rock, NJ 07452
(201) 444-0707

Livingston

Alvin Friedland, M.D.
201 S. Livingston Ave.
Livingston, NJ 07039
(201) 994-1611

Newark

Martin Buxton, M.D.
100 Bergen St.
Newark, NJ 07103
(201) 456-4300

Piscataway

Martin Weinapple, M.D.
Rutgers Medical School
University Heights
Piscataway, NJ 08854
(201) 564-4636

Plainfield

Charles Goldfarb, M.D.
Muhlenberg Hospital
Plainfield, NJ 07061
(201) 668-2028

Princeton

Kenneth S. Gould, M.D.
20 Nassau St.
Princeton, NJ 08540
(609) 924-3888

Tenafly

Charles Goodstein, M.D.
171 Devon Road
Tenafly, NJ 07670
(201) 871-4649

Upper Montclair

Joseph Daniels, M.D.
20 Tuers Place

Upper Montclair, NJ 07043
(201) 746-9151

Hardat Sukhdeo, M.D.
369 Upper Mountain Ave.
Upper Montclair, NJ 07043
(201) 643-5057

Westfield

Henry B. Ehrlich, M.D.
1 Stoneleigh Park
Westfield, NJ 07090
(201) 232-7574

New Mexico

Santa Fe

Ssu Weng, M.D.
11 Calle Medico
Santa Fe, NM 87501
(505) 982-9844

New York

Brooklyn

Stephen Zimmer, CSW
845 Carroll Street
Brooklyn, NY 11215
(212) 789-4494

Freeville

Marlene B. White, Ph.D.
George Junior Republic
Freeville, NY 13068
(607) 838-3067

Long Island

Marie Friedman, M.D.
Adolescent Pavilion
Long Island Jewish-Hillside Medical
    Center
Long Island, NY

William Davis, Ph. D.
Pederson-Krag Clinic
Huntington, NY
(516) 421-5664

New York City

Orestes Arcruni, M.D.
Payne-Whitney Psychiatric Clinic
New York, NY

Michael S. Aronoff, M.D.
60 Riverside Dr., 96-D
New York, NY 10023

William Davis, Ph.D.
473 West End Ave., 3-B
New York, NY 10024
(212) 724-5353

or Institute For Contemporary
    Psychotherapy
1 West 91st St.
New York, NY 10024
(212) 595-3444

Donald Gribetz, M.D.
1176 Fifth Ave., Room 7
New York, NY

Elizabeth Kleinberger, M.D.
1060 Park Ave.
New York, NY

Ruth LaViete, M.D.
55 E. 72nd St.
New York, NY
(212) TR3-3972

Steven Levenkron, Ph.D.
16 E. 79th St.
New York, NY 10021
(212) 794-1956

Leslie Jane Maynard, MSW
227 E. 57th St.
New York, NY 10022
(212) 421-1220

Julius Pomeranze, M.D.
340 E. 64th St.
New York, NY 10021
(212) 753-1322

Joseph Silverman, M.D.
622 W. 168th St.
New York, NY 10021
(212) 694-2500

Otto Sperling, M.D.
960 Park Ave.
New York, NY 10028
(212) 535-9070

Theodore Van Itallie, M.D.
St. Luke's Medical Service
New York, NY

Anthony Zito, M.D.
179 E. 79th St.
New York, NY 10021
(212) 628-9430

Rochester

Elizabeth McAnarney, M.D.

Robert Holkelman, M.D.
George Engle, M.D.
Strong Memorial Hospital
601 Elmwood Ave.
Rochester, NY 14642

Yorktown

Margaret Cioffi, M.D.
Westchester Psychiatric Group
200 Veterans Rd.
Yorktown, NY 10598
(914) 962-5544

North Carolina

Ashville

Jack Bonner, III, M.D.
Anne Sagburg, M.D.
Highland Hospital
Division of Duke University Medical
  Center
P.O. Box 1101
Ashville, NC 28802
(704) 254-3201

Charlotte

Jerald P. Lane, M.D.
1900 Randolph Rd., Suite 900
Charlotte, NC

K.T. Shultz, M.D.
Durwood Clinic
1351 Durwood Dr.
Charlotte, NC

Durham

Bernard Bressler
David J. Jones, M.D.
Box 3812, Duke University
Durham, NC 27710
(919) 684-5616
(919) 684-2372

North Dakota

Fargo

Russell Gardner, Jr., M.D.
700 1st Ave. So.
Fargo, ND 58102
(701) 235-5354

Ohio

Cincinnati

Sam Baird, M.D.
Jerry Kleinman, M.D.
7770 Cooper Rd.
Cincinnati, OH 45242
(513) 984-2800

Bette Gillman, MSW
Adolescent Clinic
Pavillion Building
Children's Hospital
Cincinnati, OH 45229
(513) 559-4681

Pauline R. Langsley, M.D.
60 Hollister
Cincinnati, OH 45219
(513) 721-1737

Michael Maloney, M.D.
Hugh Pettigrew, M.D.
Children's Hospital Medical
    Center
240 Bethesda
Cincinnati, OH 45229
(513) 559-4701

Cleveland

Meir Gross, M.D.
Enrique Huerta, M.D.
Cleveland Clinic
9500 Euclid Ave.
Cleveland, OH 44106
(216) 444-5822
(216) 444-5813

Robin Moir, M.D.
University Hospital
Division of Child Psychiatry
2040 Abingdon
Cleveland, OH 44106
(216) 444-3281

S.F. Wallace, M.D.
24670 Euclid Ave.
Cleveland, OH 44117
(216) 486-3003

Columbus

Janet K. Bixel, M.D.
John Larrimer, M.D.
John Krupko, M.D.
Central Ohio Medical Clinic
497 E. Town St.
Columbus, OH 43215
(614) 221-7671

Katharine Dixon, M.D.
Upham Hall—OSU
473 W. 12th Ave.
Columbus, OH 43210
(614) 421-8232

Amy Enright, Director
The Bridge (Mental Health Center)
4897 Karl Rd.
Columbus, OH 43229
(614) 846-2588

Harding Hospital
Ray Dutton—Contact
445 E. Dublin-Granvill Rd.
Worthington, OH 43085
(614) 885-5381

Ralph Henn, M.D.
300 E. Town St.
Columbus, OH 43215
(614) 221-5030

Rotraud Moslener, M.D.
220 West Bridge
Dublin, OH 43017
(614) 889-9245

Irving Pine, M.D.
3543 Olentangy River Road
Columbus, OH 43214
(614) 268-4378

Marilynn A. Strayer, M.D.
William E. Todd, M.D.
John Morcos, M.D.
Indianola Psychiatric Institute
4319 Indianola Ave.
Columbus, OH 43214
(614) 268-2860

Dale Svendsen, M.D.
Chief, Mental Health Clinic
Ohio State University
Student Health Services
1875 Millikan Road
Columbus, OH 43210
(614) 422-0149

Carl Tishler, Ph.D.
Children's Hospital
Department of Psychology
700 Children's Drive
Columbus, OH 43202
(614) 461-2000

University Hospital Endocrine Unit
410 W. 10th Ave.
Columbus, OH 43210
(614) 422-5631

Dayton

Elizabeth Wales, Ph.D.
Wright State University
Department of Psychiatry
P.O. Box 927
Dayton, OH

Delaware

Phyllis Bahrick, Ph.D.
5 Westgate Dr.
Delaware, OH 43015
(614) 363-1753

Newark

William McFarren, Ph.D.
Guidance Center
Newark, OH
(614) 345-3356

Toledo

Charles Davenport, M.D.
Joel P. Zrull, M.D.
Medical College of Ohio
C.S. 10008
Toledo, OH 43699
(419) 381-3495

Oklahoma

Norman

James M. Behrman, M.D.
900 Porter
Norman, OK 73069
(405) 329-1651

J.A. Montero, M.D.
University of Oklahoma
Box 26901
Oklahoma City, OK 73190
(405) 271-5284

Oregon

Corvallis

Raymond S. Sanders, Ph.D.
Oregon State University Health Center
Corvallis, OR 97331
(503) 752-7607

Eugene

Josephine Von Hippel, M.D.
1900 Crest Dr.
Eugene, OR 97405
(503) 343-1313

Portland

University of Oregon Medical
  School Psychiatry Clinic
Portland, OR

Salem

Eleanor Houston, Nutritionist
Wheatland Road No.
Salem, OR

Pennsylvania

Abington

Nina P. Randall, M.D.
1174 Highland Ave.
Abington, PA 19001
(215) TU7-7426

Blossberg

John Phagan
448 Ruah
Blossberg, PA

Bryn Mawr

Erwin Smarr, M.D.
936 County Line Rd.
Bryn Mawr, PA 10910
(215) 525-8778

Doylestown

Barbara A. Spear, M.D.
New Britain Rd.

R.D. #3
Doylestown, PA 18901
(215) 348-4502

Hershey

Anthony Kales, M.D.
Pennsylvania State University
Hershey, PA 17033
(717) 534-8515

Jenkintown

Daniel Freeman, M.D.
721 Upsal Rd.
Jenkintown, PA 19046
(215) 884-3568

King of Prussia

Margaret V. Conrad, M.D.
491 Allendale Road, Suite 304
King of Prussia, PA 19406

Carl F. Schuttheis, Jr., M.D.
Pediatric Associates, Inc.
491 Allendale Rd.
King of Prussia, PA 19406

Philadelphia

Ivan Boszormenyi-Nagy, M.D.
R.C. Steppacher, M.D.
John Straumanis, M.D.
Eastern Pennsylvania Psychiatric
Henry Avenue and Abbottsford
Philadelphia, PA 19129
(215) 842-4347
(215) 842-4000

John Brady, M.D.
University of Pennsylvania
Philadelphia, PA 19104
(215) 662-2825

John L. Bulette, M.D.
3300 Henry Ave.
Philadelphia, PA 19129
(215) 842-6920

John Frank, M.D.
Thomas Moshang, Jr., M.D.
Hannemann Medical College
230 N. Broad St.
Philadelphia, PA 19102
(215) 448-8500
(215) 448-7708

Leonardo Magran, M.D.
Harold Meyer, M.D.
Stephen Steltzer, M.D.
Albert Einstein Medical Center
York and Tabor Roads
Philadelphia, PA 19141
(215) 329-0700

Salvador Minuchin, M.D.
Ronald Liebman, M.D.
Philadelphia Child and
    Guidance Center
34th and Civic Center
Philadelphia, PA 19104
(215) 243-2650

Michael Pertschuk, M.D.
Hospital of the University
    of Pennsylvania
1157 Gates Pavillion
Philadelphia, PA 19104
(215) 662-2834

Stephen Risen, M.D.
219 E. Willowgrove Ave.
Philadelphia, PA 19118
(215) 448-7000

Albert Stunkard, M.D.
Andrew Winokur, M.D.
University of Pennsylvania
Philadelphia, PA 19104
(215) 243-5000

Andrew Winokur, M.D.
Hospital of the University
    of Pennsylvania
3400 Spruce St.
Philadelphia, PA 19104
(215) 662-2854

Pittsburgh

Thomas Detre, M.D.
F. Gordon Foster, M.D.
David Kupfer, M.D.
3811 O'Hara St.
Pittsburgh, PA 15261
(412) 842-6920
(412) 624-2100
(412) 624-2353

Irma L. Hausdorff, Ph.D.
5555 Forbes Ave.
Pittsburg, PA 15217

John B. Reinhart, M.D.
125 De Soto St.
Pittsburgh, PA 15213
(412) 681-7700

Rhode Island

Providence

Brandon Qualls, M.D.
333 Grotto Ave.
Providence, RI 02906
(401) 456-3860

South Carolina

Charleston

Donald E. Manning, M.D.
Steven B. Whipple, M.D.
80 Barre Street
Charleston, SC 29401
(803) 792-0211

Columbia

Alexander G. Donald, M.D.
University of South Carolina
Box 119
Columbia, SC 29202
(803) 758-2205

South Dakota

Sioux Falls

Kathleen Cody, M.D.
William Fuller, M.D.
Carl Rutt, M.D.
2501 W. 22nd St.
Sioux Falls, SD 57105
(605) 339-6785

Tennessee

Memphis

Gene Abel, M.D.
William L. Webb, M.D.
University of Tennessee
Box 4966
Memphis, TN 38104
(901) 534-6668

Nashville

Bruce Rau, M.D.
Vanderbilt University
Nashville, TN 37212
(615) 322-2423

Texas

Dallas

Carrie Arnold, M.D.
12700 Park Central, #1318
Dallas, TX 75251

Webster Blocker, M.D.
Thomas Allison, M.D.
6116 North Central Expressway
Dallas, TX 75206
(214) 369-9951
(214) 361-5947

Mark Blotcky, M.D.
4645 Samuell
Dallas, TX 75228
(214) 381-5996

Frank Crumley, M.D.
3600 Gaston Ave., #808
Dallas, TX 75246
(214) 827-9830

John E. Davis, MSW
12820 Hillcrest Road
Dallas, TX 75230
(214) 233-2030

Dianne Fagelman, M.D.
13601 Preston Road, #1001
Dallas, TX 75240
(214) 387-4747

Richard Jaeckle, M.D.
Southwestern Medical School
University of Texas Health
   Science Center
5323 Harry Hines Blvd.
Dallas, TX 75235
(214) 688-2211

Keith Johansen, M.D.
4645 Samuell
Dallas, TX 75228
(214) 381-1924

Thomas F. Johnson, Ph.D.
1600 Promenade Tower
Richardson, TX 75080
(214) 231-7311

Guy Kindred, M.D.
Lacy Edmundson, M.D.
Linda Hughes, M.D.
7777 Forest Lane
Dallas, TX 75230
(214) 661-7898
(214) 661-7730
(214) 661-7478

Dan Myers, M.D.
5206 McKinney
Dallas, TX 75205
(214) 522-7240

Dan G. Perkins, Ph.D.
13531 North Central Expressway

Dallas, TX 75243
(214) 234-1083

Edith Rossi, M.D.
8226 Douglas
Dallas, TX 75225
(214) 369-6986

Sandra Steinbach, M.D.
One North Park East, #322
Dallas, TX 75231
(214) 363-8445

Kenneth Timken, M.D.
3636 Dickason
Dallas, TX 75219
(214) 528-3041

Mark Unterberg, M.D.
Timberlawn Psychiatric Hospital
Dallas, TX 75222
(214) 381-7181

Agnes Whitley, M.D.
8210 Walnut Hill Lane, #308
Dallas, TX 75231
(214) 691-0832

Forth Worth

Richard D. Yentis, M.D.
815 Eighth Ave.
Forth Worth, TX 76104
(817) 335-8222

Galveston

Robert B. White, M.D.
University of Texas
Galveston, TX 77550
(713) 765-1281

Houston

Hilde Bruch, M.D.
Baylor College of Medicine
Houston Medical Center
1200 Moursund Ave.
Houston, TX 77030
(713) 790-4964

Dorothy Cato, M.D.
2210 Maroneal
Houston, TX 77025
(713) 666-4311

Neil Edwards, M.D.
Arthur Farley, M.D.
6400 W. Cullen, Box 2070
Houston, TX 77025
(713) 792-5530

Francis Kane, M.D.
Marc Moldawer, M.D.
The Methodist Hospital
6516 Bertner
Houston, TX 77030
(713) 790-2405
(713) 790-2661

Lubbock

Richard Weddige, M.D.
Texas Technical University
Box 4569
Lubbock, TX 79409
(806) 743-2800

San Antonio

David S. Fuller, M.D.
Lonnie K. Zeltzer

University of Texas Health School
7703 Floyd Curl Dr.
San Antonio, TX 78284
(512) 696-6223
(512) 696-6264

Utah

Salt Lake City

Claudia Berenson, M.D.
Eugene Bliss, M.D.
University Medical Center
50 North Medical Dr.
Salt Lake City, UT 84112

Richard Ferr, M.D.
Kim Peterson, MSW
Primary Children's Medical Center
320 12th Ave.
Salt Lake City, UT 84013

Vermont

Burlington

Lewis Ravaris, M.D.
University of Vermont
Burlington, VT 05401
(802) 656-3270

Virginia

Charlottesville

Ann Johnson, M.D.
Vamik Volkan, M.D.
University of Virginia
Charlottesville, VA 22901
(804) 924-2701

Falls Church

Janet Kaplan, Ph.D.
3403 Cypress Dr.
Falls Church, VA 22042

Radford

Delano W. Bolter, M.D.
Route 11, Box 3747 FSS
Radford, VA 24141
(703) 639-9301

Richmond

Prakash Ettigi, M.D.
Virginia Commonwealth University
Box 253, MVC Station
Richmond, VA 23298
(804) 770-5961

W.D. Ward, M.D.
6620 W. Broad
Richmond, VA 23230
(804) 282-9032

Orestes S. Zalis, M.D.
5855 Bremo Rd.
Richmond, VA 23226
(804) 288-7988

Washington

Pullman

Christine Haggenmacher, M.S.
Student Counseling Service
Washington State University
Pullman, WA 99164

Mimsi Wise, ACSW
Whitman County Mental
    Health Center
NE 340 Maple No. 3
Pullman, WA 99163

Seattle

Cornelis Bakker, M.D.
John Chiles, M.D.
Carl Eisdorfer, M.D.
Nicolas Ward, M.D.
University of Washington
Seattle, WA 98195
(206) 543-3300
(206) 543-3924
(206) 543-3750

Wisconsin

Green Bay

St. Vincent's Hospital
Green Bay, WI

LaCrosse

Pauline Jackson, M.D.
Larry Goodlund, M.D.
Gundersen Clinic, Ltd.
1836 South Ave.
LaCrosse, WI 54601
(608) 782-7300

Laona

Richard Kujoth, Ed.D.
5229 Silver Lake Rd.
Laona, WI 54541

Madison

Richard Anderson, M.D.
Carl Whitaker, M.D.
University of Wisconsin
1300 University Ave.
Madison, WI 53706
(608) 262-3637

Steve de Shazer, MSW
Insoo K. Berg, MSW
James F. Derks, MSW
Marvin Wiener, M.D.
Brief Family Therapy Center
8115 Hillcrest Dr.
Wauwatosa, WI 53213
(414) 453-5664

Wauwatosa

D. Meyer, M.D.
Anthony V. Machi, M.D.
Child and Adolescent Treatment
    Center
9501 Watertown Plank
Wauwatosa, WI
(414) 257-7611
(414) 257-7586

Index

Abdomen, distention of , 24, 154
Abreaction, therapeutic, 125, 157
Abuse, substance. *See* Substance abuse
Acanthocytes, 27, 28, 29
Achalasia, 33
Acid-base balance, 16
Activity, increased. *See* Exercise
Adaptation, need for, 104
Addiction:
    drug, 19, 95, 154, 171
    heroin, 19
Addison disease, 21
Adolescent girls. *See* Females
Affect, flat, 16
Age:
    of parents in anorexia, 11
    of patients, and prognosis, 13
Aggression, 12, 158
Aggressive drive:
    in bulimia, 160
    of family, 21
Alcoholics Anonymous, 95
Alcohol abuse:
    in anorexia nervosa, 16, 95, 171
    in bulimia, 100, 154, 157
Alpha-wave action, 122
Amenorrhea:
    in anorexia nervosa, 1, 4, 5, 15, 16,
        41, 172
    in bulimia, 155, 156
    and depression, 16
    and endocrine function, 121
    and exercise, 25
    and schizophrenia, 16
    and weight loss, 75, 171
Amitryptyline, 99
Amyotrophic lateral sclerosis, 32
Anemia, 6, 19, 27, 28, 29
Anergy, 70, 78, 145
Anisocytosis, 27
Anorexia nervosa:
    clinical features, 1, 6, 10, 16
    critical elements in, 169
    diagnostic criteria, 3–4, 17–18,
        45–46, 84–85

differential diagnosis, 18, 84–85
family role in, 9–13, 21–22, 81–89
forms of, 15–17
follow-up, 22–23
as functional disorder, 31
history of, 5–7
hospital treatment, 91–101
incidence of, 41
management, 15–25, 37–38
psychology, 163–175
resources for aid in, 159, 177–213
secondary, 16
theory, 9–14
therapy, 15–25, 84–88, 94–96,
        103–109, 111–118, 119–127
        129–139, 171–173
Antidepressant drugs, 99
Antigen testing, 74, 78, 145
Antihistamines, 101
Anxiety, 105, 114
Appetite, lack of, 4, 93
Arm-muscle circumference, 70, 73, 76
Arrythmias, 23, 45
Arthritis, 19
Assertive behavior, 116
Assertiveness training, 94, 107, 115

Barbiturates, abuse of, 154
Bartter syndrome, 19, 120
Behavior:
    compulsive, 12
    passive-aggressive, 107
    ritualistic, 105
    See also Obsessive-compulsive
        behavior
Behavior modification:
    and biofeedback, 136, 137
    and bulimia, 118
Behavior modification contract, 23
Behavior therapy:
    in bulimia, 159
    and hypnosis, 119
    in milieu therapy, 94
    and obesity, 165
    and weight contract, 107–108